Long Way Round

Also by John Hildebrand

Reading the River: A Voyage Down the Yukon
Mapping the Farm: The Chronicle of a Family
A Northern Front: New and Selected Essays
The Heart of Things: A Midwestern Almanac

LONG WAY

~~~~~~~~~~~~~~~

ROUND

Through the Heartland by River

John Hildebrand

THE UNIVERSITY OF WISCONSIN PRESS

Publication of this book has been made possible, in part, through support from the Anonymous Fund of the College of Letters and Science at the University of Wisconsin–Madison and from the Brittingham Trust.

The University of Wisconsin Press
728 State Street, Suite 443
Madison, Wisconsin 53706-1428
uwpress.wisc.edu

Gray's Inn House, 127 Clerkenwell Road
London EC1R 5DB, United Kingdom
eurospanbookstore.com

Printed in the United States of America

This book may be available in a digital edition.

Library of Congress Cataloging-in-Publication Data
Names: Hildebrand, John, author.
Title: Long way round: through the heartland by river / John Hildebrand.
Description: Madison, Wisconsin: The University of Wisconsin Press, [2019]
| Includes bibliographical references.
Identifiers: LCCN 2019008122 | ISBN 9780299324803 (cloth: alk. paper)
Subjects: LCSH: Hildebrand, John—Travel—Wisconsin. | Rivers—Wisconsin.
| Wisconsin—Description and travel.
Classification: LCC F586.2 .H55 2019 | DDC 917.7504—dc23
LC record available at https://lccn.loc.gov/2019008122

ISBN 978-0-299-32484-1 (pbk.: alk. paper

I want to sit by the bank of the river,
    in the shade of the evergreen tree,
And look in the face of whatever,
    the whatever that's waiting for me.

Charles Wright
"The Other Side of the River"

Contents

Long Way Round

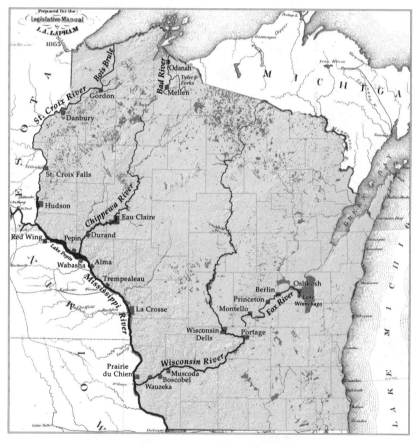

Map of Wisconsin. Background by Increase A. Lapham, 1865; foreground by Professor Sean Hartnett, Geographer, University of Wisconsin–Eau Claire, 2019.

When the weather turns summery, I'll stand at midspan and watch students launch themselves down the river on brightly colored air mattresses and inner tubes. Buoyed upon their own breath, they link arms and float face-up beneath the footbridge toward New Orleans. I envy their journey, the spontaneity and pointlessness of it. They are adrift between college and whatever comes next—a job, marriage, payments on their student debt. The flotilla slides slowly past the Fine Arts building, a tanning salon, and a Mexican restaurant. If the students kept going they might reach the Mississippi in a few days and the Gulf of Mexico by summer's end. But they never do. A quarter-mile into the voyage, they call it quits and wade ashore at the public boat landing. Shouldering their inflatable white shark or pink flamingo, they hotfoot it up the city bike path to the footbridge, back to where they started, and re-launch while the sun still shines. For the students, the Chippewa is a Round River.

The idea of a Round River goes back at least to the Okeanos of ancient Greece, a great freshwater stream that encircled the earth and flowed back on itself. The myth was an early take on the hydrological cycle, an explanation of why rivers flow continuously to the ocean yet never run dry. "All the rivers run unto the sea," says Ecclesiastes, "yet the sea is not full; unto the place from whence the rivers come, thither they return again." The North Woods has its own version of the myth in a Paul Bunyan tall tale. One spring, the big lumberjack hops aboard a log raft and heads for the nearest sawmill. Three days later the river, high with meltwater, shoots him past a logging camp that looks suspiciously like Bunyan's own. Three more days pass and another camp, identical to the first, heaves into view. He keeps going. Not until the third pass does the big galoot recognize his own red long johns flying from the flagpole and realize he's riding the Round River. That's the whole story. It's one of those elaborate jokes that works on an order of three, repeating the same details over again until the situation becomes clear to everyone but our dimwitted hero. There's no moral, no discernable theme except the obvious: to know where you are in the world it helps to remember where you've been.

In the 1940s, Aldo Leopold resurrected Paul Bunyan's river for an essay that begins: "One of the marvels of early Wisconsin was the Round River, a river that flowed into itself, and thus sped around and around in a never-ending circuit." Writers are always using rivers as metaphors for one thing or another, and Leopold was no exception. When he wrote, "Wisconsin not only *had* a round river, Wisconsin *is* one," he wasn't referring to a body of water but the flow of energy from soil to plants to animals to people. Leopold's "Round River" is an ecological parable, a metaphor for the natural world being interconnected, a closed system, and what goes around inevitably comes around. It's a fine essay but also a bit of a letdown. The first time I read it, I was terribly disappointed when the title river dried up after page one because a Round River is a beguiling idea. It's a very Zen idea: start here, paddle there, end up where you began. It's an idea that can send you scrambling for a map.

Look at a map of Wisconsin and the first thing you notice is how much blue there is, especially around the borders, which are mostly water. A riparian boundary, formed by the St. Croix and Mississippi Rivers, is all that keeps residents of western Wisconsin from waking up in Minnesota or Iowa. But rivers aren't walls; they don't divide, they connect. They cut across state and county lines, city limits and reservation boundaries, regardless of political demarcations or jurisdictions. Wisconsin has eighty-four thousand miles of rivers and streams, enough to circle the equator three times, and certainly enough to cobble together a circular route through the state. Cobbling rivers together—descending some and ascending others—is how Indians traveled from one watershed to the next. Rivers were the original blue highways, the first routes of commerce and trade, the arbitrators of great cities. Now they're more like back roads, loopy digressions from the midwestern grid, meandering past towns that didn't grow into great cities but dwindled over time to become, for lack of a better word, backwaters.

One morning I spread a highway map on the kitchen table and plotted my own Round River route. I would avoid hydroelectric dams, big cities, and reservoirs wherever possible. I would begin at home, naturally, by launching below the campus footbridge and descend the Chippewa River to its juncture with the Mississippi. There I would make the first in a series of left turns that would move me clockwise around the state. Left at the Mississippi River and down to Prairie du Chien, another left turn up the Wisconsin River to Portage with a side trip to Aldo Leopold's shack. Then east down the Fox River as far as Lake Winnebago. A long car portage north would deliver me to the Bad River and ultimately to the shore of Lake Superior. Then, reversing course, I'd turn south and somehow ascend the Bois Brule to its headwaters. There I'd lug my canoe over a historic portage trail to the headwaters of the St. Croix and descend that river to the Mississippi, make one more left turn up the Chippewa and complete the circle by arriving where I started, back home. On a map, it looked easy.

Soon I was telling colleagues at work about my plans. If my Round River was hard to envision, it's because the river constantly transformed itself. It tumbled out of loden-green forests and splashed down a staircase of rapids. Round a bend and it became a broad, slow-moving prairie river that was mostly sky. It flowed through a lineal wilderness of floodplain forests and prairie remnants. Or it was a working river, heavy with traffic, a waterway where towboats muscled long strings of grain barges past white clapboard towns terraced into green bluffs, places where I could spend the night in a hotel built for the steamboat trade. If my colleague's eyes began to glaze over at this point, I'd fall back on the romance of place-names. Who can hear the words *Prairie du Chien* or *Bois Brule* and not want to jump in a canoe?

Not everyone, it seems. A literalist pointed out that my round river had a major gap and didn't resemble a circle so much as the letter E. Others wondered why the trip wasn't more expeditionary. Why leave home if you're only going to circle around it? Why take the time and trouble to travel such well-worn, domestic rivers? Why not a far-flung river? Or, better yet, a wilderness river where animals outnumber people and the natives speak a disappearing language? In fact I'd already done a trip like that, years ago in the Far North, a summer-long drift beneath the Midnight Sun, and what I'd learned traveling alone through the wilderness was mainly that I could *be* alone, not that I necessarily enjoyed it. The real challenge in life, I learned much later, isn't solitude but staying in one place and getting along with the neighbors, whoever they might be. But who were they? Were they friendly? Did they speak a disappearing language or were they just tuned to a different frequency?

Most of my colleagues are exiles from one big city or another and generally avoid those parts of the Midwest not connected to the interstate. Like exiles everywhere, they find themselves stranded in a strange land where the customs seem simple or amusing or both, a land of few bookstores but many taverns, places decorated with antlers, where patrons usually wear camouflage clothing and seldom remove their hats. Strange, yes, but not strange enough to be interesting.

My students, on the other hand, often came from just such places, small towns with three blocks of redbrick storefronts and plenty of diagonal parking on Main Street, a defunct movie theater and one thriving convenience store—towns they'd grown up imagining as the epicenter of the universe, at least until they got to college. Higher education is *meant* to make the familiar seem strange in the same way that travel does, but sometimes the familiar shrinks in the process, gets smaller and smaller until one's hometown looks like just another hicksville situated halfway between the Equator and the North Pole, which is to say in the middle of nowhere.

My job, as I understand it, is convincing students that American literature is somehow about *them*, that certain themes in the novels we read connect to their *own* lives. Yet very little in those books point students homeward because the classic American story is leave-taking—lighting out for the territory, setting sail, hitting the bricks, jumping the back fence and heading down the long brown path. The rural Midwest, to the extent that it still appears in television and the movies, is always a point of departure, an exterior shot behind the opening credits: a water tower rapidly receding in the rearview mirror on the highway to skyscrapers and romance.

"They're very naïve," a colleague of mine once declared as we sat together at a Modern Language Association conference in Chicago. We were interviewing a job candidate who had, quite naturally, inquired about the student body. "They're not well read," she told him. "Many of them grew up on farms."

Well, my wife grew up on a farm and is one of the more complicated people I know. The complication came from having a foot in two worlds. An art major in college, she could hold forth on De Kooning and Rothko, but I'd also seen her reach into a squeeze chute, grab a bull calf's tail and bend it backwards so the calf couldn't kick her father in the face as he turned it into a steer. None of my colleagues at the university know what a squeeze chute is or care to know, nor did I until I found myself standing beside one trying to slip a rubber band around a bull calf's nuts. It was a toss-up as to who was more surprised—the calf or myself. On the farm I began to understand that there are many kinds of knowledge in the world and many ways to be naïve.

The days grew unseasonably warm. As finals week approached, signs of encouragement appeared on campus. Literally. One sign read, "You Are More Important Than a Grade." Another proclaimed, "We Believe in You!" The signs were posted by the counseling office in the mistaken belief that students are more depressed by the thought of looming exams than excited by the bright prospect of summer vacation. If anyone was depressed, it was the teachers who weren't being hired back in the fall. They were getting the axe because Wisconsin's governor had cut $250 million from the university budget, the very same amount he proposed giving the hedge-fund owners of the Milwaukee Bucks to build a new arena.

Governor Scott Walker didn't create the fault lines running through Wisconsin, he just exploited them. As politicians go, he was ahead of the curve. The politics of division certainly simplified elections. Voters only had to be told who was on the other side of a divide—urban versus rural, union versus nonunion, high school degree versus college—and vote against them. The governor's signature legislation, Act 10, stripping public employees of their collective bargaining rights, came as a terrible shock to those of us in the teaching profession. But any outrage we might have felt was tempered by the knowledge that half the state agreed with the governor, at least enough to vote him into office three times, including an unprecedented recall election. And this awareness inevitably led to a deep sense of estrangement because you couldn't be certain if the flag-flying fellow down the block who home-schooled his children and greeted you warmly on the sidewalk didn't also want to see you fired.

Now we were into another election cycle and the university seemed more isolated than ever, a small island in a fogbound sea. Then again, the whole country seemed divided. Every morning my wife and I read the newspaper over coffee and fell into a bad mood. The state news was especially discouraging: the Government Accountability Board disbanded, a developer put in charge of the Department of Natural Resources, political donors shielded from liability, a botched attempt by the governor to remove "search for truth" from the University of Wisconsin mission statement, John Doe investigations of the same governor dismissed by the state's partisan Supreme Court. On the strength of this abysmal record, our governor was considering a run for the White House.

I didn't feel angry. I felt displaced. Having lived here for thirty-odd years, I couldn't tell you what *here* meant anymore. My own assumptions about Wisconsin were mainly a physical sense of the land itself—its farms and forests, small towns and big cities—an entity held together less by geographic boundaries than by shared notions

of fairness, respect for hard work, and a belief in the common good—
the sweet notion that we're all in the same boat and might as well
pull together. What happened to that place? Where did that Wisconsin go?

One sultry evening in May when the air was heavy with the scent of
lilacs and impending summer, I walked around the block to an end-
of-semester party. After the guests made their way through the line
of corn-and-black bean casseroles and broccoli salads, the chair of
the English Department, a wafer-thin linguist, turned to the evening's
main business, handing out thank-you cards to the half-dozen staff
soon to be unemployed.

The thank-you cards were followed by hugs and sniffles and finally
an awkward silence. To keep the party from becoming a full-fledged
wake, the host handed out improvised lyrics and led the crowd in a
singalong. The song was a reworking of Gordon Lightfoot's "Wreck
of the Edmund Fitzgerald" and imagined our governor as captain of
a floundering ship.

> The legend spreads forth
> From Madison to the north
> On the big lake they call Whydyascrewme?
> Your policies don't work
> You're just a big jerk
> You've decimated our ranks—Bang! Kablooey!

We sang through all nine verses, including one surprising couplet
that rhymed "Iowa caucus" with "fuck us." By the song's finale everyone was grinning. It was the most fun the English Department had
allowed itself in years.

A flash of white outlined the backyard trees, followed shortly by a
muffled explosion of thunder then a fusillade of raindrops. Everyone
scattered for home, myself included. The rain fell in great sheets,

gushing from drain spouts and into the street, where it swirled down storm sewers and into the Chippewa.

Time to shove off, I thought. Leave my own little island and head downstream. Ho for the river! All I needed was a boat.

Chippewa River

~~~~~~~~~~~~~~~~

I

Wedged between lecture halls on the first floor of the tallest building on campus is a glass display case. In the rush between classes I've often paused to admire what's in the case: a fifteen-foot birchbark canoe. Immured in its glass case in the hallway, the canoe has no context; it's simply a beautiful object. Patches of stippled bark sewn together with spruce roots are stretched over a framework of split cedar planks and ribs. The ash thwarts are tenoned and lashed to the gunwales with rawhide strips. Nobody knows for certain how old the birchbark canoe is or who made it or where. In all likelihood, it's a ricing canoe built around 1900 on the Lac Courte Oreilles Chippewa Reservation in northern Wisconsin. The original owner could have delivered it by paddling south from the reservation, descending the West Fork of the Chippewa River until it merges with the East Fork, then portaging several intervening rapids and waterfalls until pulling out at the university just five hundred feet from the riverbank and beaching the canoe in the glass case. Of course, that's not how the birchbark canoe arrived on campus. It was off-loaded from the back of a panel truck half a century ago and for years hung suspended from the ceiling of the anthropology department until administrators decided to move it to the humanities building. The canoe was incredibly light, one of the movers told me later, and lodged between its cedar planks were stray kernels of wild rice.

All canoes are direct descendants of the Indian birchbark. For all the technological advancements—bark replaced by canvas, then fiberglass, aluminum, ABS (acrylonitrile butadicue styrene) plastic, Kevlar—the basic shape of a canoe remains unchanged: a long, narrow hull tapering up at the ends like a quarter-moon. When the architect Louis Sullivan declared that form followed function, he could have been describing a birchbark canoe. The canoe's function is to go downriver. A trip on a Round River, however, would require going both ways, upstream and down, and if I wanted to avoid a physical ordeal, I'd need a square-stern canoe with a transom to hold a small outboard motor. I didn't own one, so I called a friend.

Robert Elkins's backyard resembles a canoe livery in receivership. Elkins collects canoes the way some people collect mismatched furniture. He might stop at a garage sale to check out an oak commode or a sheepherder's stove and come away with another canoe lashed to the top of his car—an Old Town Tripper, say, or a seventeen-foot Smokercraft with a pockmarked hull that might have been used as a backstop for pitching practice. Elkins hardly seemed to care what shape the canoe was in as long as it floated, and even then exceptions could be made. At the moment, his collection was absent a square-stern but he promised to keep an eye out for me.

Elkins and I first met on a stretch of whitewater on the South Fork of the Flambeau River. I had just run the rapids in a fiberglass kayak and was drying off on a rock ledge when Elkins shot past in an open canoe. Instead of beaching his canoe after the last pitch to avoid a ten-foot waterfall as I'd done, he back-paddled, lining up the canoe with an open chute above the falls. When he dug into the water with his paddle, I sat up to watch. A husky young man at the time, Elkins had deep-set blue eyes and a reddish beard of Viking proportions. For a moment his canoe hung over the lip of the falls, cantilevered by the paddler's considerable weight in the stern. Then it dropped like a stone. By the time I reached the pool below the falls, the canoe was upside down, revolving slowly in the crosscurrents. An empty white sneaker bobbed to the surface, followed by a broken canoe paddle and finally Elkins himself. He waved casually as if seeing a friend off on a train, then rolled over on his back and slowly kicked to shore. We'd been friends ever since.

Elkins was a self-employed carpenter at the time. Previously he'd disassembled hogs at the St. Paul stockyards and more recently worked as real estate flipper and a rural tax assessor; each job, he liked to point out, paid him more money for doing less physical work— the central paradox of American labor.

Shortly after the end-of-semester party, I received a phone call from Elkins.

"Hey pal, I got you covered. Been snooping on Craigslist and found a seventeen-foot Grumman square-stern in Minnesota, up near Hibbing. It's been in a swamp the last couple years but it's in okay shape. The guy's a leech trapper and he's looking for cash."

"Leeches? How do you trap leeches?"

"You bait a bucket with chicken parts and check it once a day. Who cares? The boat's a sweet deal."

While I dithered, Elkins bought the canoe and began repairing some problems he hadn't previously mentioned, like a missing center thwart. Periodically, I'd receive e-mail updates: "Installed center thwart using a ratchet strap to pull the sides in. Just a wash/fresh paint and registration number installation is all that remains on the canoe. You really have to name the boat. I trust you, pal, so give it some thought."

Thirty years had passed since Elkins had gone over the waterfall and we'd both grown a little stiff in the joints. He'd put on a little weight, the beard had gone snowy white, and the only Viking he recalled was Kris Kringle. He showed up the first week of June hauling a boat trailer with a square-stern canoe lashed to it that bore little resemblance to the birchbark ricing canoe beyond a basic silhouette. I'd never considered naming a canoe before because it seemed a silly thing to do, smacking of sailing yachts with *Tradewinds* or *Miss Behaving* stenciled in gold script on their transoms. But the moment I saw the orange rust stains from the square-stern's swamp tenure and the flaking olive drab paint, I had my name. *Ms. Leech.*

A week of intermittent rain had the Chippewa River running high. Tea-colored water reached halfway up the landing below campus as Elkins backed the trailer down the concrete ramp. Wading into the river, I trimmed the canoe by distributing gear—a jug of drinking water, extra gas can, and an army surplus aluminum trunk filled with dry clothes, camping gear, and food—until *Ms. Leech* rode evenly in the water despite a fifty-pound outboard clamped to her transom. Then I shoehorned myself into the stern seat and yanked on the starter cord. The old six-horse Evinrude coughed blue smoke and I slipped it into reverse. Once the current caught the canoe, I put the outboard into forward and revved the throttle until the bow lifted and *Ms. Leech* planed downstream. Too late I realized that I'd forgotten to kiss my wife goodbye, so I frantically waved with my free arm and blew kisses until she and Elkins slipped from sight. Goodbye! Goodbye!

Two minutes later, I was back. *Ms. Leech* had sprung a leak. A tiny gash in her side released a continuous seltzer spray into the boat. Elkins looked surprised.

"Wow. How'd we miss that? Must have happened when I lashed it to the trailer."

After a quick trip to an auto parts store for marine putty, I patched the leak and was on my way again, a little more tentative on the throttle this time and blowing fewer kisses.

Three bridges passed overhead in quick succession. Then the city fell away until all that remained were a scattering of bluff-top homes that followed a ratio of height to mass: the higher the bluff, the bigger the house. As the land flattened out, the sky got larger, a rain-washed blue swirling with cottonwood fluff. Beneath the last bridge, I-94, the canoe hit an upwelling, a pillow of water where the current hits an underwater obstacle, and I heard a distinct crack, then another. I looked down to see that two of the aluminum ribs reinforcing the hull had cracked. *Ms. Leech* wasn't taking on water but she was nevertheless compromised. Never name a boat in bad faith.

2

Imagine an overturned bowl and you have an idea of the geology underlying the Chippewa River. The center of the bowl is the river's headwaters in Wisconsin's northern highlands, resting on the bowl's rim is my hometown of Eau Claire, and beyond lies a tabletop of outwash plain. By the time the river reaches Eau Claire, it has dropped nearly seven hundred feet, descending a Precambrian staircase of granite rapids and waterfalls that are now mostly drowned beneath hydroelectric dams. Below Eau Claire, the river drops hardly at all. The change in gradient signals a change in the river itself. Instead of a swift northwoods stream lined with birch and white pines, the Chippewa becomes a broad prairie river flowing beside cottonwoods and sand banks, blooming in early June with purple phlox and blue gentian.

To early French explorers, the Chippewa was *La Riviere des Taureaux Sauvages*, named for the wild bison herds that grazed along its shores. An American colonist changed the river's name. "This country is covered with grass which affords excellent pasturage for the buffeloe which here are very plenty," Jonathan Carver observed in 1767. "Could see them at a distance under the shady oaks like cattle in a pasture." Carver, a cartographer, had been dispatched to find the Northwest Passage by Major Richard Rogers, who believed an all-water route to the Orient commenced at the headwaters of the Mississippi. Carver was guided up the Mississippi River by Chippewa (Ojibway) Indians, who grew increasingly tense as they neared the villages of their traditional enemy, the Sioux. So the Chippewa guides suggested a detour up the west-flowing river on which their own villages were located and Carver fixed the tribe's name to his map. Three days from the river's mouth, the party reached a "buffaloe plain" where they laid over to replenish their supply of fresh meat. Carver described bison meat as "very good and tender" and pronounced the plentiful fat stored in the animal's hump as "but a little inferior to butter."

Below the Caryville bridge, the river split around a series of islands—Brush Island, Happy Island, Chippewa Island—that once held farm fields and now held switchgrass and big bluestem. The greatest concentration of tall grass prairie in Wisconsin remains along the Lower Chippewa. It's not a sea of grass, more like an archipelago of pocket prairies, two thousand acres scattered in remnants too steep or otherwise inaccessible to cultivate. A mile north of Meridean, Carver's old "buffaloe plain," I passed under a high bank with a barbed wire paddock holding a small herd of bison. I'd driven past the farm many times on my way to a fishing hole, and every time I'd do a double-take at the shaggy brown bulls, all massive hump, after miles of grazing Holsteins The bison aren't prairie remnants so much as transplants, trucked in from who-knows-where and raised for their grass-fed meat, which the farm advertises as "protein with attitude." No claims are made for the hump fat.

Herds of wild bison no longer shade under oak groves, but other, smaller wildlife persists along the river, turtles sunning on beaches and no end of birds wheeling in the sky. Rounding a bend, I startled a bald eagle on an overhanging bough. It flapped heavily into the air and landed in another tree downriver. The scene kept repeating itself. I'd get too close and the eagle would puff up its feathers and look imperious as if posing for its Congressional portrait. Then it flew downstream to another bend. The eagle never thought to fly upstream, so we kept bumping into each other, nodding sternly at each other like quarreling neighbors walking their dogs around the same block.

Shortly after passing the mouth of the Red Cedar River, I cut the outboard and glided onto a recently emerged sandbar. An immense silence replaced the din of the motor until it was filled in with the trilling of frogs, a sound like running your finger over a comb. The beach was a Rosetta Stone of animal tracks: heron, seagull, deer, coyote, turtle drag marks, the tiny calligraphy of some indefinable bird. After unloading the canoe, I puzzled over a fresh set of splay-footed tracks leading from the river until, in a moment of Paul Bunyan clarity, I recognized them as my own. Then I planted my tent on the sandbar like a flag.

America has no equivalent to the Swedish freedom-to-roam laws or *allemannsretten*, literally "everyone's right" to travel on foot across private land. Most law in the United States is concerned with protecting individual property rights, not public access. Rivers are the great exception. The Northwest Ordinance of 1787, the first law to apply to what is now the Midwest, guarantees the public free passage on rivers: "The navigable waters leading into the Mississippi and St. Lawrence and the carrying places in-between them shall be as common highways and forever free, as well to the inhabitants of the said territory, as to the citizens of the United States." Forever is a long time and while many of the "carrying places" or portages have disappeared under concrete, the rivers themselves remain open roads, the country's original form of public transportation, available to anyone with a boat. On a navigable waterway, I have the legal right to camp anywhere below the high-water mark.

I had traveled about twenty-five miles, not much further than I might have driven to a new restaurant for dinner, except river miles feel longer and I wasn't going home anytime soon. Camping is domestic life on a smaller scale and once my foil packet of dinner had been boiled and the pot cleaned, there wasn't a whole lot to do. I picked up my fishing pole and walked to the end of the spit. The sun was in the trees now, light gathering on the surface of the water so I could barely see my line. Cast, retrieve, cast again. Casting to the riffle where current met the slack water behind the sandbar, I suddenly had a strike! The line sheared upstream and into deeper water. From the weight of the fish and bulldozing run, I assumed it was a northern pike, a large one. Without a net, I'd have to beach the fish, which is what I did, walking backwards in the sand. What surfed ashore in the half-light was not a pike but a channel catfish—whiskered, goggle-eyed, and colossally ugly. While it thrashed on the beach, I pondered what to do with it. I'd already had supper and the last catfish I'd eaten had tasted like river bottom. On the other hand, what better beginning to a Huck-like adventure than a meal of pan-fried catfish? I put the catfish on a stringer, a temporary reprieve until morning when I'd see how hungry I was.

The evening's quiet was shattered by an outboard fast approaching from downstream. A planed-out jonboat with a forty-horse Evinrude flew around the bend, the Stars and Stripes snapping from its transom. A man in his thirties sat at the tiller; another seated in the bow wore a white cowboy hat and held a beer. Neither gave me a glance as they shot past, the sound of their outboard lingering long after the boat was out of sight.

A jonboat is the antithesis of a canoe—in design at least. It's all function and no form. Boxy and flat-bottomed, it's got a raked bow and nautical lines that fall somewhere between a barge and a trough for mixing cement. Jonboats are not indigenous to the Midwest. First developed in Southern bayous, they had migrated up the Mississippi River to its northern tributaries, where their shallow-draft and wide beam made a sturdy platform for shooting ducks or setting traps or just drinking while fishing. On the Lower Chippewa, they were ubiquitous.

A few minutes later the jonboat reappeared, drifting with the current and quiet as a ghost. The men stood casting at either end. "Any luck?" I called out. The old ice-breaker.

"Nah," shouted Cowboy Hat. "But we're having ourselves a time!" He took another sip of beer and drifted out of sight.

I crawled into my tent, slid into the sleeping bag and tried to fall asleep. Then I heard voices. Sounds carry on water, especially at night, and I realized that the fishermen who'd passed by earlier must have camped around the bend. Neighbors. Funny how hearing other people talk when you're alone can make you *feel* lonely even when you're not. The voices sounded younger than the fishermen had looked and there were at least four of them and while I couldn't make out what they were saying, I know a good time when I hear it. I pictured a blazing campfire, a twelve-pack of beer planted in the sand, a column of sparks rising to the stars. It was Friday night, the cusp of the weekend, and the boys filled in the quiet with a boom-box. At first they played a quavering, self-pitying country song about lost chances and lost love. Then the tune abruptly changed to something more up-tempo, a song with a fiddle, and I couldn't help but think of *The Jolly Flatboatmen*.

I first saw *The Jolly Flatboatmen* hanging in the old Terra Museum of American Art in Chicago and bought a print to tape to my office wall so I could look at it whenever I felt stir-crazy. George Caleb Bingham painted it in 1848 when the Open Road was not a road but a river, in this case the Mississippi fringed with cottonwoods and sandy banks and looking not unlike the Chippewa. Filling the painting's foreground is the broad stern of a flatboat. The flatboat was the jonboat of its time, a keelless barge steered by means of an enormous sweep or rudder. A flatboat could carry an enormous amount of freight downstream. Going upstream was another matter, requiring iron-tipped poles and strong backs. But Bingham painted his flatboat crew at play rather than at work and arranged them in an ascending order of mirth. At the base, three men sprawl on the boat's coach roof beside an open jug; higher up, two men play fiddle and tambourine; and at the apex a youth dances a jig, hat in one hand, red handkerchief in the other. *The Jolly Flatboatmen* proved so popular that Bingham kept painting different versions of it even after steamboats and railroads made flatboats obsolete. Somehow Bingham's crew never got the message. Whatever tune the fiddler's playing, it isn't "The Song of the Volga Boatman." Why such high spirits? The flatboatmen aren't peasants but working folks, self-contained and self-propelled, seeing a new country unfold around them. The painting is pure American optimism. "Feeling boxed in?" the boatmen ask. "Run out of dreams? Climb aboard!"

Now descendants of Bingham's flatboatmen were camped just downstream and growing jollier by the minute. Another song came on the boombox and they cranked up the volume, not singing so much as shouting, practically baying at the moon. *YEEEEE—HAAAA!* For all I knew, one of them might have been dancing a jig. Distance garbled the song's lyrics over the water, but I recognized the beat, an insistent, line-dancing, kick-ass tune, which the boys punctuated with peals of laughter and piercing rebel yells that made me want to join in. It was my second sing-along in as many weeks.

~~~~~~~~~~~~~~

3

The first sound in the morning was the strange, metallic bleating of sandhill cranes: *Ga-roooo . . . Ga-roooo-aaa . . . Ga-roooo-aaa!* Other birds might have sung earlier in the day but not loud enough to wake me. Cranes were my alarm clock.

Suddenly, I was hungry. I pulled the channel cat wriggling from the river, whacked its whiskered head with a canoe paddle and felt the fish stiffened. Then, using the paddle as a cutting board, I made a long incision with my knife along the fish's backbone, avoiding the sharp spines on the dorsal and lateral fins, and slid the blade between bone and flesh until two fillets came away in my hand. The fillets went into a sizzling skillet and then into my mouth. They tasted flaky and delicious and not a bit like river bottom. I washed the catfish down with a cup of hot coffee and broke camp.

Nobody was awake when I passed the fishermen's camp downriver. Their fire was still smoldering and several dead soldiers lay toppled in the sand. A second jonboat tethered to shore flew a skull-and-crossbones pirate flag.

The closer I got to Durand (pronounced *Dew-Rand*), the more boats I saw, all of them jonboats speeding upriver. They were crammed to the gunwales with fishermen in wrap-around sunglasses and camouflage caps with the bills turned backwards. Some of the occupants appeared to challenge the weight restrictions of their boats.

To approach a river town by water is to glimpse it as the town founders intended, a row of fieldstone buildings with skinny windows and flat tin roofs lining the riverbank. The boat landing below Main Street was as busy as if the first steamboat of the season had just lowered its gangplank. Once I tied my canoe off, I found out why. Durand was hosting its annual Fun Fest, a hoopla weekend that included a parade, carnival rides, classic car show, and fishing contest. The contest had begun at midnight, which explained the fishermen's camp downstream of my sand spit. They were getting a jump on the competition. A continuous line of pickup trucks backed boat trailers down the concrete ramp into the river. As soon as one boat launched, another roared in to re-supply.

"Back already?" a young woman asked as she lugged a bag of ice to an idling jonboat.

"We ran outta beer."

A registration board at the landing listed the categories: walleye, bass, northern pike, catfish, and a catch-all group called "rough fish." The largest catfish registered so far weighed in excess of eight pounds, so I was relieved that I hadn't eaten a winner for breakfast.

I bought pieces of aluminum channel at the hardware store to repair my canoe's busted ribs, then took in a craft show at the old Durand Theater. The red ticket booth beneath the marquee was still in place, but the rows of theater seats inside had been removed, replaced for the weekend with card tables manned by members of the Crazy Crafters. All the items for sale, frilly coasters and plant misters made out of canning jars, had been fashioned out of things that had lost their original purpose. The movie theater itself had been repurposed, in this case into something less grand and more temporary.

The theater's owner was a mother-in-law of one of the Crazy Crafters. I asked her when the movie theater had last shown movies. "Oh, 2012 I think. It costs $80,000 to $100,000 to convert to digital and there's no guarantee if we did convert that the community would support a theater. Most of the small towns that kept their movie theaters had financial support."

The shuttering of a movie theater used to be the death rattle of a small town, ranking up there with school consolidation and the post office closing. In Larry McMurtry's novel *The Last Picture Show*, the final movie is an Audie Murphy Western; in the film version it's John Ford's *Red River*. But nobody remembered the last show at the Durand Theater, not that it mattered. The loss of a movie theater is less ominous these days, one more vacancy on Main Street. People still watch movies; they just watch them on DVDs and satellite TV in the comfort of their own homes rather than in the collective dark of a single building.

I stepped from the cool recesses of the old theater into blinding sunlight and a wall of noise. The ambient sound of Fun Fest was the internal combustion engine: the revving of a 440 V-8 Dodge Dart at the classic car show, chrome-plated Harleys clearing their pipes as they mustered for the hundred-mile run, the throb of diesel generators that powered the carnival rides, the whine of outboards to and from the boat landing. Even the chorus of screams accompanying the Tilt-a-Whirl sounded the siren song of motorized escape.

Seeking peace and quiet, I ducked into the old Pepin County Courthouse, an enormous white wooden structure in the Greek Revival style with a columned portico and belfry. After a new, blocky government building went up, the old courthouse was re-purposed into a county museum, a repository of arrowhead collections, yellowing maps and photographs, obsolete tools, Durand's accumulated past loosely organized into separate rooms. The centerpiece is the old courtroom on the second floor. The scuffed hardwood flooring, cream-colored walls, and wainscoting made the courtroom resemble a movie set from *To Kill a Mockingbird*, but it once was the backdrop for a real-life drama with all the elements of a classic Western: a shoot-out between pairs of brothers, a wild escape, a public lynching and subsequent cover-up. Had events occurred on the other side of the Mississippi River—that is, in the West rather than the Midwest— they might have inspired a movie or an annual reenactment, an open-air performance by local citizens of the crime and subsequent punishment. On the other hand, what town celebrates a lynching?

Like other young men hoping to get in on the ground floor, Ed Maxwell traveled from Illinois to Wisconsin to pursue a career: in his case as a horse thief and petty burglar. In the summer of 1881 he arrived in Durand with his younger brother Alonzo. An arrest warrant had been issued for the pair, so when Pepin County Deputy Charles Coleman learned the Maxwells had crossed the river into Durand, he and *his* brother, Dunn County Undersheriff Milton Coleman, set off to apprehend the pair. Armed like the farmers they were, the lawmen carried shotguns loaded with birdshot. They caught up with the Maxwell boys near the town's cemetery, where they were simply outgunned. "Halt!" Milton cried out as he raised his shotgun. Ed Maxwell got the drop on the lawmen and opened fire with a Winchester repeating rifle, killing Milton and fatally wounding Charles. Before the deputy fell, he let go with both barrels, hitting Alonzo Maxwell in the face and arm with a load of birdshot and knocking off his hat. That night the Maxwell brothers re-crossed the Chippewa River in a stolen skiff and hid out in the woods until they could make their way west by foot to Lake Pepin. There they stole a bateau, paddled to the Minnesota shore, and disappeared, setting off the largest nationwide manhunt in history.

Two days after the shooting, W. H. Huntington, editor of the *Pepin County Courier*, wrote an incendiary editorial inciting the town to action: "Our community has suffered and borne too much already and it needs but a trifle to stir the smouldering [*sic*] wrath into a flame that will find suitable victims in short order. Lynch law is sometimes justifiable."

Huntington's paper described Ed Maxwell as "rather heavy set, broad across the shoulders, stout, well built, black hair, dark complexion, short black moustache, very sharp dark blue eyes, weight about 150 lbs., height 5 feet 7 inches." Four months later, when the fugitive was captured in Nebraska (Alonzo was never apprehended) and returned to Durand in leg irons, the desperado had shrunk considerably. He stood barely five feet tall and appeared, one eyewitness wrote, "pale, thin, and consumptive." He was also a talker. The night before his arraignment, Ed confided to a reporter from St. Paul that while he was "in a ticklish place" he hoped the jury might respond to a man's right to defend himself. "I believe in religion—believe in it hard—but I'd rather have my Winchester."

Here the story takes an interesting turn. For some reason, the pretrial hearing scheduled for the next morning was delayed four hours because the judge couldn't be located. During the delay, a crowd of five hundred "excited citizens," including Deputy Coleman's widow and children, gathered on the snow-covered courthouse square. When the judge finally appeared, Maxwell pled not guilty and waived a preliminary examination. According to the St. Paul reporter, the accused read a statement in a calm, almost conversational voice, admitting that he'd "killed the Coleman boys in self-defense but didn't know them from Adam." When deputies led Ed from the courtroom in manacles, they encountered a knot of men at the bottom of the narrow stairwell. "Hang the son of a bitch!" someone yelled. The men overpowered the deputies and slipped a noose around Maxwell's neck. At the other end of the three-hundred-foot-long rope a group of men stood in the courthouse yard. At the signal "Haul away!" Maxwell magically flew headfirst out the door and across the portico until he slammed into one of the Corinthian columns. A vigorous heave-ho dislodged the now limp body and it tobogganed down the snowy yard to a large oak tree where the rope slanted upwards to an overhanging branch. Another pull and Maxwell ascended into the winter air, hands still manacled, one leg iron dangling. Later, after the corpse had been cut down, bystanders chopped the rope into pieces for souvenirs.

My theory is that it was the Masons," said Terry Mesch. The director of the Old Courthouse Museum told me that nearly all Durand's early movers and shakers belonged to the same Masonic Lodge. "The late Deputy Coleman had been a Mason. Miletus Knight, the Pepin County Undersheriff, was also a Mason. So was W. H. Huntington."

After the lynching, Huntington wrote an editorial praising the mob's cool efficiency: "A regular legal execution could not have been conducted more quietly and orderly. . . . Five minutes after the body was cut down less than a dozen persons were to be seen about court house square and our streets assumed their regular every-day appearance."

"Back to my conspiracy theory," said Mesch. "A grand jury convened five weeks after the lynching to investigate and, if I'm not mistaken, Huntington may have also served on that grand jury. Nobody was indicted. A man is hung in broad daylight in front of half the county and the grand jury couldn't find anyone around here to indict, so they concluded it was a bunch of red-shirted loggers from out of town. I looked and couldn't find any court records for the grand jury. No documentation at all."

While I liked Mesch's conspiracy theory, it's hard not to see the story in a Biblical light: good seed versus bad seed, opposite pairs of brothers emerging from the same soil and taking different paths, the landowning Abel versus the nomadic Cain. Westerns always took their themes from the Old Testament.

After pestering the historian for an hour, I wondered if I shouldn't check my untended canoe.

Mesch smiled. "This is Durand. It'll be perfectly safe. I never lock my door."

I left the old courthouse to find the streets had resumed their regular everyday appearance except for the row of motorcycles parked in front of the Corral Bar. I'd seen their owners done up in leather vests and black-and-orange do-rags swaggering through town like pirates bound for the Pirate's Ball. The Cell Block Lounge at the other end of the block was cool and nearly empty. I ordered a hamburger and cold beer and divided my attention between a pair of flanking TV screens—a fishing show and college football reruns. Between the screens, hanging by a wire over the bar, was a Browning .270 deer rifle with a sign: "Win me."

4

Below Durand, the topography became more dramatic. The river valley narrowed between rising bluffs even as the Chippewa itself grew broader and shallower, braiding around sandbars and wooded islands like a Western trout stream. Then Buffalo Island split the river into two channels. The main channel skirted the perpendicular bluffs and goat prairies to the north while Beef Slough, the lesser channel, veered south toward a line of receding hills. Between these channels lay a vast alluvial plug stretching a dozen miles to the river's juncture with the Mississippi and containing within it the largest intact floodplain forest in the Upper Midwest. From the river, the Tiffany Bottoms appears as a flat, unbroken line of trees: swamp white oak, river birch, silver maple, and basswood. But for anyone slogging across it on foot, the Tiffany is a dire swamp, a Mesopotamia of cut-off sloughs and side channels, pothole lakes and interconnecting beaver canals, islands within islands and the easiest place I know to get lost.

I had a hard enough time staying in water deep enough to float because the channel kept shifting between sandbars and shoals. A brisk headwind brought a new sense of urgency as mountainous, black-bottomed clouds piled up downriver. Having spent enough time hunting in the Tiffany to know the larger sloughs by name—Beef Slough, Dark Slough, Stump Slough, Swift Slough—I headed for the mouth of Battle Slough. There was a place where I'd camped many times before, always in the fall after a hard frost had leveled the thick understory, never in summer when the brush is an impenetrable tangle of wild grape and stinging nettles and the soupy air swarms with mosquitoes.

Across from Five Mile Bluff, I ducked into a side channel at the head of Battle Island and got a terrific surprise. Instead of the dry apron of sand I'd expected to find, there was only more river. High water had completely submerged my old campsite. The only alternative was a small island across from the mouth, and even that would be a tight fit. A big driftwood log, white as a bone, separated a single patch of dry sand from the water. Everything else was mud and willows. The patch was exactly the size of my one-man tent. Other than being cramped, the campsite was ideal, sheltered from the wind and offering a fine view of both the main river and the narrow channel formed by Battle Island—the perfect spot for an ambush.

"Almost every bend on the Chippeway and Menominee [Red Cedar] rivers has been the scene of a fight, surprise, or bloody massacre," William Warren wrote in *History of the Ojibway People*, "and one of their chiefs remarked with truth when asked to sell his lands, that 'the country was strewn with the bones of their fathers, and enriched with their blood.'" Warren, the grandson of a Chippewa chief, documented the almost constant intertribal warfare in the first half of the nineteenth century as the Chippewa pushed the woodland Sioux out of their former lands. Much of the conflict took place here among the river's islands and sloughs as the lower Chippewa became a war zone, a dangerous no-man's-land between tribes. It was also a transition zone between deciduous forests to the north and open prairie to the south, abundant in game, especially whitetail deer attracted to the forest edge. The abundance of game was both a cause of the tribal conflict and a result because the constant threat of ambush meant there were no permanent villages in the area. When Jonathan Carver drew his map, he labeled this stretch of river "The Road of War."

These woods have a long memory. When I first started hunting in the Tiffany Bottoms, the jumbled terrain and blow-downs meant I almost never ran into anyone outside of my own party. That changed as Buffalo County became nationally known for trophy whitetails and wealthy outsiders bought up whole valleys and posted them. As land values rose, locals who used to hunt a relative's woodlot got pushed into public hunting grounds like the Tiffany. There they ran into Hmong hunters from Eau Claire and La Crosse. The Hmong were easy to spot in the woods: short men who hunted in family groups and often constructed ingenious tree stands out of dead branches and twine. Some locals found in these differences a reason to dislike the newcomers, but mainly they resented the competition. Recently a white bow hunter had beaten an elderly Hmong squirrel hunter senseless after the old man wandered onto private land. At his trial at the new Pepin County courthouse in Durand, the defendant took a page from Ed Maxwell and pleaded self-defense, even though he was twenty years younger and seventy pounds heavier than his victim. The judge sentenced him to two years probation.

Years before this incident, I wrote a magazine article about the conflict in the woods. I called Joe Bee Xiong, a man I'd never met, and asked to join his hunting party on the opening day of deer season. In Wisconsin this is akin to a stranger inviting himself to your wedding. Nevertheless, a week later Joe Bee showed up outside my house early on opening morning in a white minivan stuffed with relatives. We drove in the predawn dark to the uppermost portion of the Tiffany, just south of Durand, and walked single file into the frozen swamp. It was an overcast night, no moon or stars. Some of the hunters carried their rifles with the stock slung over their shoulders while others probed the dark with flashlight beams. They looked like soldiers, which many of them had been in Laos, undisclosed allies in a secret war who'd taken our side and lost their country as a result.

In all, the Xiong party took three deer on opening day, including one that I shot. We skinned them by lamplight in the backyard of Joe Bee's duplex. After the deer were butchered, Joe Bee painstakingly divided them—meat, bones, internal organs—into a dozen piles, one for each hunter. Joe Bee's brother said that if there had been twenty hunters and only one deer, there would have been twenty piles. I brought my share home in a white plastic bucket.

When Joe Bee decided to run for city council in Eau Claire, I served on his election committee without ever asking whether he was a Democrat or a Republican. In those more innocent times, it hardly seemed to matter. He won the election and served two terms on the city council though his leadership style puzzled some observers. Joe Bee often deferred his opinions until he learned what his constituents wanted done on an issue. He wasn't wishy-washy; he came out of a tradition in which leaders seek consensus rather than imposing their individual will. For a relatively young man, Joe Bee was one of the most serious people I'd ever met. He liked to laugh and make jokes, often at his own expense, but he could turn somber, even grave at times. Once when we went squirrel hunting in the Tiffany, I saw him take a spoonful of squirrel stew, whisper something in Hmong, and toss it in a bush. When I asked why, he said, "Spirits."

Over the years we drifted apart until one day I'd heard Joe Bee had suffered a stroke followed by a heart attack. When he got out of the hospital, we met for lunch at a Hmong café on the west side of town and ordered steaming bowls of pho. Joe Bee looked pale and worn out and obviously worried. Doctors told him that he had an old man's heart even though he was only in his early forties, an inherited condition reversible only with a heart transplant. Later that year, while visiting relatives in Laos, he had a second heart attack and this one proved fatal.

The photograph accompanying the obituary in the newspaper was so formal and unsmiling that I hardly recognized the man. The mental picture I have of Joe Bee isn't the convalescent who'd just been given a death sentence but a young, vigorous person in the very fullness of life. That picture was taken here at the mouth of Battle Slough in just this failing light. We'd spent the day jump-shooting ducks in the reedy potholes off Battle Slough and were sitting on a log, feet in the sand, bone-tired at the end of the day. As the sun went down, Joe Bee took out a slender flute and began to play. He was an accomplished *qeej* player, an instrument that produces a deep, sonorous sound like an oboe crossed with a bagpipe, but the notes coming out of his flute were high-pitched and unearthly in the stillness before nightfall. Nobody said anything. We just sat and listened, transfixed, as to some rare birdsong you hear once in your life and never again.

Storm clouds continued to build in the west as I boiled dinner on a gas stove and filled my thermos with hot water for coffee in the morning. Washing up, I noticed the reeds beside the tent moving in a way that had nothing to do with wind. A raccoon, I thought, attracted to the smell of food or, worse, a skunk. But when I parted the willows, I found a helmet-sized turtle, a Blanding's turtle to be exact. The black dome of her shell was flecked with yellow dots, and she had a bright yellow neck, which she pulled into her shell until all I could see was a hooked jaw and red eyes. She was female. I could tell because of her flat plastron, which also explained why she was on the move. She was heading for the only patch of dry sand to get enough direct sunlight to incubate her eggs once she'd dug a pit and buried them. My tent now occupied that spot. Having thwarted her most basic instinct, I set the turtle next to me on the sand for company.

As a child, I once kept a Blanding's turtle for a pet until it escaped and likely got squashed beneath someone's belted radials. Blanding's turtles can live a very long time, up to eighty years. A female will always try to lay her eggs where she herself hatched and sometimes gets run over on roads that didn't exist when her own life began. This Blanding's turtle was lucky in that there wasn't a road for at least a mile in any direction. Her only current obstacle was me. Very slowly, the turtle's head emerged from the shell, but if I moved, back it went. Over the course of an hour, four legs appeared and pivoted the turtle toward the willows. By the time I was ready to turn in, she was gone.

The storm held off until midnight, then startled me awake with a noiseless white flash before the rumble of thunder. Rain fell in heavy drops at first then pelting waves. Rain drumming against a tent is one of most pleasant sounds I know. But my one-man tent felt as if it was being power-washed, the sides accordioning in and out with every gust. Except for the strobe-like lightning flashes, everything was pitch dark. I counted the seconds between flashes and the explosions of thunder until they were simultaneous and I knew the storm was directly overhead. I tried to recall how close the nearest tree stood and whether it was tall enough to hit the tent if it fell, but I couldn't remember. One brilliant explosion of light briefly lit up the tent and I saw, wedged between one corner and the rainfly, the shadow of the Blanding's turtle.

Morning broke cool and damp. I stepped from the tent into a dense cloud. Fog hung in tatters over the river so that the bluffs on the far side seemed to rise like mountains out of snow. The rain had turned my canoe into a bathtub and the repairs I'd made to the cracked ribs had come loose in the bilge. Even the Blanding's turtle had abandoned me. Retreating into the tent, I poured yesterday's hot water from the thermos into a plastic cup and, *voilà*, the miracle of instant coffee!

By noon I was back on the river, puttering under a railroad trestle as a BNFS freight train rumbled overhead. A graffiti artist had spray-painted some of the boxcars before sending them out into the world. One swaying boxcar read "Jesus Lives" or maybe it was "Jesus Lies." Hard to tell from a moving boat. Ahead, the river T-boned into the looming green bluffs of Minnesota, the current accelerating as it swept over wing dams and flushed me into the Mississippi.

Mississippi River

~~~~~~~~~~~~~

5

The Mississippi isn't just a river, it's *the* river, the big mamou, the longest river on the continent, second longest in the world (after the Nile), and third in area of drainage. If rain falls west of the Alleghenies or snow melts on the east slope of the Rockies, chances are the water eventually makes its way to the Mississippi. What matters isn't the river's great size so much as its permanent location deep within the national psyche. For most Americans, the Mississippi is the first river they know by name, a name so impossibly long that its spelling marks an educational milestone. School children don't learn to spell it the regular way, phonetically, breaking the long word into shorter syllables; no, they memorize the whole train wreck of eleven letters and sing them out one at a time, an entire classroom ringing with young voices in a continuous rush of breath— *EM-EYE-S-S-EYE-S-S-EYE-PEE-PEE-EYE!* In the process, the name becomes a one-word nursery rhyme about a river not yet actually seen, only read about in books where it's linked to other, equally mysterious names—Père Marquette, Huck Finn, and a baritone stevedore named Joe—twin seams of history and myth running down the middle of the country, music by Oscar Hammerstein, words by Jerome Kern.

"And here for the first time in my life I saw my beloved Mississippi River, dry in the summer haze, low water with its big rank smell that smells like the raw body of America itself." Jack Kerouac, a passenger in a car crossing between Rock Island, Illinois, and Davenport, Iowa, at night not only managed to smell the river from the window of a moving car, he'd already acquired a proprietary interest in it. My first glimpse of the Mississippi likewise came from a moving automobile as I crossed the I-94 bridge on my way to the Twin Cities. The big river was proportioned exactly as Mark Twain described it, wide as a lake and perfect for rafting. I said as much to my passenger, who informed me that we weren't crossing the Mississippi but the St. Croix. When we reached St. Paul another twenty miles further, Ol' Man River was disappointingly narrow and brown and confined to a steep urban gorge.

This time the Mississippi didn't disappoint. It stretched a quarter-mile between the bottomland forest on the Wisconsin side and the steeply canted, green bluffs of Minnesota. For the first time on my trip I needed a chart to see where I was going. Luckily, my spiral-bound *Upper Mississippi River Navigation Charts*, issued by the U.S. Army Corps of Engineers, showed a two-dimensional view of the river, both above and below the surface. At this point, the Mississippi (robin's egg blue) curved between Drury Island (white) and the federally owned backwaters (lime green with crosshatched dark lines) on the Wisconsin side. The continuous red line running down the middle of the river was the nine-foot deep navigation channel. Submerged wing dams and closing dams were clearly marked (red dashes), as well as underwater stump fields (red dots). In addition, government daymarks (red arrowhead) showed mileage to the confluence with the Ohio River. What the charts couldn't reveal was the swirl of boat traffic on a sunny Sunday afternoon in June.

In theory, the nine-foot-deep navigation channel is an orderly, two-lane highway; upstream traffic stays to the left, downstream boats to the right. In practice, the Mississippi on a busy weekend is a free-for-all, a frenetic land-rush held on a strip of water. Parishioners who'd quietly endured an hour of church services were now getting the homily out of their systems by gunning speedboats up and down the river. I'd been warned to steer clear of the big towboats that push long strings of barges and require a half-mile to stop, but the commercial tows were easy to avoid compared to the forty-foot motor yachts powered by 440-horse twin diesels. Some of these ships had saltwater ports painted on their transoms and would not have looked out of place on the Côte d'Azur. By keeping my head on a swivel, I avoided colliding with the powerboats but not the enormous wakes trailing behind them.

A word about wakes: In 1887, British physicist Lord Kelvin delivered a scientific paper, "On Ship Waves," to the Institute of Mechanical Engineers in Edinburgh. In it he proved mathematically how ship wakes follow certain natural laws. "A wave is the progression through matter of a state of motion. The motion cannot take place without the displacement of particles." In practical terms, Kelvin meant that as a ship moves at a constant speed across deep water, it displaces some of that water in the form of two waves that radiate away from the boat in a V-shaped pattern. In "Kelvin's Wedge," each arm of the chevron angles away at a constant 19.5 degrees. The greater the displacement, the higher the wave. Eventually the wave dissipates as it travels further from the boat, but Lord Kelvin was writing about sailing ships on the open sea, not hot-rodding speedboats on a confined river where everything is in a constant state of motion.

A three-foot wave may not look daunting from the elevated cabin of a power yacht, but to anyone sitting in a canoe with ten inches of freeboard it's a tsunami. By turning my bow into waves before they smacked the canoe broadside, I could safely quarter them, but if I missed, *Ms. Leech* would ride up the green slope of water and slam into its trough. Each time that happened, her broken ribs flexed, and

I worried the next time she'd come apart at the seams. A common courtesy of navigation requires large boats to slow when passing smaller craft, but that wasn't the practice on the Mississippi, where the obvious rule of thumb was survival of the biggest and fastest. At first I thought the larger boats simply didn't see me, but as I wallowed in the wake of one particularly enormous power cruiser, its captain, seated in a glassed-in cockpit two stories above me, clearly made eye contact. Without slowing down and keeping one hand on the steering wheel and another on a tall beverage, he raised a toast, one sport to another.

I beached my canoe at the public park beside Slippery's Bar and Grill in Wabasha and placed a call to Bob Elkins. I told him *Ms. Leech* was taking a terrible drubbing. I told him about her cracked ribs and that I worried she and I were headed for a break-up. Elkins listened patiently.

"Damn. That's not good. Stay there. I'll see what I can do."

With a day to kill, I washed and shaved in the public restroom and went for a stroll. The two commercial blocks on Wabasha's Main Street are a showcase of nineteenth-century brickwork: jutting white cornices, fancy corbelled eaves, dentil molding, and arched Italianate windows on the second floor. Beyond architectural embellishments, the buildings were just old redbrick storefronts, most of them closed for Sunday. In the late 1970s Jonathan Raban, a British travel writer, took a boat trip down the Mississippi and spent a night in Wabasha, or *War-bashaw* as he pronounced it, mimicking the locals. (If there's an intrusive *R* in the Midwest dialect, I've long stopped hearing it.) Raban had the travel writer's gift for biting the hand that fed him, winking at the reader while making his hosts sound like yokels. He came away from the river town unimpressed.

"In whatever lottery it was decided which American villages were going to turn into megacities," Raban declared, "Wabasha had clearly drawn a dud ticket."

It's an unfair comparison. Small towns don't compete with big cities; they compete with each other and for the highest stakes—survival. So how does one take the measure of a small town? The number of vacant storefronts on Main Street? The ratio of self-sustaining services like a grocery or hardware store versus art galleries and knickknack shops? One simple yardstick is to track the census over time and see whether the population has grown or declined. In 1895, the date carved on the lintel over the old City Hall, Wabasha had 2,500 residents—about what it has today. By that measure, the city has neither grown nor shrunk; it's been treading water for the last century. Wabasha was holding its own despite losing businesses that once tied it to the river—steamboat traffic, commercial clamming and button factories, and grain elevators. The city had reinvented itself as a tourist destination and retirement community. The towering Big Jo Flour grain elevators along the riverbank had been replaced by new condominiums; there was a busy marina, and a new National Eagle Center where people paid to see bald eagles cavorting overhead. People were rediscovering the river as scenery rather than an engine of commerce. It wasn't the first time that the Mississippi had been offered to the nation as a tourist attraction.

The era of tourism on the Upper Mississippi River officially began at ten o'clock in the evening of June 5, 1854, when a flotilla of seven steamboats, bows wreathed in prairie flowers and bands playing on deck, departed Davenport, Iowa, with great hoopla and headed into the "impenetrable darkness." The Mississippi was at that time the West, the Frontier, the extreme limit of settlement beyond which lay wilderness, so the "darkness" referenced in contemporary newspaper accounts was both figurative and literal. The Midwest did not yet exist. Earlier in the evening, there had been fireworks and speeches on both sides of the river, including remarks by former president Millard Fillmore, the last Whig to occupy the White House. The stout, silver-haired Fillmore and nearly a thousand other politicians, journalists, clergy, academics, business tycoons, writers, and artists had been invited to tour the Upper Mississippi as guests of the newly formed Rock Island Railroad. In February of that year, the last section of track had been laid between Rock Island and Chicago, in effect linking the Mississippi River for the first time with the Atlantic. It would now be possible to travel from New York City to the edge of the frontier in forty-eight hours. Of course, this begged the question of who should want to make this journey. The owners of the railroad concocted an elaborate, all-expenses-paid media junket up the river to promote the territory their railroad had opened to the public. They called it The Grand Excursion.

At the Rock Island terminus, two trainloads of passengers from Chicago were transferred onto five paddlewheelers: the *Galena*, the *Golden Era*, the *Lady Franklin*, the *G. W. Sparhawk*, and the *War Eagle*. When more people showed up than could be accommodated, two more steam packets, the *Black Hawk* and *Jenny Lind*, were added. All but the *Jenny Lind* were sidewheelers with round paddlewheels mounted on each side, enclosed within elaborately decorated sponsons. The wheels could move independently, one put in reverse for quick turning, though with the river running high after a wet spring, dodging sandbars was not yet a problem.

The flotilla pushed single file through the Rock River Rapids and up the Mississippi, passengers on deck enjoying a light breeze after the day's heat. Shortly after midnight, a spectacular thunderstorm struck and the boats disappeared into the downpour and darkness, which was total except when a lightning flash outlined the shore. Morning broke cool and cloudy with a hazy curtain of rain. Below La Crosse, the steamboats encountered several large lumber rafts floating downriver, and the raftsmen cheered and waved their hats at the procession, one firing his rifle by way of salute. Staggered along the river were small settlements and woodcutters' camps on terraces above the river or crowded against the side of a bluff. As the flotilla passed, people emerged from rough-hewn log homes to stand along the shore and wave at the spectacle. The boats resembled a string of floating wedding cakes, two passenger decks stacked below a third hurricane deck with a glassed-in pilot house perched on top, and a pair of tall, ornately topped chimneys belching out sparks and clouds of black smoke. Forbidden to race each other, the steamboats offered other forms of amusements. Passengers on one boat listened to a lecture on the geology of the Mississippi's "mountains," while on another they participated in a mock trial, or they danced to band music or discussed politics in the bar. Meals were served three times a day. The bill of fare aboard the *Galena* offered a full range of domestic meats, fish and fowl as well as wild dishes: prairie chicken, buffalo steak, snipe and quail. Drinking water, drawn directly from the river, was often dosed with spirits.

The steamboats ran night and day. Except for long pauses in Galena and La Crosse for more speeches, they never stopped except to wood-up a couple of times as the boats burned through 20–25 cords of wood a day. One such wood-stop was at the base of Mount Trempealeau, a solitary bluff that rose out of the river like a pyramid. *La montague qui trempe a l'eau* is what early French explorers called it, "the mountain whose foot is bathed in water." The more prosaic Americans called it Montoville. As cordwood was loaded aboard the *Golden Era*, Abbie Fillmore, the ex-president's twenty-two-year-old daughter, borrowed a horse and swiftly rode up the mountain. Reaching the summit, she sat astride her mount and waved a handkerchief, setting off a salvo of steamboat whistles and cheers below. The crowd was less enchanted when a trio of Indians emerged from the woods as the boat prepared to leave. "They are hideous specimens," the editor of the *New Haven Palladium* wrote, "for their faces are painted, except the chin, so they look almost demonical." Passengers leaned over the deck railing to toss coins and sugar plums to the Indians as if they were animals in a zoo.

On the second evening, the flotilla passed the mouth of the Chippewa and into the broad waters of Lake Pepin, a few hours downriver from St. Paul and the end of the voyage. Four steamboats were lashed together so passengers could move between ships and compare accommodations. Most stood on deck and marveled at the passing scenery and debated whether the craggy bluffs along the river reminded them of the Palisades of the Hudson River or the Rhine

Valley between Bingen and Koblenz. "They are unique," wrote novelist Catharine Sedgwick, "they have no likeness—they daguerreotype new pictures on the mind." She also noted, in a private letter home, that "the drinking of these people is inconceivable."

The owners of the Rock Island Railroad never sent out a follow-up survey to determine if the junket was a success, though press coverage in the Eastern newspapers was overwhelmingly positive. Charles Dana, managing editor of the *New York Tribune*, predicted a great future for the nascent towns along the Mississippi. "There is no region on earth, I think which can sustain a larger population than that on both sides of the northern Mississippi," he wrote. "A rich soil, suited to every produce of the temperate zone, and absolutely inviting the hand of the farmer, a climate genial but not enervating, frequent streams to afford water power and fuel abundant on earth, the great river for a highway, and railroads which in forty-eight hours, land the traveller on the Atlantic—with all these advantages the entire country must become the home of one of the freest, most intelligent, most powerful and independent communities of the world."

A sign at the end of the highway bridge connecting Wabasha to Wisconsin welcomes visitors to the home of *Grumpy Old Men*, a Hollywood version of small-town life filmed mostly in the Twin Cities. The lead actors, reprising earlier roles as a pair of feuding New Yorkers, transformed themselves into midwesterners by donning red flannel shirts, bib overalls, galoshes, and Elmer Fudd hats. Wabasha embraced the movie. Every winter it holds a Grumpy Old Men Festival with a cribbage contest, minnow races at the VFW, and an ice-fishing competition in which locals dress up in red flannel shirts, bib overalls, galoshes, and Elmer Fudd hats in a case of life imitating art imitating life.

A poster from the movie's sequel hung in the men's restroom at the Eagle Nest Coffee Haus where I ate lunch. The foursome of retirees at the table next to mine wore Bermuda shorts and pastel polo shirts and didn't seem in the least grumpy. A young waitress in a full-sleeve tattoo served them coffee as they argued the merits of marijuana, not the cultivated variety but the kind that grows wild on the ragged edge of farm fields.

"Guy took some weed home and dried and smoked it."

"What?"

"I said he tried *smoking* the stuff."

"Oh."

"He said all it does is give you a headache."

The old men smiled and shook their heads.

I spent the rest of the day in the park where I'd left the canoe. It was cooler in the shade and a park bench offered a bucolic view of the Mississippi, smooth dark water with green bluffs rising in the distance; even the frenetic boat traffic looked pretty from land. The tableau on shore was constantly changing. A family of pale redheads spread a brown blanket on the grass while the youngest, a little flame-haired girl, played tag with waves as they lapped on the beach . . . one . . . after . . . another. Two young men bobber-fished from the beach, identical twins except one had a white prosthetic leg. A skinny old man climbed into a folding chair; he wore a flesh-colored Speedo and had the alarming habit of crossing his legs. None of these people possessed a boat or seemed interested in swimming, yet all seemed perfectly content to spend Sunday afternoon by the river, basking in its beauty and power.

I struck up a conversation with a man throwing a tennis ball into the water for his black Labrador to fetch. His arm was going to wear out before the dog did.

"Do you hunt her?" I asked.

"No. I'm retired military. Never stayed in one place long enough to get to know it, so I don't hunt." He sounded almost apologetic. "There's more things I like to do in Wabasha than the Twin Cities, so I moved here." He'd bought a bluff-top house next to a golf course and liked playing a round in good weather. The river was scenery to him and a place to exercise his dog. The lab was swimming around with a puzzled look because the tennis ball had sunk. When the fisherman with the prosthetic leg cast a red and white bobber about the size of the missing tennis ball near her, the lab went for it.

The park was in long shadows when Elkins rolled in towing another canoe. He tried parking his van and boat trailer at Slippery's Bar and Grill but gave up and drove around the block.

"Meet me at the boat landing at the other side of the park," he shouted.

I started the outboard and steered *Ms. Leech* up an inlet, past the marina's gas dock and slips to a boat landing where Elkins was waiting. He looked over the cracked ribs.

"Never saw that coming. All I can think is that when I ratcheted the sides in, there wasn't enough give so that's why the ribs cracked. Shee . . . it."

He backed the trailer up and slid the new canoe into the water, a seventeen-foot Alumacraft with a fantailed transom, a wider beam than *Ms. Leech*, and a factory paint job designed to blend into cattails. Elkins had bought it that afternoon from a duck hunter who'd used it as a set boat in the river bottoms near Wabasha. I wasn't going to make the mistake of naming it this time. After Elkins and I transferred the outboard and gear to the new canoe, I asked if I could buy him dinner but he wanted to hit the road while there was still light.

"You saved my life, pal."

"No I didn't," Elkins said and drove away.

That night I camped on a high island across the river from Wabasha. The next morning a deep throbbing woke me, as if the whole island was vibrating. It was the big diesel engine of a towboat. A towboat doesn't *tow*, it pushes, and this one was pushing a phalanx of nine barges upriver. As the three-story towboat passed, its white pilothouse was level with my tent. The rest of the river was deserted, the pleasure boats snug in their marina slips. After partying hard all weekend, the Mississippi had returned to work sober and resolute, emptied of all but the most earnest travelers.

6

Below Wabasha, the Mississippi enters a deep gorge, as beautiful and imposing a stretch of river as anywhere on earth, fringed with floodplain forest at the bottom and walled in at the top by towering, castellated bluffs. When travelers on The Grand Excursion wrote of "mountains" along the Mississippi, this is the stretch they had in mind. When they compared the scenery to the Hudson River Palisades or the Rhine Valley, they meant this portion of the Mississippi hemmed in with bluffs on either side. The limestone bluffs reach no more than five hundred feet above the water, yet the rise is so abrupt that they have the visual impact of mountains. The gorge runs down the center of the Driftless Area, so called because the land wasn't flattened by the last ice age and lacks the telltale layer of glacial sediment or "drift." Rushing water, not glaciers, carved the convoluted terrain, a jumble of sharp ridges and narrow, incisive valleys, and the straightest path through it, even today, remains the Mississippi.

This morning I had the whole lovely stretch of river to myself except for the passing towboat crew, who were too busy to appreciate it. With no wind or chop, I opened the throttle to see what the new canoe could do. The bow rose and the canoe planed out across the broad lake formed by the backwaters of the Alma lock and dam. It was wonderful to enjoy the scenery without worrying about boat wakes or the canoe breaking apart at the seams. Then I noticed a Styrofoam cup float past my feet followed by a candy wrapper. An inch of water lay in the bottom of the hull and I turned around to find the river spilling over the fantail transom. I killed the throttle and the backflow from the stern stopped, but the canoe kept taking on water, not enough to sink but enough for my feet to slosh around in. Suddenly I felt like Jonah, a jinx in whatever boat I set foot. Goodbye cracked ribs, hello slow leak. Ahead loomed Twelve Mile Bluff, which meant I'd only covered twelve miles since leaving the mouth of the Chippewa. I'd have made better progress walking. Bailing with one hand and steering the tiller with the other, I limped slowly toward shore.

The marina at Alma rents houseboats and dock slips, sells gas and bait, and—more importantly—makes boat repairs. The repairman diagnosed the leak in my canoe as the result of loose rivets and said the aluminum hull needed "pinging."

"Pinging?"

Pinging, he explained, is the sound a ball-peen hammer makes when applied expertly to a loose rivet. Apparently, the canoe needed a heavy dose of onomatopoeia. At any rate, he was in the middle of overhauling a jonboat and couldn't "ping" my canoe for another day, but he'd let me camp in the boatyard while I waited. I pitched my tent next to a cruiser shrouded in blue shrink-wrap and walked to town.

Because Alma lies at the foot of a steep bluff, its marina and park are located a mile north of town on land reclaimed from the river. Traffic whooshed along Highway 35 as I walked the mile into Alma in the rising heat. I passed a Kwik-Trip, Kathy Kut & Kurl, the Dam

View Bar, the lock and dam itself, and VFW Post 224. A sign in front of the VFW: "Best Town By A Dam Site." In all of Buffalo County there's only a single traffic light and it isn't in Alma. The town shares a narrow bench above the river with two parallel streets and a pair of busy railroad tracks. Traffic slowed through Alma because one of the streets was being torn up. I was hoping for coffee and homemade muffins at Kassel City Drugs, where I'd stopped a few years earlier, but when I got there the door was locked. A note taped to the window explained: "To our beloved customers: It is with heavy heart for our community that we must announce we are closing at the end of the month. Unfortunately, the Alma area no longer has enough business to sustain a pharmacy." The letter went on to list contributing factors, but they all added up to the same thing, not enough customers.

Having just left Wabasha, which has two drugstores, I found it hard not to compare Alma with its neighbor across the river. Both are county seats, river towns with old, red brick Main Streets lined with art galleries and gift shops; both compete for the same tourist traffic down the Great River Road. If anything, Alma is the prettier town, its view of the Mississippi more elevated, its lovely old homes clinging picturesquely to the hillside. But Alma is a prisoner of its own geography, hemmed in by perpendicular bluffs on one side and the river and a railroad on the other. The town's population had peaked in the 1890s at 1,428, twice what it is now. If Wabasha was treading water, Alma had developed a slow leak over the years. The only major difference between the two towns that I could see was that Wabasha had a bridge across the Mississippi and Alma didn't.

Kitty-corner from the shuttered pharmacy stood the Alma Hotel. It's one of the oldest buildings on Main Street, though I didn't realize how old until I walked inside and saw the thick limestone walls, which kept the hotel cool in the summer heat and muffled the din of road construction. There was a bar and café on the ground floor and a warren of small rooms on the second. A handwritten sign behind the kitchen counter warned "Do Not Cash Checks From . . ." and listed two names. A little tentatively, I asked the waitress at the café if it was still possible to order breakfast.

She handed me a menu and sang, "Breakfast, lunch and dinner. Every meal's a winner."

At that moment, I knew I'd come to the right place. A few minutes later she returned with a plate of fried eggs, sausage links, hash browns, toast, and coffee. She had short brown hair and an excess of energy. I asked if having Main Street torn up had hurt business.

"We're down, way down," she admitted but she wasn't worried since the hotel had weathered other storms. "This place has been operating since 1853. The bar, café, hotel. It's never closed."

The Grand Excursion hadn't stopped in Alma on its way up the Mississippi, but if it had, passengers would have seen this hotel, then called the Union House. It rented out a dozen small rooms on the second floor. Now there were eleven, one room having been converted to a shared bath.

"The rooms aren't fancy. No TV, no radio, no clock, just a bed in a small room. Most of the people come for the river and they come to fish or hunt. Most of them are older folks from Chicago. And they've been coming for years and years."

The waitress took a proprietary interest in the hotel because she owned the place. Jerri Schreiber had grown up in Alma, left town after high school, then returned to sell real estate. When she saw the Alma Hotel came up for sale, Jerri and her husband bought it.

"My dad and mom grew up in Alma, and their parents grew up in Alma as well, so I'm third generation. I lived in Minneapolis and Milwaukee after college. I moved back permanently when I was twenty-six because I couldn't live in a place where I was anonymous. If I go to the post office here, it takes me an hour because I know everyone in town."

Anyone who returns to a childhood home after a prolonged absence experiences the shrinking effect, the sense that things have gotten smaller. It's one of the sentimental traps of nostalgia. But in Jerri's case, the experience was literal. The town had not physically shrunk, but it was no longer the thriving, self-sufficient place she'd known as a child.

"When I grew up, we'd drive to Winona maybe once a month. Everything that you needed was right here in Alma. Three grocery stores, a shoe store, variety store, a hardware store. There were thirteen bars in Alma. Where the post office is, that was a bar. My dad walked to work. He was a barber. He was also a commercial setline fisherman. A lot of people made a living fishing the river then."

Commercial fishing was a family operation. After school, Jerri and her siblings would go out on a boat and put out the setlines for catfish: eight lines with a hundred hooks apiece. Bait depended on the season. Minnows cut into segments were the mainstay, but in midsummer their father would drive his truck around a field with a net to catch grasshoppers or go to the Nelson Bottoms to catch crayfish, or if a farmer slaughtered a hog he'd buy the coagulated blood in a five-gallon pail and cut it for bait. Baited lines were put out every evening and pulled the next morning at sunup. Jerri's mother had a technique for cleaning catfish, using a little baseball bat for the *coup de grâce,* then sticking one end of the bat in the fish's mouth to snap its neck, so she could pull the entrails out along with the head. Every day the family took three hundred to five hundred pounds of fish to sell in Pepin. Then in the 1970s pollution in the Mississippi worsened and the fish market plummeted.

Jerri and her husband had bought the Alma Hotel in part to keep it from closing. Running a hotel in a small town was not a simple undertaking.

"The last owner was struggling financially. The gal was losing it to the bank, and the bank said they were going to close it. I thought: It can't close. It opened in 1853, for gosh sakes. The hardest thing on a bar and restaurant are the convenience stores. Fishermen used to stop at a café. Now they get gas and grab a sandwich. People come here because they want to visit. You feel lonely, just come down here."

At that moment another customer, an older gent in a plaid sport coat, strolled into the café and called out, "Hey good looking!"

"Here comes trouble," Jerri said under her breath, but to the man in plaid she said, "You look like you've lost weight."

He patted his tummy. "I've been chasing my wife around. Hey, how's the potato salad? I hear it's pretty good."

Almost twenty years ago, the MacArthur Foundation awarded a grant to a husband and wife team of sociologists to study the depopulation of small towns in the Midwest. Patrick Carr and Maria Kefalas moved from their home in Philadelphia to a small town in northeastern Iowa, not unlike Alma, to better understand the exodus of the young, and often the brightest, from the communities that had nurtured them. After surveying almost three hundred former students from the town's high school, the sociologists came up with three categories: Leavers, Stayers, and Returners. Leavers were the people you'd expect, kids whose trajectory in life was a steady upward arc—leadership in school and sports, high SAT scores, a college acceptance letter, and never looking back. Stayers, on the other hand, entered full-blown adulthood directly after high school graduation, if not sooner; they married early, had babies, and often settled for low-paying jobs in the area. The bumper sticker "MY KID BEAT UP YOUR HONOR ROLL STUDENT" expresses exactly the resentment of people for whom education seems a divided highway with smart kids bound for opportunity and the C students headed for a dead end. In their book, *Hollowing Out the Middle: The Rural Brain Drain and What It Means for America*, Carr and Kefalas write that "small towns play an unwitting part in their own decline" by habitually grooming the Leavers to leave and the Stayers to stay. The Stayers may be hard workers but not innovators; they don't create the new jobs small towns need to survive. If there's any hope for rural communities, it's the third category, Returners. They're the ones who go out in the world then reverse course at some point and bring their acquired skills home. Jerri Schreiber was a Returner and so was Kenny Salwey.

7

Kenneth James Salwey was born on his grandparents' farmstead in Yeager Valley on a hot summer day in 1943. The valley was a separate world. To understand just how separate, you'd need to consult the 1932 topographic map of Buffalo County created by the Wisconsin Geographical Survey, state geologist E. F. Bean presiding. It's a stunning piece of cartography with azure rivers and streams and deep umber contour lines so densely packed together they look like a slice of Switzerland. The map was drawn a year before the Corps of Engineers began construction of a series of locks and dams along the Upper Mississippi that flooded sloughs and backwaters behind the Alma dam. In a sense, the map depicts a place that no longer exists. Nowhere is that more obvious than in the ridge and coulee country beyond the river where place names—Norwegian Valley, Irish Valley, French Valley, Jahn's Valley, Weisenberg Valley, Joos Valley—reveal a rural society long since disassembled. Each immigrant group claimed at least one incisive, stream-cut valley with its own church (a black square with a cross on top), one-room school (a black square with a flag on top), and cemetery (a blue square with cross inside). A child could be baptized, educated, married, and eventually buried all within the same semi-autonomous valley.

Growing up in Yeager Valley, Kenny Salwey enjoyed a mixed-sports childhood: fishing for trout in spring-fed creeks, trapping gophers for the bounty, and riding the neighbor's workhorses. During the war years, farmers continued to plow by horse instead of tractor because a team of horses was less likely to fall off a steep hillside. Salwey's formal education began with a half-mile walk to a one-room school in adjacent Waumandee Valley. After sixth grade, he matriculated to public school in Cochrane (pop. 453), then to the consolidated Cochrane-Fountain City High School, a process that had the unstated goal of moving children from their own narrow valleys into the wider world. Like other rural boys with no chance of college and a desire to see far horizons, Salwey followed up high school graduation by joining the military.

In the 32nd Infantry Division, Salwey received survival training in the rain forests of Washington State, but his real education in living off the land commenced after his hitch in the army was up. Salwey worked as a carpenter and roofer in Alma while honing his own survival skills in the nearby six-thousand-acre Whitman Swamp. He built a pair of tarpaper shacks and a floating tent camp as bases for hunting and trapping. He earned a reputation as a river guide and gatherer of wild foods and medicine, not to mention a recluse and occasional poacher. Solitary evenings he read by lantern light— Thoreau, Leopold, John Muir—writers who shaped and validated his own views of the natural world. He began scribbling observations on the square pages of bank calendars, fitting his thoughts or things he'd seen in the swamp onto the blank space surrounding the date. A reporter doing a profile on Salwey suggested he try his hand at writing a magazine column. He wrote one for five years and the collected columns became a book, the first of many. Then a British filmmaker produced a documentary about Salwey called *Mississippi: Tales of the*

Last River Rat and the loner became, incongruously, famous. Small town reputations die hard, however. When I told the ping-man at the Alma marina who I was waiting for, he immediately perked up. "Friend of mine went to high school with Kenny Salwey. Said he was a real wild man back then."

An hour later the wild man arrived in a pickup truck. A thick-chested man with a weather-beaten face and a brindled beard, Salwey was on his way to see an eye doctor.

"My left eye is going blurry. Seventy-two years old and I've gotten along without spectacles until now. My dad used to say the golden years were interesting because every morning you wake up and find something new that doesn't work."

With his one good eye, Kenny looked over my canoe.

"If it leaks when you throttle it, that means you got a seam that can't handle the pressure. I'd lend you a canoe, got eleven of them, but none is registered for an outboard. They're all in the swamp, scattered around. I put 'em all over the place so I don't have to portage. Portaging and I don't get along."

Salwey was a self-described slow-talker. He spoke in a hushed baritone so resonantly deliberate that it sounded as if he was smoking each word slowly over an open fire. He no longer lived in a swamp but in a house with his wife near Little Waumaudee Creek, not far from the one-room school he'd attended as a child. He preferred it to the larger schools that followed where kids were trained to move from room to room at the sound of a bell "like cattle." In the one-room school he'd always carried a jackknife in his pocket. He might have gotten into arguments—even fistfights with other boys who also carried jackknives in their pockets—but the knives never came out. The more people crowded together, he concluded, the less courteous they became. The same dynamic was true of the Mississippi River. Increased boat traffic on the river was one reason he kept to the backwaters.

"The thing about the Mississippi is that there's a lot that can go wrong. You have all the towboats and pleasure boats, mini-yachts I call 'em. Wing dams are wonderful places to fish but you can't hold a boat on them because of the wave action of the pleasure boats. They throw a treacherous wake because they're going so fast. There's a certain etiquette on the river. The angler knows when to go. Somehow that's not been passed down. The worst places are Wabasha and Winona because they have the big marinas. The river belongs to everyone. Now it's like the interstate. Nobody looks at anyone. They just drive. They just burn gas. I guess that's a reflection of our society. I don't mean to sound like an old curmudgeon, but some things are on the decline and common courtesy is one of them."

Kenny Salwey didn't strike me as a curmudgeon or a wild man or a recluse. He seemed, to use an old-fashioned term, courtly, and that code of manners, even more than his survival skills, made him both remarkable and an anachronism. The problem, he believed, was that people moved too fast through the world to get to know any one place, much less care about it. Kenny wore the dried claw of a snapping turtle on a leather thong around his neck. He identified with turtles. They were his totem animal, slow moving but tough, adapted to living on land and water or some combination of both.

"There have been studies," said Kenny, "where they put rubber turtles on a road and sometimes on the shoulder of the road and some people, not a lot but enough, will try and hit them. There's no respect. A rabbit or a deer can jump out of the way but turtles will hardly move. They were the first mobile homes. That's why turtles are never in a hurry. They just pull their feet inside and they're home."

The U.S. Army Corps of Engineers is charged with maintaining a nine-foot navigation channel to allow commercial barge traffic to go up and down the Mississippi. The channel and the lock and dam system help keep the region's economy afloat. At public expense, the Corps continuously dredges the river bottom and deposits the sand at spoil sites like the one between the marina park's baseball diamond and the railroad tracks running parallel to the river. The sand is available, free of charge, to anyone who'll haul it away, and there was always a long line of dump trucks waiting at the spoil site. As I walked back toward town, I saw that one of the private haulers had painted a message in red on the door of his dump truck: "I wanted to be a crook when I grew up, but the government beat me to it."

Back at the Alma Hotel, the bartender brought me a glass of beer then set a raffle ticket and a cup of dice next to it.

"There are ten dice," she explained. "You need to roll seven of a kind in three rolls or less."

What a friendly place, I thought. Every time you bought a drink, you got a raffle ticket. The drawing for the raffle would be in an hour, but in the meantime I could roll for the drink.

My first roll came up three snake eyes and a pair of boxcars. I rolled again. Another pair of snake eyes! One more pair and I'd win. I covered the cup with the palm of my hand and rattled the dice before spilling them onto the bar. A single snake-eye.

"Oh, so close," said the bartender, removing a dollar bill from my change. She was skinny and appealing in a waif-like sort of way though I was safely beyond the age of flirting with barmaids.

"Can I roll again?"

"No. You can only roll the first time you're served. You'd have to wait for the next shift and I'm working all night."

"In Minnesota, that's illegal," a male voice boomed from the end of the bar, a voice that made the last word sound like "ill eagle." "It's a stupid law because that's a personal bet. The bar isn't gambling, the bartender is. That's what happens when the government gets involved in anything—stupidity."

The evening news came on the television and I watched it with Steve, the legal scholar at the end of the bar. The bartender felt the need to keep the conversation going, so each time Lester Holt read a dispatch from the greater world, she'd comment on it. When Holt reported two convicts had escaped from a high-security prison in up-state New York, the bartender declared, "They had power tools, so it wasn't like *The Shawshank Redemption* or anything." When the escapees' mug shots flashed on the screen, two nondescript men in green prison fatigues, she said, "Look at those guys. They just look like criminals." When the TV screen shifted to footage of a Florida policeman wrestling a black teenage girl to the ground, the bartender said, "Cops can't get away with anything anymore. Everyone has a cellphone camera."

If the bartender treated the nightly news as a kind of sing-along, Steve took it as a personal affront. He glowered through most of Lester Holt's monologue, but the anchorman's shiny gray suit was what really set him on edge. "What do you suppose a suit like that costs?" he asked though he wasn't asking a question but blowing a dog-whistle to see if anyone heard it. What he really meant to say was, "Where does this black guy get off wearing a $500 suit?" Steve wasn't bothered by the suit so much as the skin underneath it. And if the innocuous Holt and his fancy threads annoyed Steve, the sight of President Barack Obama hobnobbing with other world leaders at the G-8 Summit made him positively apoplectic.

"They oughta send that guy back to where he came from."

"And where would that be," I asked. "Hawaii?"

"Ha! That's what they want you to think! When he went to college, they listed him as a foreign student."

I was trying to be nice and that was the problem. Small towns don't make small minds—Kenny Salwey was proof of that—but they'll tolerate one. Midwest Nice, the ingrained habit of meeting trouble with silence or a grin, isn't really politeness or good manners but a kind of fatalism borne of the belief that it's better to take abuse than risk making a scene. In the end, it only encourages bad behavior. There was something of the naughty boy about Steve. Like most barstool bigots, he'd probably swallowed some disappointment in life that metastasized over time into a deep sense of aggrievement. His carping about the dark Other may have been a smoke screen for his own sorry-ass existence, but doing it in public made us complicit. Nobody agreed with Steve, but then neither of us told him to shut up.

Obama was still on the television and Steve kept fuming: "Imagine being a black guy and President of the United States. Imagine killing all those little white babies . . ."

Instead of babies, I imagined turtles, a line of baby terrapins, newly hatched and staggered along the shoulder of Highway 35, slowly making their way to the river. And I imagined a car hurtling down the highway in the dark toward them with Steve, white-knuckled behind the wheel, swerving onto the shoulder to squash every . . . single . . . last . . . turtle.

When the evening news finished, the bartender drew the winning lottery ticket. There were only two of us at the bar so my chances were better than fair, but Steve held the winning stub.

"Oh, you won the Frisbee!" Jerri cried as she came in from the café and saw Steve clutching the grand prize: a neon pink Frisbee. "Too bad you weren't here yesterday. We gave away a trip to Hawaii!"

The women hooted as Steve tucked the Frisbee under his arm and stood to leave. He wasn't from Alma, I was glad to hear, not a Leaver or a Stayer or a Returner, just a big-mouth from Minnesota. When I asked why he drove across the river just to drink, he nodded sadly in the skinny bartender's direction and slipped out the door.

A perfect summer evening. Blue haze hanging over the bluffs, an orange disc of sun rolling down an incline into the cottonwoods, a train *whoo-whooing* past the ballpark every ten minutes, a cool breeze wafting off the river, carrying with it the good smell of French fries in hot oil and hamburgers on a grill.

I sat in the bleachers beside the concession stand undecided which girls' softball team to root for. Both were small-town teams in nearly identical uniforms—red T-shirt and red baseball cap—although Elmwood's had a white E stenciled on the crown and Alma's didn't. The girls seemed interchangeable as well, though not to the parents in the bleachers. The mothers in particular appeared to be attached by invisible wires to the players on the field. When their daughters walked to the plate, the mothers' shoulders would slump forward in a batting stance or twitch spasmodically in the rare case a pitch was hittable or shrug when a player struck out. Mostly, though, they called out encouragement, a chorus of hopeful voices that drowned out even passing trains.

"C'mon Maggie! Be a hitter!"

"Let's go Emilee! You got it! Two more! C'mon Emileeeeeeeeee!"

Emilee was on the mound for Alma. She'd struck out two Elmwood batters; now the count was one strike and three balls. If Maggie just waited patiently, odds were she'd get walked, but the voices from the bleachers called for direct action. "Step into the pitch," they shouted, "and swing." So Maggie did just that and . . . *thwack!* The softball rose heavily in midair then dropped to the ground and rolled into the first baseman's glove. Now it was Alma's turn at bat.

"Be ready outfield!"

"C'mon Elmwood! Let's hold 'em!"

I don't even like baseball. The pace is too slow, the players too spread out to enjoy on television. The last time I went to a major league ballpark the game bored me to tears. So why was I watching girls fast-pitch softball on a sultry evening in June and enjoying myself to no end? I suspect it's because in a small town the national pastime reverts to its nineteenth-century origins, a game played by farmers on a village green—the outfield thrumming with insects, familiar voices hanging in the warm air.

"Nice pitch Anna! Way to go! Right to the glove Anna! You can do it!"

The strawberry blonde Anna had a habit of putting her tongue against the side of her mouth when she'd lean forward to study the batter. She'd tug the brim of her cap then go into a windmill wind-up and let fly. The wild pitch beaned a big girl from Alma, who winced and limped to first base.

By the end of the third inning, I was rooting for the home team. Who wouldn't want to retire here, I thought—the narrow streets and rugged bluffs, the great river sliding past—though towns like Alma don't need another pensioner. Too many beautiful places have been given over to retirees and absentee landlords. Towns like Alma need fewer old people and more youth, which was what was currently on display here. Besides, the appeal of small-town life is precisely the generational mix, grandparents and cousins no farther than a bicycle ride away. The softball players were of an age, ten to twelve, when the circumscribed lives of aunts and uncles didn't necessarily set a limit on their own possibilities. The girls could still believe that nothing has to be given up. You could imagine a star turn on Broadway while still sleeping in your own bed at night. Sooner or later, though, they'd learn about trade-offs in life, choices to be made, and the first and most difficult would be whether to stay or to go.

"C'mon Brianna! You can do it!"

Brianna whiffed the first pitch then hit to the infield, advancing the big girl to second base. Another batter approached the plate, resigned to being walked or beaned, and let a perfectly good pitch sail past.

"Be ready Maggie! That one was yours!"

"Two runners, guys! Two runners! Outfield, get ready."

Maggie faked a bunt then pulled back but not in time.

"Two out. Throw to third!"

The girls in the outfield had so little to do they cradled their gloves like dolls and stared at the lengthening shadows. If you only watched the young players wilting in the heat, you saw only discouragement or ineptitude or, worse, an attack of yawns. But if you shut your eyes and just listened, you experienced an altogether different game. Baseball, like most games, is about time, the passage of it, and even if the players on the field were oblivious to its ticking clock, their parents in the stands weren't. They understood the game as a small segment in a much longer interval of time called childhood that they hoped, beyond hope, would go into extra innings. Years from now, if they wanted to remember Maggie or Brianna or Anna at age ten or twelve, they could reach back and recall this very game or one like it on a warm evening of a long ago summer. What you heard in the voices calling from the stands, women's voices, was a

8

In the morning, my canoe freshly pinged, I rejoined the Mississippi exactly where I'd left it—above the lock and dam at Alma. Avoiding the turbulence of the spillway gates, I skirted the bull-nosed guide wall along the shore until the lock gates were in sight. Nobody was visible outside the red-roofed lock building, so I shifted into neutral and waited. There's a bell attached to a rope recessed into the guide wall for boaters to announce themselves, but I'd brought along a handheld marine radio. Turning to Channel 14, I addressed the lock operator in a hearty imitation captain's voice: "Southbound canoe approaching lock."

Nothing. I tried again. "Southbound canoe approaching lock."

This would be my first time locking through and I didn't want to make any mistakes. Kenny Salwey had coached me on the procedure. Nothing to it, he'd said, so long as I didn't tie my canoe to the lock chamber. Then he told me an awful story about a young woman who'd made that mistake going through the lock and dam above

Winona. She'd tied her bowline to the ladder on the side of the lock chamber then watched as the chamber filled with water, and her boat was dragged down. The woman frantically attempted to cut the line with a knife only to have the blade bounce back and cut her throat. She bled to death in minutes. Immediately I regretted hearing the story, but Salwey had told it with such urgency that I assumed the girl had died earlier in the summer or perhaps the summer before. In fact the fatal accident had occurred forty years ago, a cautionary tale passed down from one generation of river travelers to another. Not wanting to become another sad story, I continued to bob in the water, occasionally using a paddle to keep my canoe straight, until a voice broke through the static: "Stand off. Be about four or five minutes."

Finally, an air horn blew and the massive steel gates slowly opened outward. I pulled on the outboard's starter cord and put-putted into the lock chamber, cut the engine, and watched the gates close behind me. The chamber was the size of two football fields laid end to end, a tight fit for a commercial towboat with a string of barges two across but absurdly spacious for a seventeen-foot canoe. A tanned face appeared over the railing and asked if I wanted a mooring line. I did. A rope was lowered and I remembered not to tie off but hold it loosely in my hand as the canoe began to drop. The water in the chamber made a sucking sound as it dropped seven feet below the high-water stain on the concrete walls. The chamber was dank and fish-smelling and now framed a blue rectangle of sky. Eleven million gallons of river had been displaced for my personal benefit. Moses parting the Red Sea couldn't have been more efficient.

"How far are you going?"

The tanned face had reappeared over the wall to haul in the rope.

"Prairie du Chien," I said with a certain amount of pride.

"We had two canoes come through yesterday," the lockmaster shouted down to me. "Not too many square-sterns though. Most of the canoeists we see are paddling all the way to New Orleans. There's supposed to be an ex-Navy Seal coming through this summer. Started up at Lake Itasca. He's *swimming* the whole river."

"Oh."

The air horn sounded, the lower gates opened, and I entered the head of Pool 5 in my motorized canoe that I now considered naming the SS *Cream Puff.*

On the Upper Mississippi, the stretch of water between dams is called a "pool." Since joining the Mississippi at its confluence with the Chippewa, I had been continuously traveling on Pool 4, at forty-five miles the longest on the river. Leaving the lock chamber at Alma, I'd entered Pool 5, among the shortest at only fourteen miles. The twenty-seven locks and dams strung along the Upper Mississippi act like stringers on a staircase to even out the four-hundred-foot drop between St. Paul and St. Louis, allowing boats to step up or down the river a pool at a time. In a sense, each pool is a separate river, separated from other segments by concrete dams that regulate its height and flow. A free-flowing river gradually changes shape and speed over its entire length from headwaters to mouth, usually running narrow and fast at the beginning where the gradient is steepest and then it broadens and slows down as the river fans out into a delta. The dams on the Upper Mississippi repeat this sequence of river morphology over and over again.

The head of Pool 5 is a vision of the pre-dam Mississippi, fast-flowing and heavily wooded along its banks, trees draped with blue herons and white egrets. It's Ol' Man River unbowed, a stretch that passengers aboard the Grand Excursion would have recognized, at least until they neared the bottom of the pool where formerly big islands had been reduced to a string of marshy atolls. Certainly they would have wondered upon reaching Lock and Dam 5 why the young river had broadened into a sluggish lake.

Winona was the largest city I'd encountered so far on the Mississippi. I might have paid more attention to its impressive skyline sliding past on the starboard side—the towering Richardsonian county courthouse with its turrets and arched windows—if not for the sudden swarm of speedboats. Kenny Salwey had warned me about cities with marinas. On a warm summer afternoon they were a minefield to anyone in a small boat. The runabouts towing water skiers and forty-foot power yachts were bad enough; more alarming from my perspective was the addition of personal watercraft. Jet skis shot from the marina with a high-pitched whine and arching roostertails. While powerboats leave a predictable wake in their paths, jet skis dispense multiple wakes that radiate in all directions. Their riders don't go anywhere, they corkscrew across the water, jump each other's wakes and generally create a stir. After one close call, I beached my canoe on a spoil island below the city and waited for the fun crowd to go home.

At sunset, the temperature dropped and the Mississippi became a different river—placid and deserted, its shoreline utterly wild. Of course, this wildness was wishful thinking. Highways and railroad tracks lined either bank, but they weren't visible from the river. After the traffic jam beside Winona, the quiet was palpable. I threaded my way through a narrow channel formed by a mile-long rock causeway built to carry railroad tracks up the middle of Pool 6. Had a train streaked by at that moment, it would have appeared to be running on water.

The setting sun cast the Minnesota shore into a cool shadow even as it threw a slanting shaft of church light across the river onto Mount Trempealeau. Rising four hundred feet above the river, it isn't a mountain but an isolated bluff cut off by the mouth of the Trempealeau River. Now the whole of it, from the oak canopy at its foot to the goat prairie at its peak, was bathed in a painterly glow. For a moment I had a sense of déjà vu because I'd seen this identical view in a nineteenth-century painting by Alfred Thompson Bricher, *On the Mississippi near Winona, Minnesota—Shower Clearing.* The artist must have set up his easel on a Minnesota blufftop and looked downriver. What he saw then was what I was seeing now, minus the elevation. When I first saw Bricher's painting in a Winona museum, I'd dismissed it as so much Romantic varnish applied to the landscape. Yet here it was—same luminescent light, the same variegated foliage—as if no time had elapsed between Bricher's passage and my own. Just then, and I couldn't make this stuff up, an enormous flight of geese flew *over* Mount Trempealeau. Only they were much larger than geese with long white wings that beat so slowly and rhythmically the birds seemed to be rowing across the sky. It was the sort of detail even the most shameless of Romantic artists would have rejected as too improbable. With the camera in my head, I took a snapshot of the birds then hurried to get off the river by nightfall.

Those were pelicans," the ruddy-faced man at the bar said in a slight German accent. "American white pelicans. They migrate up from the gulf this time of year. They're clumsy and awkward on the ground, but in the air they're absolutely graceful."

I'd lugged my duffel bag from the marina to the Trempealeau Hotel in the dark. The restaurant was closed but the owner, Joerg Droll, the man who'd identified the pelicans, let me order a hamburger from the kitchen. I ate it at the bar where Joerg and a young bartender were watching the NBA playoffs. Joerg owned the Trempealeau Hotel with his wife, Amy. They'd met in Berlin where she'd worked in marketing for an internet company and he edited a magazine. The couple moved to the states and lived on both coasts before heading inland to Amy's old stomping grounds. She'd bartended at the Trempealeau Hotel in college and when it came up for sale they bought it. Like the Alma Hotel, it was old, built in 1868, and there were small rooms upstairs, but the Trempealeau Hotel drew a younger, more upscale crowd from nearby La Crosse and Winona. The restaurant offered farm-to-table cuisine with dishes like Ribeye Marchand Du Vin in a wine and shallot reduction sauce, and there were summer concerts under the stars. Had I arrived two weeks earlier, I could have ordered jerked chicken at the hotel's annual Reggae Festival.

Like most Europeans, Joerg's first glimpse of the Mississippi River came in the pages of a Mark Twain novel. He'd read *Die Abenteuer des Tom Sawyer* as a ten-year-old until the cavern scene with Injun Joe frightened him so much he put the book aside. In middle school he took up the novel's more complex sequel.

"When you're from Germany and you're not familiar with American geography and read *Huckleberry Finn*, you think the Mississippi River only goes through the South. I had no idea it went through the Midwest as well. It's very different from a river like the Rhine, which is deeper and carries no sand or silt so there are no river bottoms. Here you really feel like you're getting away from civilization."

From the hotel's front door Joerg could look down the street at three-story white tugs sliding past. He confessed that whenever he saw one, he felt a tug of wanderlust; the crewmen reminded him of Huck and Jim on the raft, living on the river, waking every day to different scenery. I ordered another beer and dusted off my old lecture notes. Twain had written *Huckleberry Finn* in fits and starts, I told Joerg, uncertain as to whether he was writing a boy's adventure story or a morality tale. The split runs through the novel, playing a runaway slave's journey for laughs in one chapter and dead serious in the next. Like most great novels, *Huckleberry Finn* gets some things right and other things wrong. Twain is embarrassing on race, for instance, but spot-on about the competing impulses in American life: the desire for stability versus the attractions of unrestricted freedom. For Jim the two are linked. He has to flee home to win back his wife and children. But Huck, who has no family, dabbles in both impulses. He has no destination other than the river itself and every time he leaves it and settles into something like normalcy—among the Grangerfords, for instance—things turn violent. So the novel's central question becomes whether absolute freedom is worth the ensuing chaos and bloodshed. Twain sidesteps the answer at the end by retroactively freeing Jim and having Aunt Sally adopt Huck so she can "sivilize" him, but for his countrymen the question remains open.

"In this country," said Joerg, "especially *this* part of the country, people are willing to give up some control in exchange for personal freedom. I was back in Germany two weeks ago, and for western Europeans the amount of gun-related violence is something we couldn't justify. I had enough exposure to weapons when I was in the military. A rifle with a sixteen-shot, nine-millimeter magazine is for a professional soldier. Why a civilian would want one is beyond me."

We both agreed that the country seemed in the midst of a malaise, fearful of decline, paralyzed by partisan politics, torn as usual between conflicting visions. As a émigré, Joerg had the benefit of the outsider's perspective.

"It's hard enough to run a democracy even if you work with the opposition, but it's impossible if you won't compromise. The middle class is declining. That's been the trend for the last thirty years. In some ways it's an education problem. If everyone has to take out loans to finish college, you're going to thin the ranks of the middle class."

We were comparing American and German education systems when Amy Droll pulled her husband away to drive home, leaving the bartender and me to watch the playoffs. On the television screen, ten heavily tattooed, oversized men galloped up and down a basketball court. The Cleveland Cavaliers and Golden State Warriors were even at a game apiece. In the final seconds, with the score tied, a bearded LeBron James, looking like a muscular, black Abraham Lincoln, stole the ball as time expired.

"I used to live in Fort Meyers," said the bartender, "so I like LeBron. He plays hard. I was a fan when he was with the Heat. The problem with Florida is there's no community, you know? Only shopping malls. The only thing I miss there are the winters. I *hate* the winters here."

The bartender didn't announce last call but simply locked up. When he left, I was alone in the hotel. I staggered upstairs to a tiny room at the end of a hallway. It was neat as a pin with just enough space inside for an old-fashioned iron bedstead and wooden dresser.

9

The next morning I left my room key on the dresser and walked downstairs to an empty hotel except for a cleaning woman. While she mopped I dawdled around the restaurant looking at a wall of old photographs. Many were cyanotypes from the previous century with the greenish-blue cast of blueprints. Some bore captions. "Lydia Spier (holding rattlesnake) on First Peak w/ 'Badance Rock' in background." In the picture a woman in a calico dress holds a limp rattler between her outstretched hands like a jump rope. The chagrined look on her face suggests she'd been put up to this stunt. A bigger mystery was the river in the photographs. Was that skinny ribbon of water really the mighty Mississippi? In one picture, Trempealeau's Front Street looms above a bare riverbed crowded with shoeless boys. The old, undammed, free-flowing Mississippi was a different river altogether from the one I'd been traveling; it was crooked and stuffed with sandbars, shoals, and snags. It ran flood high in spring then dropped to an average depth of three feet. In a dry summer a person could wade to the other shore.

I locked through Lock and Dam 6 and followed the river past a raft of forested islands toward blue bluffs along the Minnesota side. The head of the pool looked wild and newly minted, so I was caught off guard when Amtrak's *Empire Builder* came screaming along the western shore. Passengers in the dining car on their way to Chicago could glance over their morning coffees to see a man in a small canoe waving at them.

Traveling the Upper Mississippi, I was continuously whipsawed between two vastly different rivers that share the same bed and, more or less, take turns flowing. One is a mechanical wonder, a segmented canal engineered for commerce and regulated by the federal government. The other is Ol' Man River as he's always been, "sullen, untamed and intractable," a force of nature and a great migratory flyway. I couldn't make up my mind which I preferred—the wild river or the working river. A purist would be lost on the Mississippi. The irony is that both are human constructs, the natural river as much as the canal, equally the result of government committees and bureaucratic compromises and one man in particular, now mostly forgotten, whose life amounts to another sad story.

Winona had a reputation as a wide-open town during Prohibition and attracted wealthy Chicagoans looking to escape city heat and the Volstead Act. One of them was a hard-drinking, cigar-chomping outdoor writer and ad man named Will Dilg. In an era when newspapers followed blood sports as closely as baseball and football, Dilg was a celebrity. His sporting columns drew from the same inkwell of hyperbole as his advertising copy. The bass popper he devised and named for himself was "the greatest lure ever invented for a fly rod." His friend and fishing guide Bill Pohlman was "the king of the Upper Mississippi boatmen." And as for the Mississippi itself, "Nowhere on earth is there so beautiful a river." Photographs of Dilg recall the vaudevillian Jimmy Durante, a thin, balding man with a bulbous nose and salesman's sideways smile.

As he did most summers, Dilg arrived in Winona in July 1921 to spend the month fly fishing for smallmouth bass. On this trip, Dilg was accompanied by his wife Marguerite and their four-year old son. The Dilgs had a complicated relationship—married, divorced then remarried—but they shared a passion for fly fishing and their child. Dilg kept a houseboat moored to a slip in the Winona marina. *The Golden Day* had an open porch on the stern end and cozy quarters below deck for the family of three. Dilg hired Pohlman to pole the houseboat upstream so they could fish the sloughs and backwaters of what is now Pool 5.

On a day when the temperature soared into the nineties, Dilg and Pohlman went off in a skiff to fish while Marguerite and the boy remained aboard *The Golden Day*. As she prepared lunch in the galley, Marguerite thought she heard a splash at the other end of the house-boat. She went on deck to check on the four-year-old but couldn't find him anywhere. Hearing Marguerite's cries, Dilg and Pohlman quickly rowed back to the houseboat. At first the men assumed the missing boy had crossed a plank to shore so they searched the woods. When they couldn't find any sign of him, they probed the river. Finally, Pohlman located the boy's body under the houseboat. He must have fallen from the plank into the river and the current trapped him under the hull. A motor launch brought the body back to Wi-nona and the bereaved parents returned by train to Chicago.

Dilg never wrote about his son's drowning. A year after the ac-cident, he edited a book with the unfortunate title *Tragic Fishing Moments*, a collection of humorous fishing anecdotes in which the greatest tragedy is that the fish gets away. The closest Dilg got to ac-knowledging the loss was a line in the book's preface to a generalized American boy:

"Those of us who have known the golden age of angling in this country realize that our game fishes are rapidly disappearing, and that the American boy . . . is in danger of losing his heritage of sport afield and astream."

Dilg was referring to the accelerating loss of sloughs and back-waters along the Upper Mississippi. Under the Swamp Land Law of 1850, states had the right to acquire "swamp and overflow" land from the federal government, ditch and drain it, then sell it to private developers. The Corps of Engineers had done exactly that to the Trempealeau River Bottoms downstream from Winona, and there was no reason to believe remaining wetlands along the Mississippi wouldn't share a similar fate. That winter Dilg and fifty-three wealthy and influential sportsmen met at the Blackstone Hotel in Chicago to form an organization dedicated "to promote all things piscatorial" including the preservation of lakes and rivers. They named it the Izaak Walton League after the seventeenth-century English angler and overwhelmingly elected Dilg as its first president.

The organization's initial challenge was stopping the Corps of Engineers from draining the fifteen-thousand-acre wetland on the Upper Mississippi known as the Winneshiek Bottoms. Dilg toured the Wisconsin side of the bottoms with a plant physiologist who concluded it had little value as marginal farmland but was irreplaceable as habitat for fish and waterfowl. Barnstorming the Midwest, Dilg spoke at small town sportsmen's clubs and fraternal organizations up and down the river. His speeches combined Main Street boosterism with an apocryphal vision of the future: "The Upper Mississippi bottoms are America's most prolific spawning grounds for black bass and for all warm water game and food fishes. . . . Veritably, these river lands offer you and your boy and posterity the greatest sport to be found on this planet. . . . But it's going to GO— it's going to be destroyed—these river lands are going to be drained all the way from Lake Pepin, Minnesota to Rock Island, Illinois. And when these river bottoms are once drained, THEY ARE GONE FOREVER."

With the Winneshiek Bottoms project tied up in court, Dilg traveled to Washington, DC, to seek a more permanent solution. He lobbied President Coolidge, another fisherman, to declare the entire Upper Mississippi River a national wildlife refuge and later, he hoped, a national park. The park concept didn't fly but the next year, 1924, Congress passed a bill authorizing the purchase of lands and islands along 261 miles of the Mississippi, and Coolidge signed it. Dilg had almost single-handedly prevented the wholesale drainage of bottomlands along the Upper Mississippi and created the first migratory bird refuge authorized and paid for by the federal government. Under his leadership, the Izaak Walton League grew to a hundred thousand members in two short years. For a time, Dilg seemed unstoppable, an unlikely successor to John Muir. Then everything fell apart.

A year after his triumph, the Izaak Walton League's board of directors ousted Dilg as president. He had been a great fundraiser but a terrible accountant and often spent more than he took in. He could also be abrasive and confrontational. Marguerite filed for divorce a second time, citing "desertion, non-support, and cruelty," and this time the divorce took. The following year, Dilg was diagnosed with throat cancer. Informed by doctors that surgery could extend his life at the cost of losing his voice, the ad man declined.

A final indignation came a few years after Dilg's death when Franklin Roosevelt's administration began construction of an extensive lock and dam system on the Upper Mississippi that flooded many of its bottomlands. The original bill creating a refuge prevented all development along the river, public and private. However, the Secretary of War, who oversaw the Corps of Engineers, had inserted a provision in the final draft that prohibited "any interference with the operations of the War Department in carrying out any project now or hereafter adopted for the improvement of said river." In less than a decade, those words would transform Dilg's river so much that even "the king of the Upper Mississippi boatmen" would need a chart to navigate.

10

A week's travel had left me with a sunburn and a ditty bag of dirty laundry. I passed under an old railroad swing bridge, a marvel of nineteenth-century technology, a mile and a half long with an iron truss span mounted to a turnstile that could pivot ninety degrees to allow boats to pass underneath. It didn't need to pivot for me. By now I reckoned the *Empire Builder* was halfway to Chicago while I was only a mile or so above La Crosse. Sunlight pulsed off the water in blinding sheets as the Mississippi split around a wooded island. I took the left channel and almost ran into another vision of the river's past, *The La Crosse Queen*. A tour guide's amplified voice preceded the sternwheeler, while behind her threshing paddlewheel the city's hazy silhouette arose. A public beach across from the city was packed with glistening bodies, only a few of which ventured into the cordoned swimming area to escape the heat. Hooking around the island, I docked at the Pettibone Boat Club. The marina attendant agreed to let me park my canoe for a few days and recommended a covered slip because rain was in the forecast. Given the cloudless blue sky, I thought he was overly cautious. The next day it rained four inches.

I took a break from the river and moved into my daughter and her husband's house in La Crescent for a few days of clean sheets and home cooking. Their home was perched on a sloping hillside that had once been an apple orchard. After supper I could take my drink out on the deck and look beyond the tops of remnant apple trees to the river and La Crosse. For a young family, La Crescent was an ideal location, a place where they could have it both ways—the intimacy of small-town life with the economic opportunities a highway bridge connected to a mid-sized city afforded.

One morning before leaving for work in the city, my daughter mentioned that her friend's husband was employed at the lock and dam in Genoa, the next one downriver, where he worked the swing shift. Would I like to meet him? My encounters with lock operators had necessarily been brief and impersonal, a businesslike voice at the other end of a mooring rope. A conversation in a lock chamber was like trying to make small talk at a border crossing. So given an opportunity to see the operation from topside, I jumped at the chance.

Flying above the lockhouse at Lock and Dam 8 is the flag of the U.S. Army Corps of Engineers: a three-towered white castle on a scarlet field. The banner is a reminder that the facility, while not a fortification, is overseen by the military in light of the Mississippi's strategic importance to the nation's flow of commerce. The leadership of the lock and dam system is active duty military. They wear uniforms and salute and can be deployed to war zones like Afghanistan. B. J. Nissalke is a civilian though he looks the part of a noncom, short red hair and a trim physique. As a lock and dam operator, he is in charge of Pool 8, the twenty-four miles of Upper Mississippi between Genoa and La Crosse. His job involves two separate but interconnected tasks. The first is fine-tuning the dam to keep the upriver water level in Pool 8 at a minimum nine-foot depth in the navigation channel for boat traffic. His second task is operating the lock so boats can negotiate the eleven-foot difference in elevation between pools.

When I arrived in the early evening, Nissalke was engaged in the latter. The towboat *Stephan L Colby*, name spelled out in red letters against a white cabin, was in the process of locking through on her way upriver. She was pushing a phalanx of fifteen barges, three across and five deep, the equivalent in carrying capacity to a freight train two and a half miles long. Since the lock chamber could only accommodate nine barges at a time, the *Stephan L Colby* pushed that number into the chamber; a crewman uncoupled them, then the tow backed away.

Nissalke raised the water level in the lock chamber eleven feet to the height of the upriver pool. Another man hooked a cable to the barges so a mechanical "mule" could move them through the open miter gates. As the second load of barges reached the upriver level, Nissalke barked into a walkie-talkie. "Hey Travis, you copy? Could you give this guy the green light?"

To me, he said quietly: "This guy's got fifteen barges and they're all empty. He'll leave them upriver until harvest time then he'll carry oats, soybeans, corn, wheat, whatever downriver."

The barges the towboats pushed, Nissalke explained, were either *boxes* or *rakes*. The difference was in their shape and position.

"Barges that are straight across are called 'boxes.' The ones with a raked front end like a skiff are called 'rakes,' and usually placed at the head of a tow because they have less resistance to the water or ice. You can't put two boxes together because ice gets between them. So we require ice-coupling. That means putting a rake in front of a box or rake to rake. Right now we're flowing at 20,000 cubic feet of water per second, which is normal. During flood stage we've been as high as 125,000 cubic feet per second. Imagine pushing a string of barges upriver against *that* kind of current. When those barge lines blow, they sound just like a 20-gauge shotgun."

After the *Stephan L Colby* disappeared into the night, Nissalke turned to his other responsibility, the dam. Every morning, he receives an order by computer from district headquarters in St. Paul to set the water level in Pool 8.

"Every dam has a target elevation to maintain. Currently we're at 630 feet. That's our pool water, not our tail. The order might say, 'Go for five feet on the roller gates.' So we'll open one foot on five roller gates. If the river gauge gets too high, we're going to open on our own."

The popular image of a dam is a V-shaped concrete plug between high canyon walls, electric lines trailing into the desert. But the dam at Genoa, like the twenty-six other dams strung along the Upper Mississippi, isn't a miniature Hoover Dam. It's a low dam, wider than it is tall, and it doesn't generate hydroelectricity or provide much in the way of flood control. Its sole purpose is holding back enough water to maintain a reliable nine-foot deep navigation channel. When water is released, it's released at the bottom of the dam through a roller gate, a steel cylinder that sits on a concrete sill. The Genoa dam has five roller gates, each eighty feet long, along with ten smaller tainter gates. To show how they worked, Nissalke led me across a catwalk on the lock's upriver miter gate to the parapet of the first roller dam and inside the structure itself. A reduction gear system resembling a giant set of bicycle sprockets raises or lowers the roller gate. Nissalke pushed a button and the needle of an enormous metal dial moved to 2.5 feet as the roller gate at the bottom of the dam rose the same distance. Thus was the Father of Rivers, at least Pool 8, brought to heel.

As a canoeist I've always disliked dams on principle. Dams don't tame rivers; they drown them, and what remains of a free-flowing river once it's given up the ghost is a flaccid imitation of moving water called an impoundment. But I have to admit that I found the rumbling interior of the Genoa dam pretty exciting. The lock and dam system had transformed the Mississippi but also kept it a working river, which meant the towns along the river were still relevant.

"This is all original from the 1930s," said Nissalke, pointing to the concrete walls. "They built the dam with hand-made forms. The pilings and all the cribbing, the pre-structure, were trees cut from the hillsides. In places you can still see planks in the walls."

For most of the nineteenth century, the federal government's obligations toward the Mississippi River amounted to clearing snags, submerged logs, and other debris from the main channel. After the Civil War reinforced the river's strategic importance, Congress appropriated money for the Corps of Engineers to maintain a four-foot-deep navigation channel by building thousands of brush and rock wing dams and closing dams to divert more current into the river's main channel. But this self-scouring approach required constant dredging and the channel was still too shallow for most commercial vessels. In the interim, railroads and the opening of the Panama Canal had killed off most commercial boat traffic on the Mississippi because it was cheaper to ship commodities from one coast to another via rail or ocean-going vessels rather than through the middle of the country. Finally in 1930 Congress took up a proposal for a nine-foot channel to be achieved through a series of locks and dams. Passage of the measure was not a slam-dunk. In favor were midwestern farmers and manufacturers who wanted an alternative to the rail monopoly on shipping. Opposed were the railroads as well as Will Dilg's Izaak Walton League, which feared that dams would flood most of the wildlife refuge established only a few years earlier. An editorial in the *Winona Republican-Herald* warned that the "nine-foot channel-slackened river would become a giant sewer, a death trap for fish and a menace to public health." But the Mississippi already was a giant sewer and one benefit of a lock and dam system was that it would force communities on the river to develop water treatment plants.

As the Great Depression worsened, the nine-foot channel was eventually sold as a New Deal public works project. For all the grousing one hears in river towns against big government, it was a massive stimulus package by the Roosevelt administration that kept those same towns in business. The project was the equivalent of building twenty-six small-scale Hoover Dams, each costing about $8 million and employing hundreds of workers, most of them unskilled. First cofferdams had to be built to redirect the river to the old Raft Channel while workers hammered together forms to hold the concrete for the locks. The four miter gates, weighing eighty tons apiece, were constructed on site. Then the dams were built pier by pier. In the small river towns where the workers were quartered, business boomed, especially in taverns. In May 1937 the bottom of the Genoa dam's fifteen gates closed and the lock was open for navigation. Last year more than sixteen million tons of cargo passed through it, not to mention an average of about forty canoes.

When Samuel Clemens grew up along the Mississippi in Hannibal, Missouri, in the 1840s, he wanted nothing more than to become a steamboat pilot, a job that offered good wages and a degree of glamor—all without having to leave the river. Had Clemens spent his childhood in the little town of Dresbach, Minnesota, at the end of the twentieth century, as B. J. Nissalke did, he'd probably have aspired to work for the Army Corps of Engineers. A job as a lock and dam operator with the Corps is relatively well-paying, requires technical skills, and doesn't force applicants to choose between meaningful employment and life on the Mississippi. While steamboat pilots had to read a wild river in all its mutations, lock and dam operators are responsible for smoothing the river out and making it behave. Starting as a seasonal employee, Nissalke worked summers at the lock and dam in Lynxville while taking classes at Winona Tech. At the end of one summer, instead of laying him off, the Corps deployed him to Gulfport, Mississippi, to clean up the aftermath of Hurricane Katrina. It was the first time he'd seen the southern end of the Mississippi.

"It's a totally different river down there. Places right off shore drop away to ninety feet. Ocean-going vessels can come up as far as St. Louis."

Nissalke preferred his home stretch of the river. He was a Stayer, someone who had married his high school sweetheart and lived close to where he'd grown up, not in Dresbach but La Crescent, another river town.

I asked him to define the term. What was the difference between La Crosse and its neighbor La Crescent?

"See, La Crosse is on the river, but it's too big. A river town's got to be small like Alma or Trempealeau or Genoa or Brownsville. People have a sense of pride if it's a river town. Ninety percent of the people I know either duck hunt or fish or catch willow cats for bait."

"What's a willow cat?"

"All it is is a baby catfish. They're slimy and they'll sting you too, just like a catfish, but people like 'em as bait. Me, I'm more a bass fisherman."

On his days off, Nissalke liked to fish the weed beds along the old Raft Channel, the river's original main channel that runs from Brownsville to Genoa.

Nissalke struck me as the sort of person Huckleberry Finn might have grown into, so I asked what he thought of Clemens's novel. I was surprised when he said he'd never read the book. I didn't think it was possible to matriculate from an American high school without reading *The Adventures of Huckleberry Finn*. Then again, Nissalke probably would have found the book redundant. The last book he'd read was the memoir of a Marine sniper in Vietnam.

Electric lights had come on when we climbed out of the dam structure and into the cool night air. The parapet walls were cast in a strange amber light swirling with the shadows of mayflies and moths. The river below was lost in the darkness except for mist and the boiling sound of the tailrace. We threaded our way back across the closed miter gate to the lockhouse where Nissalke took a seat behind a computer terminal.

"Let's see where the *Stephen L Colby* is now," he said and pushed a button. "She's just below Winona and moving at 4.4 knots."

Every commercial vessel in the country carries a transponder aboard that allows the Corps to track its location, direction, and speed in real time. Nissalke hit another key and enlarged the map on the screen to cover the entire river system. It was a planetarium show in reverse. Instead of stars and planets in the night sky, the map showed a dark country speckled with the white blips of towboats and pink bars of locks and dams. A constellation of blips was blinking downriver.

"Look at all the boats by St. Louis. The *Lee Ann Ingram*, *Tauraus*, *Père Marquette*. They're all bunched up so there must be something wrong. In high water, they might not get under bridges though I doubt that's the situation here."

Nearly all the vessels Nissalke admitted to the lock chamber were motorized, from big diesel towboats to my square-stern canoe. Occasionally, though, a free-floating craft would break the routine. Nissalke retrieved a three-ring binder from storage to show me a recent rescue report. At 7:15 on a warm summer evening, he received a radio call that a person in an unspecified boat had been swept into the dam from upstream and was clinging to a safety line. The boat was a small blue inflatable raft and its sole occupant was intoxicated. After sealing three of the closest roller gates, the lock operator threw a rope to the man and called the local fire department, which dispatched a crew with a rescue boat.

"All he had was a case of beer and a carton of Marlboros. Here's a picture of him being arrested."

The fellow in the photograph, rail thin beneath a striped polo shirt, looked more agitated than relieved. His blue raft was the sort my students used to float beneath the campus footbridge on hot afternoons. I'd often wondered how they'd fare if they just kept floating and now I knew.

~~~~~~~~~~~~~~

II

The problem with taking a break in a journey is that soon enough *there* becomes *here* and you settle in. I'd gotten used to my daughter's cooking and my son-in-law's home-brewed beer. Every time I looked from their deck to the Mississippi, the river looked bigger than I'd remembered even as it seemed more remote. It was becoming an abstraction. Finally one morning I packed my bag, got a ride to the Peabody Boat Club, and reclaimed my canoe from its sheltered slip among the heavy cruisers.

I had considered taking the old Raft Channel, the route steamboats and lumber rafts had once used on the river between La Crosse and Brownsville, but my chart showed it flanked by submerged stump fields. So I stayed between the red and green buoys of the navigation channel instead. Below Brownsville the river yawned into the bottom of Pool 8, an enormous lake whose mirror-smooth surface was a rippling archipelago of clouds. In the real sky, turkey vultures soared on thermals above the twin smokestacks of the Genoa coal-fired power plant.

I didn't recognize the lock operator who threw me the mooring rope, and as soon as the miter gates opened I puttered through them and into the head of Pool 9. I was lucky to lock through when I did because a towboat was heading upriver behind a load of barges, mainly boxes with three rakes in front. It was the *Lee Ann Ingram*, whose white blip I'd seen flashing the other night on the lock house computer screen. I waved to a figure in the pilothouse as we passed, one skipper to another.

The sky turned gloomy below the little town of Victory, so I made a beeline for the nearest campground. It turned out to be a county park across from the mouth of the Iowa River and behind yet another Battle Island. A long expanse of manicured lawn had been cut out of the floodplain forest and developed into a cloverleaf of trailer hook-ups. There were, however, a few isolated tent sites right on the water, so I took one, pulling my canoe high enough on the beach so it wouldn't roll in the backwash of passing tows. I pitched my tent on the gravel pad and made a nice cup of instant cider fortified with brandy. The park had pushed back the bottomland forest rather than obliterating it. Beyond the mowed lawn and gazebo, the land reverted to a jumble of overgrown woods and cut-off sloughs, a scene out of the Hudson River School of landscape painting—wilderness confronted by cultivation. Out of the corner of my eye I spotted something moving in the nearest slough, a sharp V cutting through the slack-water slough as it headed toward the river. When it drew directly across from me, the V submerged, detonating the water with a fierce tail whap! A beaver then. It surfaced and whacked again, a loud implosive sound like a large rock dropped from a great height. Tail-whacking was a territorial gesture meant to dislodge me from the campsite. Perhaps the beaver remembered when the park had been swamp because it kept cannonballing the river even after I retreated into my tent and long into the night.

Morning broke sodden and overcast, the tent speckled with mayflies. The air felt thick and damp as a sponge. I walked to restrooms at the center of the park to fill my water jug. A heavy dew had fallen on the clipped grass and more rain seemed in the offing. It was still early enough that nobody was stirring in the trailer loop. Next to the empty playground swings stood a smooth limestone marker shaped like a tombstone. The lettering was old and weathered but still legible.

> Head of Battle Isle. On the eve of Aug. 1, 1832, Blackhawk and his men with a flag of truce went to the head of this island to surrender to the captain of the steamer *Warrior*. Whites on board asked, "Are you Winnebago or Sacs?" "Sac," replied Blackhawk. A load of canister was fired at once, killing 22 Indians suing for peace.

The marker was the work of Dr. C. V. Porter, a local historian who'd erected similar limestone markers in the 1930s along the route of Blackhawk's long retreat. A new metal plaque next to Porter's stone offered a disclaimer: "The State of Wisconsin recognizes Dr. Porter's markers as part of Vernon County history but does not condone the language or prejudicial references used on some of the markers." It was hard to see grounds for offense. If anything, the doctor had been discreet with regards to what took place at Battle Isle, which had not been a battle by any measure but a one-sided massacre.

*M*a-ka-tai-me-she-kia-kiak, Black Sparrow Hawk, was born in 1767 at a time when the Sauk and Fox controlled a wide swath of the Mississippi River from the mouth of the Wisconsin south to the Missouri. Blackhawk's birthplace, Saukenuk, was the very heart of that vast territory. The tribe's eponymous village (present-day Rock Island, Illinois) was perfectly located on a point of land between the Rock River and the Mississippi; there were plentiful fish below the rapids, hundreds of acres of corn and squash under cultivation, and long-standing enemies within striking distance. On a journey to St. Louis in 1804, Blackhawk learned that a treaty signed under fraudulent circumstances had ceded all Sauk land east of the Mississippi to the United States, including Saukenuk. He refused to accept the loss even after his tribe moved to the west bank of the river. In April of 1832, at the age of sixty-five, Blackhawk led his band back across the Mississippi in a futile attempt to reclaim, as he put it, "my towns, my cornfields, and the homes of my people." It was a bitter homecoming. At Saukenuk the old warrior found the tribe's lodges razed and their cornfields fenced in or ploughed under. Illinois's governor declared Blackhawk's return an armed invasion and ordered the military to pursue the Indians up the Rock River. What followed was a war of skirmishes and scalpings on both sides. Blackhawk's band numbered less than five hundred warriors and faced thousands of militia and regular troops. The alliances Blackhawk had expected with other tribes and the British never materialized and without supplies the Indians were soon starving. Blackhawk's long retreat was a series of brilliant holding actions in which the outnumbered Sauk fought off pursuing troops while gradually moving women, old people, and children back toward the Mississippi.

On August 1, Blackhawk's band reached the river just south of the mouth of Bad Axe Creek and began felling trees for rafts to cross into safety. Late that afternoon, the steamboat *Warrior*, a six-pound cannon lashed to its bow, dropped anchor just offshore. Blackhawk ordered his braves to lay down their weapons. Wading knee-deep into the water, he held up a piece of white cloth on a pole and asked to come aboard and shake hands with the captain, whom he'd met before and trusted. The slaughter began as a breakdown in communication. Nobody on the steamboat spoke Sauk and nobody on shore spoke English. For several tense minutes words passed back and forth between a Winnebago translator aboard and a Winnebago in Blackhawk's party. Suspecting a trap, the captain of the *Warrior* ordered his men to fire. The load of canister from the six-pounder cut through the Sauk on shore like a scythe through tall grass. When the steamboat finally left to refuel, Blackhawk urged the survivors to follow him north to Chippewa country, but most remained behind believing safety lay just across the river.

The next day was worse. Militia reached the bluffs above the Sauk camp and fired upon the Indians as they ran desperately across sloughs and through bottomland woods to the riverbank only to find the *Warrior* steaming upstream. Caught in deadly crossfire, scores of Indians including women and children dove into the water to be shot by sharpshooters or drowned. In the aftermath of the massacre, *The Galenian* (Illinois) newspaper heaped praise on the *Warrior* for "the coolness and gallantry of all on board."

Having escaped to a Winnebago village, Blackhawk agreed to surrender to the Americans at Prairie du Chien. From there he was taken in shackles to Jefferson Barracks near St. Louis, where he posed for the artist George Catlin. Caitlin's portrait shows Blackhawk in a suit of plain white buckskin with a string of wampum beads in his ears and along his neck. His head is shaved in the Sauk style with only a short topknot painted vermillion. Slender and standing only about five and a half feet tall, he has high cheekbones and a somber, down-turned mouth. In one hand he holds a hawk's tail-feathers, which, according to Catlin, he fanned himself with constantly.

The following year, the prisoner was taken on a tour of Eastern cities, including the capital, where President Andrew Jackson admonished Blackhawk to follow the counsel of Keokuk, a more malleable Sauk leader. The tour was meant to impress upon the old warrior the power and technology of the nation. Blackhawk saw great puffing steam locomotives, silver coins stamped at the United States Mint, the ascent of a hot air balloon, and a fireworks display, which he thought interesting but "less magnificent" than a prairie fire. Everywhere he went, the old warrior drew enormous crowds eager to see the savage who had caused so much trouble. But he returned to Iowa a man without power or position in his own tribe and was regarded by many Sauk as a bitter reminder of a lost war.

Shortly before his death in 1838, Blackhawk was invited to address a Fourth of July celebration at Fort Madison in Iowa. The table of dignitaries sat on shady bluff overlooking the Mississippi River. While the gist of most of the speeches concerned the nation's greatness and its limitless future, Black Hawk was offered as visual proof of its contentious past. When it was time for him to address the crowd, the old man needed a cane to rise to his feet. He paused before he spoke, a silence that grew long enough for people to take notice.

"I was once a great warrior; I am now poor. Keokuk has been the cause of my present situation, but I do not attach blame to him. I am now old. I have looked upon the Mississippi since I have been a child. I love the great river. I have dwelt upon its banks from the time I was an infant. I look upon it now. I shake hands with you, as it is my wish, I hope you are my friends."

12

The great cantilevered truss bridge connecting the Winne-shiek Bottom to Lansing, Iowa, is named the Black Hawk Bridge. I had a good view of it outlined against gray skies from Shep's Riverside Bar and Grill. The lunch crowd evenly split between the horseshoe-shaped bar and the dining room were mostly elderly. I picked my way through the salad bar and sat down at a window table. A scattering of mayflies gazed back from the other side of the glass.

Lansing's Main Street, four blocks of redbrick, false-front buildings sloping to the river, was lined with flagpoles. A row of Old Glories drooped in the midday air. Most of the storefronts had black-and-white placards in their front windows, courtesy of the Main Street Association, that read "This Place Matters." A newspaper revealed the Iowa primary in full swing and our governor ahead in the polls. The theme of his campaign was "Unintimidated." To get his theme across (and appear less dorky) he was crossing the Hawkeye state on a Harley-Davidson Road King and talking tough on immigration. He called for deporting illegal immigrants and celebrated the "real America," which, to a lot of people, looks a lot like Lansing, Iowa.

I walked to a Carquest Auto Parts store at the far end of Main Street to buy a quart of outboard motor oil. The store was a converted movie theater with a marquee that asked, "READY FOR SPRING? GET YOUR MOWER TUNED UP." Behind the parts counter, a yellowing poster of Kirk Douglas in a cowboy hat, all teeth and six-guns, glared down from the engine belts. I asked the parts manager the last time a movie played there.

"Must have been when I was in high school because I saw *Jaws* here and that was, what, 1975?"

If Blackhawk ever returned to the Upper Mississippi, he'd feel right at home in Prairie du Chien, even though the only time he spent there was as a prisoner at Fort Crawford. Today he could lug the gear from his birchbark canoe up Blackhawk Avenue, past the Blackhawk Sportsbar to Highway 35 and Blackhawk Motors where he'd find Jeep Cherokees in the lot inventory and perhaps a Winnebago on trade-in. America has a special place in its heart for Indians defeated in lop-sided battles. Friday nights, the old warrior could join fans of the local high school football team chanting from the bleachers, "Blackhawks! Blackhawks! Blackhawks!"

I settled among the motel and fast food franchises along the highway into the ranch-style Brisbois Motor Inn. Named for an eighteenth-century French-Canadian fur trader, the motel was currently managed by a Yugoslavian immigrant. Evenings I binge-watched a cable TV show called *Fat Guys in the Woods*. It featured a buff outdoor expert teaching a group of obese urbanites how to survive in the wild and I found the show addictive. It was the reality show parallel to early American captivity narratives in which Indians yanked Puritans from their comfortable settlements and led them deep into an alien wilderness where they were subjected to ordeals of the flesh. In colonial literature, such ordeals led to spiritual redemption; on the TV show, they led to weight loss and male bonding. The fat guys occasionally joked and high-fived each other as they roasted a ratty-looking squirrel around a campfire but none of them appeared to be having much fun.

Mornings I'd sleep late then check the hydrologic flow on the Wisconsin River, the next leg of my trip, by calling an 800 telephone number. A recorded voice would announce water levels at different towns along the river. The first morning I called, the gauge at Prairie du Sac read 27,845 cubic feet per second. One cubic foot per second equals about 450 gallons per minute. Above 17,000 CFS, all of the sandbars on the Lower Wisconsin (where I intended to camp) would be underwater. Days of heavy rain had the Wisconsin running unseasonably high, so each morning I called and waited for the river to drop.

Weather is the *lingua franca* of the Midwest. Even more than sports, it's a neutral subject, something we have in common. Over breakfast at the Hungry House Restaurant next door, I watched the weather channel on a flat-screen TV mounted over the counter. "I need cheese for my fried onions!" the waitress commanded through a slot in the kitchen wall. She refilled my coffee cup with one hand and rested the other on her hip. We were both watching Tropical Storm Bill spiral up the Gulf of Mexico in all the colors of a psychedelic sunset. The camera cut away from the satellite image to a meteorologist on the Texas coast standing knee-deep in pounding surf.

"The weather sure is getting funny," the waitress observed.

"Think we'll catch a break?"

"Well, today's supposed to be real nice."

"And tomorrow?"

"One of the forecasters said rain tomorrow, but I don't remember if he said rain in the day or rain at night. That's the only job I know where you can be wrong half the time and not get sacked."

The sun was shining as I left the café and walked back toward the river. Away from the highway traffic, Prairie du Chien is a town of quiet neighborhoods, shady mulberry trees, flower beds decorated with homemade whirly-gigs, boat trailers in driveways, and American flags on front porches. The air hummed with the cicada-drone of lawn mowers. Almost every other block had a semi-permanent garage sale. I stopped at each of them because a garage sale is the most democratic of institutions, allowing anyone to paw through their neighbor's castoffs. In this country we don't redistribute wealth; we redistribute crockpots and ice skates, Christmas ornaments and plastic baby furniture, old board games, stacks of romance novels and ugly leather jackets. Garage sales are also a good place for a stranger to loiter in a small town because shopping looks purposeful; whereas wandering around a quiet neighborhood in the middle of the day on foot without a leashed dog or some other clear reason suggests a vagrant or someone with too many DUIs. Having left one garage sale, I smiled at a woman pulling a child's wagon up the sidewalk and said, "Good morning." Alarmed by a stranger with a two-day growth of beard sweating heavily in the summer heat, she quickly pushed on.

A block later, two guys bent over a car yelled at me from their garage.

"HEY! Come over here! Hey, how ya doing?"

A friendly town, I thought, but it turned out to be a case of mistaken identity. Apparently I resembled a sweaty, unshaven friend of theirs. Having broken the ice, they invited me to look under the hood of their car. I know nothing about engines, I explained. When I added that I was waiting for the water level on the Wisconsin River to drop so I could canoe up it, the men looked at me in a new light. Giving directions is also a *lingua franca* of the Midwest.

"Go downstream about five miles south of town then turn left at the mouth. You can't miss it. Boy, that river's got a current! Four or five miles an hour depending on the water level. Not many people go up. I've only been up a few miles from the mouth."

"Keep an eye out for speedboats," said the older guy, warning about something I already knew. "They'll swamp you and wave going by. Those sons of bitches don't slow for nobody."

The neighborhood ended abruptly at a bridge over a sluggish slough to St. Feriole Island, the old Fourth Ward in the second oldest city in Wisconsin. Forty years ago, the island had been a tree-lined neighborhood like the one I'd been walking through until a record-breaking flood convinced the Corps of Engineers to tear down all the houses and relocate residents to the mainland. Now it was a city park and only the trees remained, mostly elms arching over an empty grid of grassy blocks. This morning, though, the park had new residents. Crossing the bridge, I was surprised to find the grass dotted with white canvas tipis, a reminder of Prairie du Chien's earliest neighborhood.

Until the mid-nineteenth century, a floating population of fur traders and Indians resided on St. Feriole Island. Twice a year that number swelled with Sauk, Potawatomi, Winnebago or Ho-Chunk, Chippewa, Sioux, Ottawa, Iowa, and Menominee, not to mention French *coureurs de bois* and American traders. The Indians came first in October to receive credits from the traders for the furs they would trap; the following May they would rendezvous at the island to deliver the pelts and generally have a good time. "This place is a Very Handsum one," a Yankee fur trader named Peter Pond wrote in 1773. "The Plane is Verey Smooth Hear. All the traders & All the Indians of Several tribes Meat Fall & Spring."

I had arrived on the island in time for the Prairie Villa Rendezvous, the largest fur trade reenactment in the Midwest and yet another instance of things that go around coming around again. Pickups and vans pulled into the park and families spilled out with bundles of canvas and pine lodge-poles to erect more tipis and marquee tents where vendors would soon be hawking everything from beeswax candles to homemade root beer. The Rendezvous wouldn't start for another day, however, so the reenactors I met in the registration tent were still dressed in blue jeans and T-shirts instead of buckskins and calico.

"Tomorrow morning, everyone has to be in pre-1840s costume," Sindee Gohde, one of the organizers, told me. "Anything that's not primitive must stay in the parking lot. Of course that doesn't apply during registration. What goes on in the tipi, stays in the tipi."

The year 1840 was a significant watershed for the reenactors. It marked roughly the point in time when silk began to replace beaver in the manufacture of top hats. The change had a devastating impact upon trade that had been built on beaver pelts, the soft under-hair of which could be compressed into a lustrous felt and shaped into men's top hats. The beaver hat was a necessity for fashion-conscious men in the early nineteenth century in the same way that Ugg boots were for women in the early twenty-first. The search for beaver brought the first Europeans into the Upper Mississippi Valley to trade blankets, copper kettles, rifles, and glass beads to the Indians for the lucrative pelts. And the economic relationship spawned social ties as traders married into tribes to cement good relations while Indians saw in the same bond an opportunity to achieve technological parity with their enemies. Working together, traders and Indians decimated the beaver population in the Upper Great Lakes. At about the same time, silk emerged as a substitute for felt in the manufacture of men's hats, so the fur traders found themselves out of a market while the Indians lost their only allies. The settlers who replaced the traders had no use either for fur-bearers or the Indians who trapped them. So the pre-1840s could be viewed as a golden era, a brief hiccup in history when Indians and peripatetic whites mingled together at St. Feriole Island on something like an equal footing.

For the reenactors, the annual Rendezvous was a week of time travel in another respect, a trip not just back to the early nineteenth century but to the carefree days of their own youth.

"When we first got started," Sindee reminisced, "it was just guys. There weren't too many women. The guys would drink and sleep it off. Then women started showing up and the Rendezvous turned into a family-oriented, pet-friendly sort of deal."

Many of the reenactors had been coming to the Rendezvous for forty years. I could imagine how it must have looked back then, an encampment of long-haired young people for whom a fringed buckskin shirt or calico dress would not have been a sartorial stretch. Over the years, as they married and had children of their own and then grandchildren, the gathering must have become a yardstick for measuring one's own trajectory through time. The reenactors struck me as being less like old hippies and more like the 4-H club families I know, joking and reminiscing in the livestock barn before the opening of the county fair.

Sindee explained that when the Rendezvous began, there was little competition with other historical reenactments. But in recent years some reenactors had jumped ship to other eras: Renaissance Fairs, Civil War encampments, and, more recently, a War of 1812 reenactment. The latter was held in the same park and used the same black-powder rifles but required participants to perform infantry drills in blue wool coatees, white leggings, and plumed hats.

"The 1812 reenactors are getting the younger people," she lamented. "Of course, now they've got a video game of the War of 1812. Maybe that's what we need? A video game."

"Depends on what part of history you're interested in," said a thickset bearded man with a variegated ponytail down his back. "I read books on mountain men. I shot muzzle-loaders for eons. I trapped and hunted anyway so the Rendezvous was something I felt comfortable with. Besides, I spent my time with the military and I'll be damned if I want to play soldier on weekends."

He wore a bear-claw necklace and a death's head tattoo peaked from under the sleeve of his black T-shirt. He looked less like a fur trader than an extra in a 1960s biker film. Watching me write his words down in my notebook, he said, "Ask me a question and I'll give you an answer. And if I don't know the answer, I'll lie to you."

"Okay. What's your name?"

"Do you want my real name or my trading name? My real name is Butch Smith. My trading name is Bugling Elk. Back in the day when I was hitting the bottle good, I was a loud talker so they gave me that name."

The next morning I carried my gear down from the motel to the St. Feriole Island marina and went looking for Bugling Elk. Overnight several blocks of pyramidal tents had sprouted beneath the park's shade trees, and the air was now redolent of wood smoke and fry bread. I found Butch Smith, aka Bugling Elk, and his wife Norma on Fisher Street, drinking coffee in front of their tipi and setting out trade goods. Everything in sight was pre-1840s except for Butch's cell phone and cigarette lighter. He and Norma had married at the Rendezvous on a similar summer day twenty years ago. Today was their wedding anniversary.

Butch sat down on a folding wooden chair and lit a cigarette.

"I grew up on this island, a block and a half from here. Right where we're at was Dan Ackerman's store. Over there where those cars are parked is where my grandparents lived. My great-grandparents lived on what was Brisbois Street. This is old home week for me."

When Butch was a child St. Feriole Island held 160 houses along with two taverns, two grocery stores, and a lumberyard. Neighborhood life revolved around the Mississippi River, especially commercial fishing and harvesting freshwater clams for the button factories. When Butch was a small boy, his mother took him out in the family boat one warm summer day, anchored in a side-slough, and threw him over the side. He thrashed his arms wildly until he stood up. The water came up to his waist. That was Butch's first swimming lesson. He was a lackadaisical student in school but a great scholar of the river. At twelve, he got his first hunting license and teachers soon found they could tell when duck season opened and closed by Butch's absences.

"I dropped out my junior year and Uncle Sam got me. Spent just over two years in Vietnam. In Vietnam the people in one valley spoke a different dialect than in the next valley. I can still speak a little Viet, but it's not the choice words. Ended up with a Purple Heart and a disability."

Butch came home from the war to find his neighborhood changed. After more flooding, long-time residents had begun to move ahead of the Corps of Engineers resettlement. Butch stopped cutting his hair and started working on the river. A new market for freshwater clams had emerged in Japan where the shells were ground into beads and inserted into Akoya oysters as seeds to produce cultured pearls. Butch dove for clams tethered to the end of fifty feet of hose connected to an air compressor. The water was so dark and murky that he had to crawl along the bottom feeling for the clams that lay in long veins off the main channel. The clams had fantastic names: Elephant Ears, Wabash Pigtoe, Maple Leaf, Washboard, Pimpleback Sheepnose, Monkeyface, Wartyback, Heelsplitter. The Washboard was the big money-maker because it was so large, up to a foot long, and thick. Then one year a virus wiped out most of Japan's Akoya oysterbeds and the clamshell market dried up.

By then Butch, who'd always admired Indian beadwork, was sewing beaded patterns and selling them at the Rendezvous. Traditionally, beadwork was the province of women, not thick-handed old warriors, but Butch clearly had a knack for it. He arranged a dozen or more strips of beadwork on a display table. He picked one up and burned off stray threads with his lighter. Some of the traditional patterns were recognizable, a star or a rattlesnake, but the cumulative effect of the beadwork, if you took in the whole tabletop, was something out of the school of Geometric Abstractionism.

"The patterns I use are all original to certain tribes. The Nez Perce has a diamond shape. This one is Sioux. These two are Crow. This piece is supposed to be lake and mountains. Most of the stuff I got here is Woodland Crow. They did a lot of alternating blocks of the same color. The Woodland is hard to do because you're changing colors a lot. The Indians had their Sunday-go-to-meeting clothes and that's what the beads are for, but they'd always sew an off-bead in their work to show they weren't perfect. They weren't God."

Before European traders supplied them with glass beads, Indians along the eastern seaboard had used small white shells called *wampumpeage* in Algonquin. Colonists shortened the term to "wampum" and mistakenly translated it as "money," but the value of such bead-work or wampum belts wasn't so much as currency. These pieces were mnemonic devices to mark a ceremony or recall a treaty. They were a means of remembering.

Butch pointed to a beaded strip with a block pattern of alternating red and yellow bars.

"The Pacific Theater ribbon for military service has the same colors. Yellow and red. Same as the South Vietnam flag."

As I got up to leave, he reached into a wooden box and handed me a fringed leather pouch of buttery-soft buckskin. It was beautiful. The first act of generosity I experienced on the trip but not the last. I didn't know what to say, especially as this was his wedding anniver-sary and I had no gift to give in return. Flustered, I asked Butch if he thought I'd have any trouble getting up the Wisconsin River.

"There's a good current right now. She's running fairly high. You shouldn't have to worry about hitting any sandbars."

Wisconsin River

~~~~~~~~~~~~~~

13

The confluence of great rivers has engendered many a great metropolis, but no Pittsburg or Geneva had sprung up at the juncture of the Mississippi and the Wisconsin—not even a Cairo, Illinois—just a notch between pleated bluffs and a mouth of wooded islands. At four hundred miles, the Wisconsin is the longest river in the state, but its delta is so spread out and screened behind thick floodplain forest that I couldn't tell at first which channel continued down the Mississippi and which led up its tributary. Finally I turned left between islands and headed up a channel that was a lighter shade of green.

For the first time on my trip I was going against a current instead of with it. The sight of the landscape flowing backwards left me feeling light-headed. Initially my six-horse outboard was more than a match for the current, but the further the delta fell behind me the more I felt those four hundred miles of river push against my bow. I couldn't run full-throttle without water pouring over the transom, so I had to reach an equilibrium between the river's momentum and my own. The shoreline was a peripheral blur, silver maple and basswood in the bottoms and white oak and black walnut on the bluffs, forests stacked upon forests, each canopy a different variety of green. Sweepers leaned into the river and snags and deadheads stuck out from it, slowly nodding up and down with the current.

Butch Smith was right about not hitting sandbars, at least for the first few miles. But once I was through the notch in the bluffs the river broadened out, grew shallower and broke into multiple channels. Sandbars are the tip of the iceberg, the fraction that shows above the waterline; the submerged part is a shoal. Shoals block channels or hide them and, because they're underwater, are hard to spot, a thin line or dimpling on the surface that I invariably saw too late. Choose the wrong channel and you'd run aground and face a long pull upstream. I ran aground so often that I began to miss the Mississippi's nine-foot channel with its comforting red and green buoys that made navigation simple rather than a game of chance. The outboard would shudder as the prop dug into hard sand or kicked out of the water followed by my paddling to deeper water or else getting out and lining the canoe. A chart would have been useless since the sandbars and shoals on the Wisconsin aren't fixed but move downstream with the current, sometimes as much as eight hundred feet in a year.

"The River on which we embarked is called *Meskousing*. It is very wide; it has a sandy bottom, which forms various shoals that render navigation very difficult. It is full of Islands Covered with Vines."

Père Jacques Marquette, S.J., the first European to lay eyes on the Wisconsin River, devotes only a few lines to the discovery in his 1673 journal because he was looking for a bigger river, the Mississippi. A devotee of the Blessed Virgin, the priest intended to name the mother of all rivers the Conception but in the end went along with what the Indians called it, which simply meant "big river." Marquette seems not to have given much thought to the tributary that led him there or what its name might mean.

The Wisconsin River's name, and by extension the state's, is a linguistic puzzle. Marquette's fur trader companion, Louis Joliet, labeled the river *Miskonsing* on the map he drew a year after the expedition. Later, another Frenchman, Rene de LaSalle, misread Marquette's cursive *M* as *Ou* when he printed the name on a map of his own travels. When the territory came under American control in the 1820s, politicians replaced the vowel with a consonant as *Ou* became *W*. Even after the word's spelling and pronunciation became fixed, there remained the greater question of its meaning. Indian place names typically describe the geographic feature they represent, a kind of aural map to aid the traveler. The meaning of *Meskousing* depends entirely on which Indian language it originally came from. Some scholars contended that it was a Chippewa word meaning "the small lodge of a beaver" or "grassy place" or perhaps the more grandiose "gathering of waters." There were so many contenders that one cynic suggested the word's meaning depended on which Chippewa you asked on any given day. Other scholars argued for a Sauk word meaning "holes in the bank of a stream in which birds nest." Or a Menominee word for "River of flowery banks." Or a Potawatomi word meaning "toward where it is cold." One amateur linguist thought it wasn't an Indian word at all but a corruption of a French phrase meaning "the place from which one comes down," that is, "rapids." All of these meanings work at some level, but they ignore the context in which Père Marquette first heard the name. In recent years the linguist Michael McCafferty has argued persuasively that because the priest was guided from Lake Michigan and up the Fox River to the portage by Miami Indians, it only makes sense that *Meskousing* is a Miami word, in which case it means "this stream meanders through something red." The "something red" was the russet sandstone dells a few miles upriver from the portage. So Wisconsin is named for a rhetorical misunderstanding: an English misspelling of a French version of a Miami Indian word. No wonder the state has an identity crisis.

As a freshman, I attended a Jesuit university in Milwaukee named for Père Marquette. In the library hung a wall-sized painting of the explorer-priest standing upright in a birchbark canoe before a rapt audience of Indians. The painting struck me even at the time as pretty hokey. As a reader I've always been less intrigued by the journals of explorers than the works of travel writers who followed much later and had more time for introspection. For that reason, Reuben Gold Thwaites was a man after my own heart. Before starting my voyage, I'd checked out a copy of Thwaites's *Down Historic Waterways* from the university library. The book's binding had been reinforced with tape and the due dates stamped in the back began in the 1930s. Thwaites was secretary of the State Historical Society of Wisconsin, where he edited *The Jesuit Relations* and wrote a full-length biography of Marquette. A photograph of him shows a bespectacled man with a weak chin and the sad moustache of a Victorian parson. In 1887 the scholarly Thwaites embarked on a Walter Mitty adventure to retrace Marquette's route by going down the Fox River and later descending the Wisconsin. On this final leg he was joined by his wife, referred to in the book as W— (For *wife?*). Her name was Jessie. The couple set off from Portage in a thirteen-foot lapstrake canoe that drew five inches of water and was rowed rather than paddled. It was equipped with oarlocks, a spritsail, attachable keel, and a canvas awning that could be fitted over a pair of steel hoops in bad weather. Heading downriver, Mr. and Mrs. Thwaites quickly ran into a rain shower, the first of many. They hardly slept the first night, kept awake by every snapping twig and rustling wind until daybreak. Throughout all this, W— remains a good sport while her husband comes across as a constant worrywart.

In the book's introduction, Thwaites warns the would-be canoeist not to travel alone and, if camping, to bring along a large party, "for two persons unused to this experience would find it exceedingly lonesome after nightfall, when visions of river tramps, dissolute fishermen, and inquisitive hogs and bulls, pass in review, and the weakness of the little camp against such formidable odds comes to be fully recognized."

"Gloomy" is a word that appears frequently in Thwaites's account. Maybe it's a reflection of the bad weather, the incessant fog hanging over the river, or the late summer storms arriving every other day. Or maybe he's just an overprotective husband. Traveling alone can sharpen one's fears, especially at night, but I think Thwaites's worries multiplied precisely because he'd brought W— along with him. Instead of drifting into other people's lives, he remains part of a couple, beset by a landscape he'd only read about in books, so that Marquette's "savage-haunted wilderness" becomes the abode of unspecified fears and things that go bump in the night, the phantasmagorical river tramps, hogs, etc.

Rowing down the Wisconsin, Thwaites and W— found that many of the settlements that had flourished during the steamboat and lumbering eras were already, by the late nineteenth century, fading into ghost towns. Yet the couple were themselves harbingers of a new era. Landing at an isolated farm or settlement, the couple frequently drew a crowd of gawkers who came to see something entirely unique on the river, self-propelled tourists.

Down Historic Waterways ends, logically, with the couple's arrival at the Mississippi River and the requisite nod to Marquette and Joliet, but that's not the climactic scene, not for me anyway. That scene occurred on the next-to-last day of their voyage, when Thwaites and W— encountered one more storm. Unwilling to spend another night beneath wet canvas, they rowed up the mouth of the twisting Kickapoo River through a bottomland swamp until they encountered a fisherman in a punt who led them in the pouring rain to Wauzeka. They left their boat by the railroad trestle, walked up a muddy track, and settled into a comfortable little hotel for the night. In the morning, though, Thwaite turned a critical eye on the town. "Three saloons disfigure the main street, and in front of them are little knots of noisy loafers, in the evening, filling up the rickety, variously graded sidewalk to the gutter, and necessitating the running of a loathsome gauntlet to those who may wish to pass that way. . . . . There are few large cities where one can see the liquor traffic carried on with such disgusting boldness as in hamlets like this, where screenless, open-doored saloons of a vile character jostle trading shops and dwellings, and monopolize the footway, making of the business street a place which women may abhor at any hour, and must necessarily avoid after sunset."

Thwaites's reaction to the town is so unexpected and so over-blown that I couldn't help wondering if it hadn't been preceded by some unrecorded event. Had one of the "noisy loafers" said something rude to W— as the couple paraded to the hotel in the rain? Had he been embarrassed in front of his wife? It's as if all Thwaites's worries on the trip had suddenly materialized on the muddy streets of one small hamlet.

Running low on gas, I turned up the mouth of the Kickapoo where it angled through woods on the north bank. The little river was cloudy and smelled of wet clay. The swamp behind it cast the skinny trees in a greenish light. I asked a pair of fishermen in a jonboat how far upriver Wauzeka was, and they said, "Just past the railroad bridge." A few more curves in the river and I slipped under the trestle and motored slowly past a pole building of yellow school buses to a boat landing.

Rueben Gold Thwaites had followed Père Marquette down the Wisconsin River and now I was following Thwaites. Whatever had set him off about Wauzeka a century and a quarter ago was nowhere in evidence. The streets were wide and paved, lined with chaste white houses, and the only saloon in sight was a corner tavern called Carol's Bar and Grill. How pleasant it would have been to fall in with "little knots of noisy loafers"; unfortunately, the bar stood empty in the early afternoon, so I walked Front Street to the BP convenience store instead. Like most small-town gas stations, its "conveniences" were more like necessities: food, shelter, clothing (sunglasses), and fuel. I made an all-purpose stop, topping off my five-gallon gas jug and washing up in the restroom. Then I ate a microwave hamburger for lunch and an Eskimo Pie for dessert.

Back on the Wisconsin, I'd hoped to make Boscobel by suppertime, but traveling against the current changed my timetable and I ended up camping on a sandbar for the night. It was a bare, convex little island with damp edges and a high spot a few feet above the water. I pitched my tent between emergent willow shoots and a standing dead tree severed halfway up the trunk with two upturned, broken branches. In the dusky light, the dead tree had the silhouette of a cactus, but once the sun disappeared it morphed into Edvard Munch's *The Scream*. Cocooned in my tent, I listened to the marine radio forecast, a 40 percent chance of showers, and wondered if the river would rise overnight to reflood the island. I felt lonesome because my own W— was at home instead of sharing this little sandbar with me. I wanted someone to worry about besides myself.

About two in the morning I was startled awake. The rain hadn't arrived but something—or someone—was splashing in the water. It was probably a deer coming down to drink or a raccoon wading for clams. But on a moonless night too dark to see beyond the tent's mosquito netting, my mind filled with gloomy thoughts of rabid skunks, feral hogs, and river tramps!

~~~~~~~~~~~~~~~~

14

Like most small towns along the Lower Wisconsin, Boscobel is set almost a mile back from the river to avoid flooding. The digital thermometer on the bank read 78 degrees. Unlike many river towns, its population had doubled since the turn of the last century. Boscobel's main street looked prosperous, wide enough for diagonal parking and lined with limestone-fronted, fully occupied storefronts. The town possessed everything necessary for self-sufficiency—its own hospital, pharmacy, grocery stores, restaurants, high school, and nearby state prison. The unseen Wisconsin River factored into this prosperity by serving as the take-out point for canoeists floating the sixty-mile stretch from Sauk City. On my walk into town I'd passed a canoe livery with a pole shed stuffed with rental canoes and kayaks though I'd yet to see any paddlers.

"That river, boy, it's always changing," said the short order cook at the Unique Café. "You can go out in the morning and by late afternoon the channel's changed. Where there's an island that splits the channel, boy, that's a bad spot."

The café was kitty-corner from the post office and the hotel where the Gideons hatched the idea of leaving Bibles in dresser drawers. Its walls were decorated with tinplate advertisements for old soft drinks, seed companies, and gas stations, including a Mobil Oil Pegasus. The waitress who served my eggs and sausage was the cook's daughter. Her jet-black hair was shaved on either side of a ponytail and she wore a T-shirt that read "Home of the Lousiest Food in Town."

The breakfast was quite good. "So what's with the T-shirt?" I asked.

"Oh, a woman wrote in the local paper that the food here was lousy, so we're running with it."

Dawdling over coffee, I struck up a conversation with a young man at the next stool. He was hard to ignore in a neon yellow T-shirt with a pink Cookie Monster in front. He introduced himself as John Knoble, logger.

"My family's all loggers, my father and grandfather and now me."

"And what is it you log?"

"Red and white oak, cherry and maple mainly. Myself, I'd say my favorites are a toss-up between walnut and maple. Popple too. It makes up about 90 percent of what we cut. Kiln-dried popple can last fifty years without cracking. If the market's crap for popple, the logger loses his ass. Then there's piss elm. Piss elm's a weak, garbage wood with crooked grain, but if you know how to log it, it makes a beautiful hardwood for floors."

I'd never heard the expression "piss elm" before and thought Knoble just didn't care for the tree. Turns out it's a colloquialism for the American elm, *Ulmus americanus*, a tall and stately tree with the unfortunate trait of smelling like urine if burned green. A poem to that effect once appeared in *The Times* of London:

> Elm-wood burns like churchyard mould,
> E'en the very flames are cold.

Loggers, said Knoble, got a bum rap when environmentalists accused them of clear-cutting whole forests. He said he didn't clear-cut anything but popple and anyway select cutting big trees was better in the long run because it opened up the canopy for smaller trees, especially hardwoods that need a combination of shade and sun. Whereas you could take a whole popple stand down because it grows better in direct sunlight.

I've noticed that people react in one of two ways to seeing their words written down in a notebook; they either clam up or talk faster. Knoble was the latter. I had a hard time keeping up with his torrent of information.

"We bring a dozer in, cut a road through the woods, then bring up a skidder and logging truck. I started running skidder when I was thirteen. My grandpa bought that skidder new, so it's really old. We put three engines and four housings in it. Paint it once every two years. The better you take care of things, the longer they'll last. We have a sawmill at the farm with a housing that's all old railroad ties. We run it off the PTO on the tractor. You run it wide open or not at all. It was 112 years old when we bought it. I'm 32, so it's got to be close to 132 years old."

I did a quick calculation. If he was correct, his sawmill first buzzed in 1884, a long time ago even for a machine, but Knoble talked so constantly and in such good humor that it would have required more effort not to believe him.

"Logging's always been my passion," he said finally. The problem at the moment was that Knoble was out of work. Insurance for a logging operation runs high and for the time being he was dry-docked.

He gave me a ride back through town in the rising heat to the landing beside the Highway 61 bridge. Then Knoble drove over the bridge to his sawmill and I went under it in my canoe. On my trip through the state, I had assumed that people would be either diffident or close-mouthed to a stranger, but conversation came easily once you located someone's passion, whatever that might be, and sometimes that passion proved contagious. As the river spread out among green islands and yellow sandbars, I found myself trying to see the trees for the forest, picking out sawlogs, the ones with the widest girth and straightest trunk, and wondering how many board feet of lumber they might produce or if they'd smell like piss when cut.

15

On occasion I took on passengers: an iridescent dragonfly and a zebra-striped butterfly landed on my canoe's center thwart for a time. Each needed a breather, evidently, and I was grateful for the company until they zipped away. Later, running close to a high bank on the north side of the river, I spotted a bird in the drink, wings stretched out uselessly, slowly sinking. Swinging the tiller hard, I came about and scooped up the bird with my paddle. Deposited on the floor of the canoe, the bird made a jittery passenger, eyes shut, shivering in the warm sunlight. Its wings were a greenish yellow, like a goldfinch's, only its body was larger, some kind of warbler perhaps. It was, in fact, a blue-winged warbler, a migrant bird that winters in Central America but nests in the Midwest. This was probably a fledgling that had crash-landed on her maiden flight.

Once the warbler dried off, two beady eyes opened and she began to chirp. The chirping did not sound like warbling but more like a complaint. *Tsick . . . tsick . . . tsick.* I began to imagine that when she settled down, the warbler might show some gratitude for my intervention, perhaps imprint on me and become my companion for the duration of the trip. As I was thinking this, she ruffled her feathers and launched herself over the gunwales. She didn't get very far before she fell back into the river. Rescued a second time, the warbler started *tsick . . . tsicking* again and seemed less like a pirate's parrot than the Ancient Mariner's albatross. A harbinger of bad things ahead. I started looking for a place to set my passenger free and off my hands.

I beached the canoe on a sandbar and the warbler must have concluded we'd reached our destination because she suddenly took flight, heading not across the wide river but the narrow channel closer to shore. The fledgling's wings beat furiously and I was sure she'd make the woods even as she kept losing elevation. Then, a few short yards from safety, the warbler went into the drink and, as if to prove third time's the charm, slipped under the surface.

When the National Wild and Scenic River Act was passed in 1968, the National Park Service offered to include the Lower Wisconsin River, but the state declined in large part because most of the valley was already in private hands. Instead, a political compromise was reached to allow for a measure of local control while preserving the aesthetic of a wild river. The Lower Wisconsin State Riverway encompasses ninety-five thousand acres, half public land and the rest privately owned, a big chunk of land if concentrated in one spot, but not when it's stretched over the ninety-two miles of free-flowing river between the hydroelectric dam at Sauk City and the Mississippi. It isn't wilderness but feels wild in stretches, despite the whine of trucks along the screened shoreline. If a canoeist left the river and struck off on foot, he'd quickly run into a cornfield or a road or a logger like John Knoble. So the wilderness aspect of the Lower Wisconsin is an optical illusion, but the same canoeist, narrowly confined to the river and its sandbars, could honestly report a sense of wildness. Wildness doesn't require scale, only the realization that nature is calling the shots. On almost any river a traveler is open to the vagaries of weather, to the river's rise and fall, and to the possibility, no matter how remote, that on a bad day the water can kill you.

The headquarters for the Lower Wisconsin Riverway Board is in Muscoda, halfway between Sauk City and the Mississippi. The town announced itself on the side of a water tower. It looked like Boscobel's poorer cousin, half the size of its downriver neighbor, with empty lots between storefronts that gave Main Street a gap-toothed look. At least the town has a functioning movie theater, I thought. On closer inspection, though, the double feature advertised in block letters on the marquee of the Muscoda Theater turned out to be the names of people who'd fallen into arrears.

OWES FOR BACK RENT AND UTILITIES
JASON —, SHERRY —, DIANE & WILLIAM —,
TRAVIS —

The offices of the Lower Wisconsin Riverway Board were in a handsome redbrick building with white cornices.

"Is it Mus-ko-dah?" I asked the board's secretary. "Or Musk-oh-day?"

"Musk-ah-day. Lots of folks get that wrong. Same as saying 'Goth-um' instead of 'GO-thum.'"

She had a cheerful smile and certainly had me pegged as an outsider. (I'd have pronounced the next town upriver like the city in Batman comics.) I told her I was impressed with the scenery along the Wisconsin River, and she gave me a handful of brochures that were mostly regulations for private landowners and loggers. The nine-member board did not prohibit development so much as mitigate its impact so improvements were "visually inconspicuous" from the water.

"It's only buildings within sight of the river. So far we haven't had any problems with individual landowners. Most of them are happy to go along."

A landowner could build a cottage within the Riverway as long as it was a certain distance from the shore, didn't exceed the height of the forest canopy, and was painted a color chosen from a palette of greens, browns, and grays.

Then we talked about my trip.

"Canoe season really hasn't started yet, has it?" she asked, though it was a statement more than a question. "And the weather hasn't exactly cooperated. Showers one day, showers the next. We've had a lot of rain so the river's been *way* up."

When I complained that the river didn't seem up to me because I kept running aground, the secretary's tone changed.

"We've got a saying around here. The Wisconsin is a fun, beautiful river, but you gotta respect it. There was a little girl up in Go-thum who drowned this spring. They didn't find her body for a couple of months. Then there was a whole family down in Boscobel. This was, oh, fifteen years ago. And four of them drowned. One went after the other. And you know why? They never had the money to go to the public pool SO THEY NEVER LEARNED HOW TO SWIM!"

The story of the family who'd drowned together in the Wisconsin had become part of the river's mythology, lingering long after the event because the scene of the tragedy never goes away. The facts were these: On a hot August day a mother took her three children to cool off at a boat landing south of Boscobel. The fourteen-year-old was wading in waist-deep water when he lost his footing on the shifting sand and yelled for help. A cousin tried to rescue him, but broke free when he pulled him under. The ten-year-old girl and nine-year-old boy waded in to help their older brother and were swept away in the current. The mother followed and was swallowed up as well. The next day searchers found one body sixty feet from the landing, the mother's a half-mile further, and another two miles away. The river carried the daughter's body the farthest, five miles downstream of the landing.

After Bogus Bluff, a limestone cliff riddled with fissures, the valley opened and the river got shallower. I shifted from bank to bank to stay in the main channel, sometimes using my paddle as a sounding pole to keep from running aground on shoals. The Pine River came in from the north, just before the Gothum boat landing. I wasn't planning to stop except that I caught sight of something bright red suspended in a tree. It was the color of a stop sign, so I stopped. Even before landing I guessed what the red something was, a stuffed bear in a Santa Claus outfit. Two white teddy bears had been placed in the crotches of other trees above a wreath of plastic flowers.

So this is where it happened, I thought, the most recent tragedy, the place where the little girl from Gothum had drowned in the spring. The rudiments of the story hardly differed from the family drowning except for the number of victims. A five-year-old and an older sister had been dropped off at a babysitter's house not far from the river. Children who grow up in the country don't stay cooped up in houses on warm spring evenings, so the girls walked to the boat landing. At first the five-year-old must have been content playing in the sand. Then she put her foot in the water just to feel the sensation of it moving. Then she waded out a little farther and, at some point, came to a drop-off and fell in. The other children linked arms to form a human chain and walked into the river as far as they could and reached out with a stick. But the current swept her downstream.

That was the story the teddy bear in the tree was meant to tell. Whoever had placed it there must have done so not only to remember what happened but to feel the pain all over again. Coming here would keep the hurt alive as well as the memory, an emotional scab laid bare every time you looked—and it was impossible not to look. In the Southwest, I'd come upon *descansos* along highways, a framed photograph of the dead draped with flowers and rosaries at the very spot of the accident. This was somehow worse. There was no photograph or name to attach to the loss, just toys—the sort that any child has—and if you tried to picture their owner, the child who drowned, the face that came to mind was your own child's.

~~~~~~~~~~~~~~~~

16

Rounding a bend near Lone Rock, I spied a shimmering white raft floating high on the water in the distance. It looked large and round enough to hold a party, a party raft then. As I drew closer, however, the raft frayed along the edges until the solid mass dissolved into snowy feathers and bright orange bills and my eyes re-focused until I recognized what lay ahead—a circle of white pelicans standing together in shallow water.

The pelicans I'd previously seen flying high over Mount Trempealeau at sunset had looked impossibly graceful angling across the sky. But the fifty or more enormous pelicans jammed wingtip to wingtip in the shallows merely looked strange, something drawn from a Lewis Carroll bestiary, a gathering of Jubjub birds or frumious Bandersnatches! A group of pelicans is called, among other things, a "scoop" because that's what they do when they congregate to feed, corral small fish together in the shallows then scoop them up with their pouched bills. But these pelicans weren't feeding. They stood in a tight circle, wings folded, tangerine bills tucked against white chests, staring off in different directions. Since they weren't feeding, their scoop must have been a purely defensive formation, useful for fending off predators by appearing as a puffed-up mob rather than a collection of individual birds.

The pelicans stood four feet tall and since I was sitting in a canoe, we regarded each other at eye level. At first they tolerated my approach but grew agitated as the canoe drew nearer. Then a few birds broke off from the group, hopped twice and flapped heavily into the sky. Once airborne, the white pelicans became graceful again. They spread their nine-foot wings and revealed long, ink-black primary feathers underneath, the ones that allow them to fly. I wondered where the pelicans would spend the night. Later I'd ask the same question about myself.

In the afternoon, I encountered my first rental canoe heading downriver. It was occupied by a family of four: Dad looking resolute in the stern, a small boy and girl in the middle, and Mom in the bow, gripping the neck of her paddle in a choke hold. All of them wore stiff new orange life jackets. We hailed each other like passing ships at sea.

"That looks easier!" Dad called out as he paddled past, sweat streaming from his brow.

"Not if you're hitting sandbars!" I shouted over the drone of my outboard.

Not only were these the first canoeists I'd seen on the Wisconsin River so far, they were the only black people I'd seen the entire trip. Soon other boats appeared on the river, red canoes and yellow kayaks, all racing vigorously downstream. None of the paddlers drifted with the current but dug into the water with vigorous strokes and hardly ever waved in passing. At first I thought it was because I had an outboard motor and was heading in the opposite direction. Then I realized that it was the start of the weekend and people were racing to find a campsite. Later in the summer when the Wisconsin dropped, there would be no end of sandbars to camp on, but with the river running high they were at a premium.

At the head of every sandbar I passed was a nylon tent with a folding chair planted on the beach like a flag. Not wanting to compete for limited space, I kept going. An hour later I tied my bowline to a tree in front of the Riverside Resort above Spring Green. I was looking forward to a hot shower and a cold drink, not necessarily in that order. The registration desk was in the gift shop of the resort's new lodge-style main building. The cheerful, pretty girl behind the desk filled out a form and asked if I required an electric hook-up.

"No. I've just got a tent."

"That'll be $42.20."

"Excuse me?"

"$42.20," she repeated, less cheerfully. "That's with tax. The rate goes up on weekends."

I'd spent less than that for a room at the Trempealeau Hotel, but the girl showed me how the camping rates broke down by season, day of the week, and type of accommodation: Cabin, Cottage, Full Hook-up RV—Big Rig, Full-Hook-up Riverside Sites, and finally Tent. It was the weekend and the resort was packed, plus I didn't want to get back in the canoe. So I forked over the money and the girl spread a color-coded map of the resort's grounds on the counter. It resembled a plat map for a new subdivision, with looping roads and cul-de-sacs, a big outdoor pool and designated green spaces. Clustered around the roads were two hundred sites. The tent loop, indicated by little brown pyramids, was off to the east, far afield of the swimming pool and other amenities. The girl circled one of the little brown pyramids with her pen.

"Here it is, number 26. It looks a long ways away, but it isn't."

Then she moved on to another customer.

She was wrong about number 26. It *was* a long ways off, especially for someone on foot hauling a duffel bag of camping gear. Still, the walk provided a good introduction to the resort. It was a temporary city, at least on weekends, with a bigger population than many of the unincorporated towns I'd passed along the river. The resort was laid out like L'Enfant's hub-and-spoke design for the nation's capital; the main building and restaurant formed the central hub from which everything else radiated. The first ring was composed of swimming pool, playground, and shuffleboard courts. Next came the more expensive cottages and log-sided cabins with river views. These were followed by acres and acres of RVs: travel trailers, pop-ups, larger fifth-wheels, and truly mammoth motor homes. Each vehicle occupied a small rectangle of thinning grass with a picnic table on a concrete pad and a fire pit. A few of the residences were semi-permanent and had signs hanging from them: "Welcome to Camp Rum-Muk" and "Wayne & Shirley." Some had satellite dishes and air-conditioning units on their roofs; others had crank-out awnings and slide-out walls. All came equipped with an incredible assortment of bicycles, lawn chairs, flotation devices, and the occasional golf cart. And except for detail work, almost every one of the RVs was blazing white, something to do with the effect of UV rays on pigment, heat reflection, and so forth. But it did seem strange on the Lower Wisconsin, where permanent structures must be camouflaged by muted colors, to see so many RVs gathered by the river like a herd of white elephants in a dry season.

The RV loop came to an end when the speed bumps stopped and the pavement turned to gravel. The road was bordered by woods on one side and a soybean field on the other and it dead-ended, far from the restaurant and swimming pool, in a hinterland of tent sites. Most were unoccupied and site 26, thank goodness, lay in a circle of shade. While I was glad not to sleep cheek-by-jowl beside a RV with a humming generator, it was hard not to conclude that tent campers were being excluded from the fun. I shook my tent out of its bag and started fitting fiberglass wands together when a van pulled up and spilled out a noisy load of college kids, the type who might ignore quiet hours (11 pm to 8 am) in favor of strumming a guitar. Unpacking a new tent from its box, they puzzled over how to put it up.

The lopsided ratio of RVs to tents mirrors the future of camping. The percentage of young Americans who tent camp, like my new neighbors, is dwindling, while the number of households who own a recreational vehicle steadily increases. My own notion of camping derived from *The Boy Scout Manual*, fifth edition. It informed scouts who wished to obtain the camping merit badge that a total of twenty nights must be spent "under the stars or in a tent you have pitched." Not to be a reverse-snob about this, but spending an entire summer encased in an RV would earn you zero merit badges.

Having recently left the Rendezvous in Prairie du Chien, I was struck by the differences between the two encampments, the reenactors in their canvas tipis and the RVers in their aluminum land yachts. The one celebrated eighteenth-century self-sufficiency and the frontier's cultural mix; the other spoke of consumerism and an overriding concern for security. The demographic profile of the average RV owner—median age forty-eight, married, white, annual household income of $62,000—means that an RV campground has a sameness to it, as if an entire suburban neighborhood had been uprooted and transplanted in the woods. A more apt metaphor might be circling the wagons, a defensive formation against asymmetrical attack. A recent article in *RV Daily Report*, "Meth-Addicted Trio Lived in Forest, Stole Camping Fees," implied that national forest campgrounds were scary places and one would court disaster by sleeping in one, especially without the protection of a hard-shell. None of this matters except for the long-term implications for public lands. The traditional camper needs an open expanse of land or a free-flowing river full of sandbars on which to pitch his tent. The RVer requires only a parking space and electric hook-up.

As night came on, I retraced my route toward the central hub of the restaurant. The tent area was mostly dark but the RV loop was a cheerful constellation of small campfires. In almost every space a family had left the comfort of their land yacht to sit in lawn chairs around a wood fire, their faces aglow its light. The blazing fire wasn't necessary for cooking—an on-board microwave or gas range took care of that—it served a more iconic purpose, to assure the family that they were, in fact, camping.

The line for the Friday night fish fry at the resort's Bar and Grille extended to the door. The dining room was full, so I sat at the bar looking out a huge picture window at the last shimmer of lilac-colored light on the river and later, when darkness became total, at my own morose reflection. There's a difference between solitude and loneliness. Most of my time on the river I felt as self-contained and happy as one of the crewmen of *The Jolly Flatboatmen*. To feel alone, you first have to be made aware of it, and loneliness, if it struck, usually came when I was ashore and in a crowd of people talking and laughing as if they all knew each other.

To avoid looking at myself in the picture window, I watched television. A pyramid of three flat-screen TVs were arranged above the bar: local news, a baseball game, and Bill O'Reilly at the top. The sound was turned off—not that I could have heard anything over the roar of diners, but it was easy enough to see that the livid O'Reilly was getting himself all worked up. A Fox News crawl explained that nine churchgoers had been gunned down at a black church in South Carolina. O'Reilly was giving a good tongue-lashing to his guest, a UCLA law professor calling for new gun laws. Bill was clenching his teeth, waving his hands, the blood rushing unevenly to his head. The baseball game, by comparison, seemed to be played in slow motion. The camera cut to footage of the young shooter being arraigned, a gangly beanpole with a bowl haircut. He looked as harmless as a youth counselor at Bible camp. I finished my drink and tried to get the waitress's attention but she was too busy to notice.

17

Early the next morning, I untied my canoe and slipped quietly away from the resort. A purplish sunrise and high-masted clouds made for a promising start to the day. Then the weather changed, a slanting drizzle pushed along by a cool north wind. By the time I reached Ferry Bluff, the sky cleared and the land to the south flattened into wooded bottoms. Somewhere behind a maze of comma-shaped islands lay the nude beach at Mazomanie. It was a state natural area in more than one way, drawing sunbathers from nearby Madison. For decades the beach had been a cultural lightning rod that, depending on who you listened to, symbolized either the state's liberal tolerance or a steady drift toward depravity. "Just a bunch of old queers from Madison," I'd heard a man on a barstool say in a tone of bitter disappointment. Reports of illegal drugs and public sex had caused the DNR to close access to the beach except on summer weekends. Locals talked of replacing it with a public shooting range.

I was curious about Mazomanie beach. My own experience of skinny-dipping had been limited to a brief sojourn in California during my early twenties, a period I associated with batik bedspreads and the overwhelming smell of patchouli. What would one look like in the Midwest? Maybe it was the raw wind or my perspective from a passing canoe, but the beach at Mazo didn't look nude so much as naked. The sunbathers, pale and presumably goose-bumped, looked as if they had never been in the sun before. From a distance, I couldn't tell whether they were men or women or if the dark triangles below their waists were pubic hair or Speedos. Sprawled motionless on the buff-colored sand, arms flung over their heads, the sunbathers looked as if they'd died where they'd fallen.

We've pretty much given up on June," said the woman who ran the canoe livery in Sauk City. "People want to camp on sandbars and when there aren't any because the river's high, business slows down."

To my mind, the Wisconsin River had more than enough sandbars and shoals, but I didn't mention this to the livery owner, who was kind enough to let me store my canoe with her rentals. The hydroelectric dam at Sauk City meant I couldn't go any further up the Wisconsin without a lift and I'd have to wait for my ride. The woman pointed up the road to the nearest motel, a row of 1950s-style white rooms lined up along the highway with patio chairs on the walkway so guests could smoke and contemplate the traffic. A list of motel rules was framed inside the door:

NO GUESTS PAST 9:00 PM.

NO PETS, NO FISH, NO BAIT

OR GAME IN THE ROOM.

I hung my damp clothes on the bedstead to dry and called Bob Elkins.

The next day Elkins trailered my canoe around the Sauk City dam and deposited it at a boat landing across from Portage. Two miles to the east lay the Fox River, the next leg of my trip, but before leaving the Wisconsin River I wanted to visit a place along it that I'd only read about, a place that was, in a literal sense, the wellsprings of the Round River.

The Wisconsin may have been running high elsewhere, but above Portage it was stacked with hidden shoals. An island split the river into shallow channels clogged with driftwood and whole trees, one of which had snagged a deer carcass, its antlers tangled in the branches. The shoreline was unrelentingly flat with no landmarks except the Baraboo Range rising far to the west. I assumed that I'd be able to recognize what I was looking for from the river, but as the miles passed I began to worry that I'd already missed it, in which case I'd end up at Wisconsin Dells.

In the dwindling daylight, I pitched camp on a sandbar and de-termined to resume my search the next day. After supper, I heard voices and spotted a family walking along the opposite shore. Shouting over the water, I asked if Aldo Leopold's Shack was nearby. They'd never heard of it.

"Is it a big building?" the man shouted back. "We drove past a big building on the way here. *Who* did you say owned it?"

I found it hard to believe that a local wouldn't know the where-abouts of what many people, myself among them, consider the equivalent of Thoreau's cabin at Walden Pond.

I first read *A Sand County Almanac* over the interminable darkness of a subarctic winter. I was a graduate student at the University of Alaska grading papers for a professor who'd assigned Leopold's book to his freshman composition class. Initially I wasn't thrilled with the choice. Like a lot of young people who come to Alaska in their twenties, I had nauseatingly purist views about nature and no interest in anything short of untrammeled wilderness. What a surprise, then, to be caught up in a book about a landscape that had been thoroughly trammeled. In the depths of the Great Depression, Leopold bought eighty acres of worn-out farmland, "corn stubble, cockleburs and broken fences" along the Wisconsin River, for back taxes. Then he set out to restore the land to health. Arranged around a calendar year at the Shack, the book read like a midwestern version of *A Swiss Family Robinson*: the resourceful father leading his family as they build a shelter out of salvaged materials, plant trees and wildflowers, cut firewood, count migrating waterfowl, and harvest wild food.

At the time I was building my own log cabin in Alaska and Leopold's Shack seemed like a blueprint for the kind of life I imagined for myself: self-sufficient and rooted to the one good place where I could raise a family and watch the seasons turn. Things didn't turn out as planned. I abandoned the cabin, then Alaska, and finally my first marriage collapsed. In retrospect, the problem wasn't so much my lack of survival skills as maturity. Leopold was forty-eight years old when he took on the Shack. He wasn't a young man trying to find himself in the wilderness but a middle-aged professor in the grip of obligations—professional and familial. Behind Leopold's simple stories of banding birds or tracking wildlife in the snow is a complex philosophy that boils down to one idea: Land is a community. As citizens of that community, we are responsible for the whole as well as the parts, and whatever mark we leave on the land, good or bad, tells us who we are as a people. Reading *Sand County Almanac*, I realized that a meaningful life isn't about finding the one good place, it's about trying to be a good citizen of wherever you find yourself.

Once the morning fog lifted, I set off again. This time I tilted up the outboard and paddled through the shallows standing up so I could see over the riverbank. I felt a little ridiculous to be paddling gondolier-style past cottages with martin houses and white docks extending over the water. A Labradoodle mix raced down from one of the docks to bark at me, its owner in close pursuit. The woman balanced a cup of coffee in one hand and a leash in the other.

"Excuse me," I said, exasperated "Do you happen to know where the Leopold Shack is? I'm pretty sure it's around here but I can't seem to find it."

She pointed with her coffee cup upriver. "It's right there. Where that big birch tree is. You can leave your canoe here and walk there if you like."

"Thanks, but I really want to arrive at the Shack by water."

It was a silly response to a gracious offer but what was I supposed to say? Admit that I was on a journey because I'd read an essay about a metaphoric river whose source lay just upriver?

At the big birch there was nothing to see but a sand flat and a tangle of oaks and cottonwoods. I left the canoe on the beach and headed inland bushwhacking through shoulder-high blackberry brambles. Away from the river, the heat grew more intense, the air sticky and thrumming with insects. And still no Shack. Finally I broke out of the woods and followed a shady two-lane blacktop to a handsome new complex known as The Leopold Center. The buildings were constructed of recycled materials, native fieldstone, and locally milled pine from trees the Leopold family had planted in the Thirties. There were solar panels mounted on the overhanging roof and an elaborate gutter system to water a rain garden of prairie forbs. It was all very impressive and consistent with Leopold's philosophy but also a little disorienting to anyone who'd read the book and was looking for a simple Shack. Inside the complex, among the black-and-white photographs and other exhibits, I found a reminder of Leopold as a struggling writer. It was a typewritten rejection letter from a New York publisher: "As you probably know, volumes of essays are difficult to sell and we do not feel that a volume of essays on outdoor topics would find a wide enough market to warrant our use of paper at this time."

In 1944, publishers had to contend with wartime rationing, so turning down a manuscript because of a paper shortage wasn't the slam that it might appear. Still, it must have been hard for Leopold to swallow because the little volume represented a lifetime's work. The real brush-off was labeling it a collection of essays on "outdoor topics." Leopold would have been all too familiar with that attitude, the assumption that our real lives are separate from nature and any writer who placed them on an equal footing must necessarily be an "outdoor" hack. I wondered if the editor had even read the book.

Four years after that first rejection letter, Leopold received confirmation that Oxford University Press wished to publish *A Sand County Almanac*. A week after receiving the good news, Leopold drove up to the Shack from Madison with his wife Estella and youngest daughter. Spring had arrived full-blown: geese flying over the river by the hundreds, pasque flowers in bloom, a new shipment of pine saplings waiting to be planted. On that breezy April day the wind carried an acrid whiff of smoke from a neighbor's trash fire. Flames soon spread to the dry marsh grass. Leopold, worried about his pine plantation, asked his wife to guard the road with a broom where he thought the fire might cross it. Then he dispatched his daughter to call the fire department while he attacked the line of knee-high flames with a portable water pump. A short time later, he suffered a fatal heart attack. Neighbors found Leopold on his back, hands folded across his chest, the fire having passed lightly over his body.

"He was here with his wife and Estella Jr.," Dakota Johnson told me as we strolled outside the building. "He saw smoke and came down the road to help his neighbor put out a grass fire. The Center is almost right where the fire had been. It's one of the only building spots out of the floodplain."

Tall and lanky in worn-out jeans and a frayed baseball cap, Dakota Johnson is site manager for the Leopold Center, which means he thins trees and sets prescribed fires to protect its prairie breaks and oak savannahs. Johnson seemed personally acquainted with every tree on the property. As we walked back down the road and turned off into wild meadow, he tossed plant names over his shoulder: "This is bee-balm or wild bergamot. This tall grass is big bluestem. I see worm-wood, ox-eyed sunflower, Indian grass, clover, wild indigo, butterfly weed."

The meadow, Johnson explained, is what remains of the original cropland on the Depression-era farm Leopold bought in 1935. The previous owner, a bootlegger, had planted corn year after year with no rotation until he wore the soil down to the same alluvial sand as the riverbank. Leopold restored the bare fields to an earlier stage that didn't require plowing by planting prairie grasses and wildflowers. Driving up Highway 12 from Madison to the Shack on weekends, he'd stop along the roadside and the family would dig up the wild grasses and forbs to replant here. In the spring, they'd burn the old growth. The meadow is the second oldest prairie restoration in the world. The oldest is at the Arboretum at UW–Madison and Leopold started that as well.

At the edge of the open meadow, beneath a stand of tall white pines, stood the Shack. Places that loom large in one's imagination tend to shrink in the light of day, but the Shack really was small—smaller than any of the cottages I'd passed along the river, small enough to tuck inside most of the motor homes at the RV camp-ground. It was one story with a gable roof, a single padlocked door, and board and batten siding weathered a dark gray. The boards must have been sawn locally because their width varied wildly. In old black-and-white photographs, the Shack stands next to a seasonal slough with the main channel clearly visible in the background. In the eighty-year interval between the photographs and today, the slough had filled in and trees screened the view of the river. When the Leopolds built the Shack, it had stood in the open; now it lay in a deep pool of shade from pines the family had planted as saplings.

Johnson unlocked the door. It was dark as a tomb inside until he latched the window by the door open and the whitewashed walls flooded with light. The single room didn't have a musty, cottage smell because it was so bare: a table, benches, log irons in the field-stone fireplace.

"When the Leopold kids heard Dad say he'd bought a place on the Wisconsin River," said Johnson, "they imagined a cottage on the water. They got up here and it was a chicken coop knee-deep in chicken shit. The first thing they had to do was shovel it out."

The family's initial trip to the Shack was early spring so the frozen chicken shit had to be broken up with a pickaxe before it could be spread on the planned garden. When the weather warmed, the Leopolds returned with building tools and lumber. They cut out windows, laid a plank floor, mixed river sand with mortar to build a brick chimney with a massive limestone hearth, and added a lean-to sleeping room. Still, I wondered how a family of seven squeezed inside the Shack at the end of the day.

"They'd pick up pieces of wood out of the river during spring flood, bring them back here and make stuff out of them. They built benches along the wall for seating. They built two sets of bunks. They slept two to a bed and some people slept on the floor. They almost always had a dog, usually a German shorthaired pointer named Gus. There were multiple Guses. Bet you can't guess what that is." Johnson pointed to a piece of wood on the top beam with a circle of rope attached. "It's a hawk roost. Carl had a pet hawk and it would perch there at night. Estella Jr. had a squirrel and a pet crow."

Johnson made the Shack sound like the Peaceable Kingdom, but Leopold had originally bought the land for hunting. There's a photograph of young Nina Leopold walking to the Shack carrying a picnic basket and guitar under one arm and a 20-gauge shotgun in the other. The shotgun was for pheasants and the guitar and picnic basket for nightly singalongs by the fire.

One of the tools hanging neatly on the Shack wall was a crosscut saw. I wondered if it was the same saw that features prominently in the chapter "The Good Oak." On a crisp winter day, Leopold and his wife leave the warmth of the Shack and tramp through snow to a lightning-killed oak, which he and Estella (the "chief sawyer") cut into firewood with a crosscut saw. As the saw blade cuts through the oak's growth rings, Leopold counts backwards through the up-and-down ecological history of Wisconsin—the establishment of National Forests (1927), the killing of the state's last marten (1925), the Supreme Court abolishing state forests (1915), the demise of Wisconsin's last cougar (1908), its last passenger pigeon (1899), its last elk (1866).

Leopold built unlikely alliances—farmers, hunters, bird watchers—around the premise that their mutual stake in the land's health outweighed narrow interests. He also shifted wildlife management away from game wardens and into the hands of professional biologists who could be expected to take the long view. "Harmony with the land is like harmony with a friend," he wrote. "You cannot cherish his right hand and chop off his left. That is to say, you cannot love game and hate predators; you cannot conserve water and waste the ranges; you cannot build the forest and mine the farm. The land is one organism."

What would Leopold think of his home state now that the saw was cutting in the opposite direction? The head of Wisconsin's Department of Natural Resources, a former developer, had dismissed most of the agency's scientists and put a gag order on the rest. Enforcement of water pollution violations was down and permits for filling in wetlands were up. At the behest of our governor, the state legislature had passed bills that allowed open-pit mining at the headwaters of rivers and established a hunting season on timber wolves. It was all terribly, terribly discouraging.

Johnson lowered the shutters and plunged the Shack's interior back into darkness. We stepped through the doorway into blazing sunlight and Johnson walked me back to my canoe. He'd grown up nearby in the small rural community of North Freedom, where his family were practicing conservationists and revered Leopold. After earning a degree in wildlife ecology, he interned at the Center and was now in charge of its 1,600 acres.

"Every pine you see planted on the land was planted by the Leopold family," Johnson said, pointing out a mature stand. "They planted thirty thousand pines over the years."

Collectively, the trees are known as the "Leopold Pines." So protective was Aldo of his plantation that he'd have the family burn narrow fire-lanes every spring between the pines and the meadows in case of a wild fire. It was this concern that had sent him racing to the neighbor's grass fire on the last day of his life. The pines, said Johnson, were an important part of the Leopold legacy.

The more important legacy, I thought, was Dakota Johnson.

~~~~~~~~~~

18

Scarcely ten miles up the Wisconsin River from Leopold's Shack lay its antipodal twin—Wisconsin Dells. One celebrated man's interconnection with land, the other our dominion over it. If the Shack was all about the natural world, the Dells was about simulacrum, the synthetic, the cheesy. Not that I minded. Once a summer when my children were young, I'd pack them and a few neighbor kids in our car and drive to a water park at the Dells. At the admission gate we'd exchange money for plastic wristbands, splash on sunscreen and hot-foot it along the walkway to various water slides. The water park even had a version of the Round River, a concrete moat of turquoise-blue water called the Lazy River that ran in a continuous loop. If a child was too little to swim, I'd crook him or her in my arm and spend hours riding an inner tube down the Lazy River. I loved it. The smell of chlorine mixed with SPF-30 mixed with sun-baked pavement. The happy whoops and shrieks of people plunging down vertiginous water slides or bobbing in the fake surf of the wave pool. Someone's off-key crooning to a karaoke machine at the Tiki Bar.

All of the sounds slightly muffled by the water in my ears. Together the child and I would float merrily down the manmade stream as it looped through the park past picnic tables, past elevated lifeguards, sunburned faces as impassive as totems, past my older children and their mother wrapped in beach towels. Then we'd come around and there they'd be again, unchanged, as if summer itself ran on a tight loop and would go on forever.

I had planned to skip the Dells this time. It wasn't on the itinerary of my Round River trip. Returning to the scene of some past happiness is always fraught with emotional booby-traps. On the other hand, I would be negligent if I made a pilgrimage to Leopold's Shack on my tour of Wisconsin and skipped the schlock just upriver. Besides, it was raining.

There's something inherently sad about a summer resort town on a rainy day—lines of umbrellas, wet sidewalks, parents searching desperately for alternatives to the promised fun. Broadway, the main street in Wisconsin Dells, offers plenty of indoor amusements: Ripley's Believe It Or Not Odditorium, Wizard Quest, Zombie Outbreak, Dairyland Fudge, Nig's Bar ("Have a Swig at Nig's"), and Wild Fun Zone with 3-D black light mini-golf and a King Kong–sized gorilla on its roof. But even newer attractions looked less appealing in the drizzle, their garish, carnival colors—chiefly canary yellow and flamingo pink—fading as they bled into the puddled street. Everything bespoke bad timing and thwarted plans.

"Memories that last a lifetime" is a marketing slogan in Wisconsin Dells as well as an implicit threat. I realized this sitting in a Mexican restaurant off Broadway when four little girls in pink party dresses arrived at the next table for a birthday celebration. The party reminded me of ones I'd thrown for my own children when they were the same age. The birthday girl sat behind a stack of gifts and balloons while her mother circled the table in high heels snapping pictures with her cellphone so the memory of the moment would last a lifetime.

Nostalgia is an ache in the heart for what is unrecoverable. The only cure is to try something new. So when the rain let up, I bought a ticket for a boat tour. In all my previous trips to the Dells, I'd never actually seen its original attraction, the sandstone rock formations along the Wisconsin River. I thought it might be pleasant to be a passenger and let someone else steer for a change.

A young crewman slipped the mooring rope from its bollard and the *Joliet* eased backwards from its dock above the Kilbourn dam. Built in 1908, the hydroelectric dam had turned the Upper Dells into an impoundment. When the sun came out, I joined other passengers on the upper deck as we steamed through a narrow palisade of yellow sandstone topped with pines.

"Those little round holes you see are the summer homes of bank swallows. They migrate here from Venezuela and eat twice their weight in mosquitoes every day!"

Sara, our tour guide on the *Joliet*, shared this fact over the boat's speaker system, and I dutifully wrote it down. Sara had blond braids and narrated the boat trip by torqueing her flat midwestern vowels into relentless cheerfulness. Approaching Blackhawk Island, Sara retold the tragic flight of the Sauk leader in the same peppy voice she'd used to describe Chimney Rock as a "stack of pancakes."

"Black Hawk was an Indian. . . . He surrendered in 1832 to save his people. . . . Unfortunately, they starved to death during the winter." As the boat joined the main channel, Sara shifted to a lighter subject. "There used to be a rest-stop on Blackhawk Island. They said it was a cathouse, but I just haven't been able to figure out why they put a pet shop on the island!"

Groans only encouraged her.

"Omigosh!" Sara cried out as we slid past a low and horizontal rock cropping. "That's not an alligator. *That's a Rockadile!*"

Even when there was nothing much to see, Sara found something to say. Every rock cropping came with a funny name or an apocryphal story.

"On your left is Romance Cliff, seventy-five feet above the water," boomed Sara over the hum of diesel engine. "This is where the Native Americans held their wedding ceremonies and, according to legend, an Indian maiden once leaped to her death."

Sara was reciting from a memorized script that had hardly changed in a century and a half. Before boarding the *Joliet*, I had purchased a facsimile of an 1879 Dells tour book, which laid the groundwork for all subsequent narratives. "It seems certain that, in the long gone ages when true love still found a foothold on earth," the tour book says of Romance Cliff, "some desperate, lovelorn Indian maiden must have clasped her dusky lover in her arms, sung the wild death-song of her tribe, and leapt from this romantic precipice into the surging tide below." The language was more overwrought and hokey than Sara's but the message was the same: Take a beautiful stretch of river, add a little bling, a little showbiz, and what you get is pizzazz! The old tour book was "fully illustrated" with engravings of photographs by Henry Hamilton Bennett, the man who put Wisconsin Dells on the map.

H. H. Bennett, a sawed-off Mark Twain with the same overhanging ledge of a moustache and skeptical eyes, bought a tintype studio in Kilbourn City after the Civil War and taught himself the new art of photography. Even a one-horse town could support a portrait studio, but Bennett soon tired of taking pictures of squirming children and anxious newlyweds. Leaving his wife in charge of the studio, he'd row up the Dells in a skiff equipped with a darkroom tent and look for picturesque views. Other landscape photographers headed west to capture the geological wonders of the newly established Yellowstone National Park; Bennett stayed close to home.

Bennett's scenic views turned the Western landscape on its head—buttes, canyon, weathered cliffs that sink below the horizon rather than tower above it. His photographs don't elicit a feeling of open space so much as nature confined. As Ruskin once stated, composition is the arrangement of unequal things. In Bennett's photographs people aren't dwarfed by the landscape. They dominate it. They peer down at the river from Visor Ledge or they picnic by the mouth of Witches Gulch or they stare out from Diamond Grotto. They don't *do* anything. They're not pioneers or cowboys; they're something new—tourists. Bennett posed them stiffly to provide a sense of scale and of Victorian civility in contrast to the "weird, wild" rock formations. Dressed in their Sunday best—feathered hats, parasols, bustles, waistcoats, neckties—they gape at the landscape as if it was a diorama in a museum.

A rock is finally just a rock, so Bennett named many of the sandstone formations he photographed and because a name needs a story to explain it, he created or rehashed romantic narratives to fill in the blanks. Tourists didn't see a water-eroded cleft in limestone; they saw "Black Hawk's Cave," last hide-out of the Sauk warrior, or the improbable "Black Hawk's Leap," where he jumped a horse across the river, or "The Squaw's Bed Chamber," a name that has thankfully been retired. Bennett didn't just document the Dells with his photographs; for all practical purposes he invented the place.

At Witches Gulch we disembarked from the *Joliet* and followed Sara up a boardwalk into a shady side canyon of dripping, moss-covered sandstone. The change was atmospheric—the afternoon light, filtered through overhanging ferns, turned emerald. The air felt refrigerant and damp. In order to photograph the canyon, Bennett had cleared it of windfalls and built the first boardwalk into the gulch. I found the canyon still beautiful, almost sublime right up to the point where the boardwalk ended in a well-lighted concession stand, another Bennett first.

The *Joliet*'s final stop—and the farthest point I got up the Wisconsin River—was the natural rock amphitheater at Stand Rock, scene of Bennett's most iconic photograph. In 1886 Bennett developed a rubber-band-powered shutter capable of freezing motion. To showcase this new technology, he photographed his son Ashley jumping from Stand Bluff to a narrow sandstone column beside it. The distance was roughly five feet. A plaque at the base of the bluff reproduced "Leaping the Chasm at Stand Rock." In the photograph the teenager hangs suspended in time and space, arms flung forward, legs parted, head tilted slightly downward toward the slightly lower tabletop. It's a striking photograph even now but more impressive once you know the backstory. According to Sara, Bennett required seventeen takes to get the perfect shot, which meant his poor son had to jump back up to the bluff after each take.

By the close of the nineteenth century, tourism to the Dells was up, fueled largely by Bennett's own promotional efforts, but his photography business declined. The development of roll film meant visitors took their own pictures with what Bennett called "cheap snap shot cameras." Tourists don't want art; they want memories. And the river's sandstone formations weren't the only draw. There were billiard parlors, croquet lawns, dance pavilions, a caged sea lion exhibit. The final blow was a proposal to build the largest power-generating dam west of Niagara Falls that, promoters said, would turn Kilbourn City into a manufacturing center. Bennett led the opposition. In a letter to state legislators he argued against the dam, saying that "one of Wisconsin's beauty spots should be preserved for the people and not sacrificed to the greed of commercialism." He was making an argument that preceded Aldo Leopold by forty years, but in Bennett's case it was a matter of too little, too late.

When the *Joliet* returned to its home dock, I complimented Sara on her running monologue and ability to turn erosion into romance. I asked what she was majoring in at college. My initial guess was theater, but I was wrong.

"Political science."

"And what do you plan to do after graduation?"

"Work on somebody's campaign."

I wished her luck, not that she'd need it.

Fox River

~~~~~~~~~~~~~~~

19

A great divide runs through the middle of Wisconsin, though it's hard to see in a place where all things appear equal. Throw a carpenter's level across the middle of the state and the bubble would tilt upward from the Mississippi River to the center of Wisconsin then slant downwards to Lake Michigan. Since leaving Prairie du Chien, I had scaled the equivalent of a fourteen-story building and would soon descend a sixteen-story river to the east. Sitting squarely on this invisible ridge, indeed because of it, is the city of Portage. A hydrological divide suggests thin air, not an elevation of 794 feet above sea level. Nevertheless, Portage rests on the summit of a narrow strip of land between two major watersheds. Rain falling on the west end of town flows to the Wisconsin River and on toward the Gulf of Mexico; rain on the east side flows to the Fox River then on to the Atlantic. The area's original occupants, the Ho-Chunk Indians, called this marshy ground *Wan-wan-o-rah* or "The Place Where One Takes Up His Canoe and Carries It on His Back." Early French explorers called it a *portage*, a word that means roughly the same thing. Walking a footpath between the rivers, Père Marquette counted the portage at 2,700 paces, roughly two miles. The Ho-Chunk understood the value of a route between drainage systems and charged subsequent travelers a toll to use it. Later, white settlers built a wagon road over the route and eventually dug a canal but not before evicting the Ho-Chunk from their own land. Frederick Jackson Turner's father, editor of the Portage newspaper at the time, applauded the move: "When all this is considered we think there is very little occasion for shedding any tears over the cruelty of removing them. They will be vastly better off than they now are, leading a strolling vagabond life among the whites, getting a muskrat for Monday, a turtle for Tuesday, a few berries for Wednesday, begging for Thursday."

Having no intention of taking up my canoe and carrying it on my back, I rode through the streets of Portage in Bob Elkins's van, my square-stern rattling behind on a boat trailer. The old canal, terminus of the Fox-Wisconsin Waterway, still runs through the downtown, but its iron gates are welded shut, the stagnant green water coated in duckweed and snags. Elkins followed the canal's route out of town and through the flat countryside by keeping an eye on the line of elms that border it. We passed cornfields, bumped over railroad tracks, and turned down a gravel road that dead-ended beside the old Indian Agency House, a two-story white frame house built in the year the Ho-Chunk signed the first of several treaties displacing them.

The day had turned into a steam bath. By the time Elkins and I wrestled the canoe down a grassy bank into the scummy canal, I was soaking wet. I bolted the outboard to the stern, loaded the canoe, then motored down the last weedy stretch into the Fox River to resume my own strolling, vagabond life.

The Fox was the fourth link in the Round River route I had cobbled together. Compared to the other rivers, it was an infant stream, barely a few miles from its birthplace and no wider than my canoe was long. Further down, past Lake Winnebago, the Fox is much larger and staggered with locks and dams as it flows through a highly industrialized valley, but here it was clear and intimately proportioned as a trout stream. The upper Fox flows through a bucolic landscape of rolling farmland and small towns. It was going to be a nice change of pace. No going against the current, no hidden shoals or jarring boat traffic, just a pleasant ride on a warm summer's day.

As the river wound through a tall grass meadow, the smooth surface of the water reflected everything around it—meadow, solitary swamp oaks, a cerulean dome of sky—and beneath the reflection strands of seaweed wavered in the gentle current. A doe drinking at the river's edge perked up at the sound of my outboard then bounded off through the high grass, her summer coat a red pennant against the green meadow.

Then the outboard changed pitch, shuddered and quit with a puff of blue smoke. I tilted the outboard out of the water and saw the problem. Seaweed had tangled around the prop in a thick, shiny knot. I cut away the knot with a filet knife and restarted the outboard. A few bends in the river later, the same thing happened: a straining, a smoky cough and I was drifting with the current. Once again I cleared the seaweed and yanked the starter cord. This time nothing. More yanks, more silence. Obviously the spark plug was fouled. All I had to do was clean it. But when I removed the engine cowling and dug through my tool pouch, I discovered that I'd brought my motorcycle spark plug wrench, not the one for the outboard, and it was too small. A tiny error but one that unreeled a string of consequences. No wrench meant I couldn't remove the spark plug to clean it, and without a spark the outboard wouldn't start, and that meant a long paddle to the next hardware store.

A square-stern canoe with fifty pounds of useless outboard hanging from it is not easy to paddle. The reliable J-stroke, using the blade as a rudder at the end of each stroke to align the canoe, didn't work. The only way to keep my bow pointed downstream was to paddle on alternate sides: three strokes on starboard, three strokes on port. I had brought an outboard so my canoe trip wouldn't turn into a physical ordeal and now that's exactly what it had become.

When French voyageurs paddled this very route in much larger birchbark freight canoes they didn't complain about it, they sang. Expected to keep a pace of fifty-five strokes a minute, the men synchronized their strokes by singing in chorus. So important was rhythm to this enterprise that paddlers were sometimes hired for their voices and song lists as well as their arm strength. What did they sing about on those long voyages? Lost loves? Homesickness? Better wages? I only knew one voyageur song.

> Alouetta, gentille alouetta,
> Alouetta, je te plumerai.

French being the language it is, I'd always assumed Alouetta was someone's sweetheart, a girl left behind in Sault St. Marie or Montreal; in fact the literal translation is "lark." The lyrics enumerate how the little bird is to be plucked in preparation for cooking, beginning with the lark's bill, then moving on to the eyes, the head, neck, wings, and so forth. "Allouette" is not a love song but a recipe.

The only songs I know by heart are the ones I'd memorized while riding in someone's car to high school. They were mostly Beatles tunes. To liven up the otherwise melancholy "Eleanor Rigby," I would substitute the names of old girlfriends, so that's what I did now, accompanying myself with paddle splashes.

Car-o-lyn Kra-mer (three strokes)
Picks up the rice in the church where a wedding has been (three strokes)
Dah . . . Dah . . . Dah . . . Doo-Dum.
E-liz-a-beth Greene died in the church (three strokes)
And was buried along with her name (three strokes)
Dah . . . Dah . . . Dah . . . Doo-Dum.

Singing took the edge off paddling and how perfect that so many old girlfriends had names of exactly five syllables! The list, however, was pathetically short and soon I was repeating myself and wondering if any of those long-ago girls even remembered my name. Much of the shoreline on the upper Fox was low and marshy, the stub-ends of farms or cottages with deteriorating docks and a rowboat sunk in cattails. Because it was private land and there were no sandbars I worried about where I'd camp for the night. Past the County O bridge, the river entered a National Wildlife Refuge. (A metal sign stuck in the reeds said so.) One side of the river remained swampy, but the other bank rose high enough to hold a stand of white oaks with a grassy opening between them. It made a pretty campsite, wood anemone and purple gentian growing in the knee-high grass. As soon as I crawled inside, the tent felt cozy and home-like. The swamp across the river grew luminous at sunset as the last bar of golden light climbed a distant line of trees. Night settled in and everything became the sound of itself. A sandhill crane bugling from the darkness and another crane answering. The plucked banjo string of a bullfrog. Somewhere in a far-off pasture a cow mooed her sweet goodnights. Then I ruined the mood by switching on my marine radio. The National Weather Service announced in a computerized baritone that a trough of low pressure was moving east across the southern half of the state with strong thunderstorms expected by morning.

The great thunderstorms in particular interested us, so unlike anything seen in Scotland, exciting awful, wondering imagination," John Muir recalled in *The Story of My Youth and Boyhood*. "Gazing awe-stricken, we watched the upbuilding of the sublime cloud-mountains—glowing, sun-beaten pearl and alabaster cumuli, glorious in beauty and majesty and looking so firm and lasting that birds, we thought, might build their nests amid their downy bosses; the black-browed storm clouds marching in awful grandeur across the landscape, trailing broad gray sheets of hail and rain like vast cataracts, and ever and anon flashing down vivid zigzag lightning followed by terrible crashing thunder."

Muir's father had been a Campbellite preacher in Scotland, and Muir transformed this religious zealotry in his own life into a romantic view of nature—the terrible and beautiful combined to form the sublime. That's where Muir differed from Leopold. Strange that the country's two great naturalists should have lived in such close proximity, each by a river, though at different ends of the century. Of the pair, I preferred the matter-of-fact scientist. Muir was too rhapsodic. He considered all creation the wondrous hand of God, even when it was throwing lightning bolts at him.

Muir's childhood farmstead lay no more than a mile from my campsite. I'd have looked for it except that I awoke the next morning to find the air heavy and still, the sky darkening in the west. Quickly loading the canoe, I shoved off and followed the river out of the wildlife refuge and into the ten-mile bulge of Buffalo Lake. I was hoping to beat the storm to the next town. The temperature kept dropping as a brisk wind pushed ahead of the cold front. The canoe crawled across the lake. Lightning branched across the sky and I quickened my pace to four paddle strokes per side and no singing. Rain began to fall in widely spaced drops at first, then continuous white sheets. The next lightning bolt hit the horizon simultaneously with an explosion of thunder

Being caught in an electrical storm didn't feel rhapsodic so much as scary. I was terrified lightning would seek the tallest object on the lake, which at the moment was my aluminum canoe. I hunched my shoulders to make myself as small as possible and paddled furiously on, all the while looking for a place to get off the water. A row of darkened cottages loomed ahead in the storm light, a kitchen light burning in one of them.

A barefoot, shirtless man in paint-splattered jeans opened the door. His bearded face slowly composed itself from sleep to wariness as he took in the breathless stranger standing on his doorstep in the pouring rain with no car visible. What did I want?

"My outboard," I said, gesturing toward the dock. "I think it's the plug. Would you happen to have a spark plug wrench?"

"Spark plug wrench?" he repeated. "I was just using one yesterday. Now where is it?"

Nothing appeals to a man with tools more than another man's mechanical ineptness. And Nick—that was his name—was a man with tools, so many that he'd lost track of some of them. Throwing on a brown flannel shirt without buttoning it, he stepped into the downpour. He pulled back a tarp covering the bed of his pickup and rummaged through a toolbox until he found a wrench, which he quickly put back in the box.

"No. That ain't it. Let's try the shed."

Nick had a handsome, young face, but he shuffled to the shed like an old man. Inside, it smelled of spilt engine oil and old canvas. When Nick turned on the single bare bulb, we stood in a clutter of tool boxes, red plastic gas jugs, a blue propane torch, orange extension cords, tailpipes, aerosol cans, and engine parts—all clustered around a motorcycle frame.

"The frame is '86, so I guess it's an '86 Harley. I've rebuilt plenty of Harleys for people, also Nortons, BMWs, Triumphs, but not my own. This'll be my own chopper."

Nick rambled on about various motorcycles until he remembered the reason he'd come into the shed in the first place. He pulled a socket wrench from one of the tool bins.

"Here it is. This is the one I use for the weed-whackers. See if that's the right size."

I retrieved my spare sparkplug from the canoe, but it was bigger than Nick's socket.

"Okay. Let's see. Three-sixteenths is what I'm thinking."

He came up with a three-sixteenths socket that did, in fact, fit. I ran back to the dock, ratcheted the spark plug from my outboard and handed it to Nick.

"I'd say it's fouled but good. You're probably running too rich a mixture. No wonder you couldn't get a spark."

Nick cleaned away the carbon build-up with a wire brush. Then he ran a sheet of fine-grit sandpaper between the electrode and the ground until both gleamed. He still wasn't satisfied.

"That gap don't seem right. Let me check it."

From his pocket he pulled an enormous keychain dangling with all manner of things not keys, including a spark plug gapper.

"I like setting my outboard plug at thirty-two. Yours is set at like twenty-five or twenty. I can barely see the gap."

Fitting the gapper between the electrode and ground, he tapped the plug on the floor until he had the right distance. Then he screwed the plug into one of the weed-whackers, pulled on the cord, and it whined to a start.

"Okay. That's it. Want to come inside and have some coffee? I got a fresh pot."

It might seem funny that we could spend half an hour gabbing about wrenches, especially given the Midwest's reputation in other parts of the country for being tightlipped. But what people take as restraint is really a matter of utility. The language I hear (and use) at the university puts a premium on abstraction, on words used to contextualize, to wrap every possible thing in an idea and then into yet another idea. Visiting my in-laws, I'd learned that conceptual language wasn't in much demand on the farm because it didn't deal in a precise way with the world of things—draw bars and wire cutters and anything else my father-in-law needed from his toolbox behind the tractor seat. His preference for the concrete, for the word that expresses the thing itself and not a shadowy equivalent, was all part of being useful. A useful person in his book was someone who could name what was broken and fix it. By contrast, a visiting son-in-law who dealt largely in abstractions, who contextualized but did not solve problems was no help at all.

Nick's kitchen was warm and well lit inside and all the more comfortable because outside the rain was still pouring down. I sank into a chair with my cup of hot coffee and hoped not to move.

"You're lucky you stopped here," said Nick, "because these are all summer places. What I mean is it's a ghost town around here except on weekends."

My real luck, I thought, was Nick. When I praised him as a good troubleshooter, Nick brushed it away.

"Nowadays it's hard to find people who care about their work. It's more important for them to get paid than do a good job. That's why I work on my own. If I can learn to do something myself, I'd rather do that. I fix cars and bikes, do plumbing, electrical work, machinery, asphalt paving. About the only thing I haven't done is masonry and I'd like to try that. Now I'm not working and the whole time I'm painting and working on my father-in-law's cottage."

A woman popped her head out of the bedroom while we sat in the kitchen drinking coffee. "Well, I wondered who you were talking to out here." Leah poured herself a cup of coffee and the three of us settled in front of the television to watch *Let's Make a Deal*. A small square in the corner of the screen showed a radar image of the storm raging outside. The violet blobs tracking east across the radar screen were much more mesmerizing than the game show.

"You're welcome to stay here if you want," Leah said. "Pitch your tent in back or just stay inside. We got an extra bedroom."

I imagined myself settling in for the summer, a distant cousin overstaying my welcome at the family cottage. But when the rain stopped, I walked down to the dock and bailed the water out of my canoe. I installed the newly cleaned spark plug with Nick's socket wrench, gave a yank on the starter cord, and the outboard sputtered to life. Now I really had to leave. Nick hobbled down to see me off. When I asked if he'd hurt his leg in a motorcycle crash, he smiled shyly and shook his head.

"It's a degenerative disease, bits of bone fragments floating around my back. I'm supposed to have surgery in the fall, put in pig bone and plastic discs. There's a chance it won't work and I'll be paralyzed. So I'm taking time off. Twenty-nine years and I've never taken a vacation. I've never even seen the Mississippi. I want to go there this summer. I'd like to see the Grand Canyon. I want to go to

Sturgis but not on the interstate. I'll take back roads and two weeks to get there."

We shook hands and I handed the socket wrench back. Nick said to keep it.

"Might come in handy down the road. Don't worry about me. God looks out for me as he looks out for you. I believe that everything comes around."

20

The old lock at Montello had been removed and a new dam installed. Not counting bad weather, it was the first obstacle I encountered on the Fox River. It also meant my first portage. The square-stern canoe was too heavy to carry even unloaded, so I dragged it across the grass to the spillway and lugged, in descending order of weight, the outboard, gas tank, aluminum trunk, and water jug. By the time my gear was reassembled in the canoe, I was exhausted.

Below the dam, the Fox snaked through a great flat expanse of marsh that yawned into the open water of Lake Puckaway. The lake ran nine miles long to its eastern outlet. Navigating a large body of water in a small open boat isn't difficult unless a wind comes up. In the tall grass of the marsh, there hadn't been a hint of a breeze, but out on the lake I ran into a stiff, south wind that minced the surface into triangular whitecaps. It became impossible to keep the canoe on course without taking a terrific pounding from the waves. So I tacked north and hoped for a lull, but the tailwind only increased. At this point I gave up any thought of reaching Puckaway's outlet and just stayed on course with the waves. The canoe began to surf on their crests, a sensation that felt like being propelled forward by a mob, unable to stop or turn or do anything but keep up until I could make landfall. None of the cottages looming above the fast-approaching shore looked particularly inviting. Then I spotted a beacon glowing a patriotic red, white, and blue above the breaking waves. It read PABST BLUE RIBBON.

"It's murder out there," I announced as I walked into Mike and Cathy's Good Ol' Days. The tavern was empty except for the bartender and two customers, who all looked out the picture window at the choppy lake and nodded. "I can't make headway in this wind, so I wonder if I could pitch my tent in back tonight."

The bartender made a quick phone call to the owner to confirm. "Sure. In back or in front. Don't matter. Cathy gets here early in the morning to do her work but we don't open till ten." Then he added, "Can you believe this place was two deep at the bar yesterday?"

I couldn't believe my luck. I had chanced upon the traveler's trifecta: shelter, food, and beer. I ordered the dinner special, broasted chicken, and ate at the bar.

The Good Ol' Days seemed like a time capsule sealed in the 1980s: varnished knotty pine walls, red vinyl tablecloths, generously priced taps, the tunes on the jukebox. Everything was comfortably familiar, not so distant in time as to be antique but the recognizable past, twenty years back or so, a golden oldie to remind us of who we used to be. The sense of déjà vu only increased when an updated version of *The Newlywed Game* came on the TV above the bar. I hadn't seen the show since college, yet here it was in all its remembered salaciousness: young married couples grilled by a leering host. The one change in the reboot was that the host was no longer Bob Eubanks but a hefty young black woman.

"What would your wife say is your worst and best physical feature?"

"My . . . uh . . . stomach," the groom sputtered. "That's my worst feature."

"And your best?"

"My . . . manhood."

Channeling Eubanks, the host hoisted up her eyebrows, turned to the audience—including the four of us in the bar—and leered into the camera. "and can you tell the audience your *last* name again?"

"It's . . . uh . . . Johnson."

"So, Mr. *JOHN-SON*, why am I not surprised by your answer?"

The television audience roared while the bar remained quiet as a tomb. Finally, one of the other customers said, perhaps for my benefit, "Lake's calm now."

We all looked out the front window where the sun setting over Lake Puckaway was as neon red as the bar's "Open" sign. But it was too late. Calm waters or not, I was in for the night and ordered another tap.

The bartender looked like a young Brad Pitt who'd grown a dark beard, put on a few pounds, and covered himself with tattoos. He caught me looking at his forearms.

"How many altogether?" I asked.

"Eighty-four. And I'm not even finished. I'm getting one done on my chest of Simba." He gestured over his T-shirt where the young lion's head would go. "But it costs a lot."

"How much?"

"Fifteen hundred dollars."

"That's quite an investment in ink."

"Yeah."

"What was your first tattoo?"

He thought a moment then turned over a muscular left arm. "That'd be this one. I did it myself."

I couldn't read the upside-down inscription.

"It's my last name. I did it with a sewing needle and pen ink. I didn't know there's other ways."

The bartender had grown up in Oxford, thirty miles away. This corner of Wisconsin is dotted with small towns named by Yankee settlers for the Eastern cities they'd left behind—Princeton, Cambridge, Amherst—names that call to mind ivy-covered campuses. The largest employer in Oxford is a federal medium-security prison.

"There's just a couple bars and a restaurant in Oxford," the bartender said. "People grow up there and they never leave."

"What about you?"

"Me? I've been all over Wisconsin and Florida. I lived in Florida the last couple of years. Went to college in Orlando."

He'd liked the sunny weather but the experience had been mixed.

"In Florida you're either rich or you're poor. There's no middle class. There's neighborhoods in Orlando that if you're white and you go in there, you're taking your life in your hands. And it's hard to get a job because of the Spanish. The Spanish take the jobs because they're willing to work for four dollars an hour. Nobody will hire you in Florida if you can't speak Spanish, and I don't, so I came back and tend bar a couple nights a week. I can't do factory work. It's just too boring."

No doubt it would be frustrating to travel all the way to the Magic Kingdom only to discover the people there speak another language. I could have reminded the bartender there are neighborhoods in Milwaukee that are also Spanish-speaking. A generation earlier, when I lived in Milwaukee, that same neighborhood spoke with a Polish accent, and before that it had been German-speaking. That's the nature of immigration. It arrives in waves and people only see the wave that's coming at them, not the one their own relatives rode in on. After a wave breaks, it disperses and yesterday's ghetto becomes today's ethnic food destination. But I didn't say any of this because it would have been snarky to dismiss someone's personal complaint with a history lesson. For most people the past ends where memory begins; the rest is ancient history. The tough news is that while change is inevitable, like the tide, it doesn't lift all boats. If you want to avoid change, at least temporarily, you couldn't find a better place to do it than *Los Viejos Tiempos*. The Good Ol' Days.

When two men in nylon jackets sat down, the bartender had to get back to work. "Hey," he said in mock surprise, "customers!"

I pitched my tent behind the tavern in the grass next to some horseshoe pits. More cars pulled into the parking lot and I crawled inside my sleeping bag. Neighborhoods are where you find them, and I was glad to have found this one even if only for a night. Through the tent walls, the red, white, and blue of the Pabst Blue Ribbon sign glowed in the darkness. Usually it takes my body a while to adjust to the hard ground, but tonight I slipped easily into sleep, warmed by the knowledge that twice in a single day absolute strangers had taken me in.

~~~~~~~~~~~~~~

21

"Of course they took you in," I heard an inner voice insist. "You're a middle-aged white man in a canoe!" (Actually, a friend *did say* this after my trip was finished, reminding me of certain privileges that might be overlooked in parts of the country where everyone looks alike.) She was expressing an attitude, widely held at the university where we both work, that recognizes some divisions while ignoring others that are either less obvious or haven't yet worked their way into the curriculum, like the widening gulf between people who work with their hands and those who don't.

I had embarked upon the Round River hoping to circumnavigate my home state and discover who my far-flung neighbors might be. Three hundred miles into the trip, I could report that the countryside looked even more beautiful from a canoe than a car and the people who lived there were, with few exceptions, exactly who I'd thought they'd be—hardworking, welcoming, and generous to a fault. They reminded me, in short, of my in-laws. As with so many midwestern families, a farm was the common core, the point of origin that linked us together even though hardly any of my wife's relatives actually farmed. On weekends our children played together in the barn or sledded down the same hills, but after high school they went separate ways, some to college, others into the military or full-time jobs. They discovered that opportunity in this country is neither infinite nor equally distributed. We never discussed politics because nobody wanted to ruin a Thanksgiving dinner or a graduation party in someone's garage. After my father-in-law, the last farmer, passed away, the gatherings at the farm got fewer and more tense as rifts appeared. In the end, we divided into separate camps. "I wish it could be like it was," a nephew once lamented, "when we all got along." He was talking about our extended family but might as well have meant the country at large.

What surprised me on this canoe trip was how little politics came up. Maybe people just weren't interested or maybe, like my in-laws, they wanted to avoid a potential argument. I was surprised because politics was something my friends and I inhaled with our morning coffee; it was a daily source of both amusement and moral outrage. Our assumption was that politicians were the problem and voting them out of office would solve it. Lately I'd begun to think that politics are more of a symptom of what's wrong the same way a spike in fever signals an underlying illness.

A few years back while the state legislature debated Act 10, I rode a bus down to Madison with some colleagues and joined tens of thousands of other state workers—high school teachers, prison guards, parole officers, highway maintenance men—to protest. It was February and bitter cold as we marched around Capitol Square, banners aloft, in the falling snow and dim winter light. Seeing that great mass of humanity revolve slowly like a wheel around the domed capitol, I thought, we *can't* possibly lose because the whole state is behind us. The scene, somebody went so far as to say, looked like the storming of the Winter Palace—a very poor analogy, as it turned out. A Ghost Dance was more like it.

One afternoon, I took a break from the marching to watch a pathetically small counter-demonstration by the Tea Party. Later I talked with one of them, a skinny, middle-aged woman in a worn-out coat. We'd both left warm homes in other parts of the state to petition our fellow citizens, but the distance between us that afternoon seemed planetary. I asked why she supported Act 10. Screwing her face into equal parts anger and disappointment, she said, "I don't have a pension! I don't have health insurance! Why should they?"

The woman didn't question why she had no benefits or job security, only that "they" did, "they" meaning me. It was a variation on the fable of Boris's goat. In the failing days of the old Soviet Union, a joke made the rounds that perfectly expressed that country's sense of fatalism. There were two peasants, the story went, Boris and Ivan. In nearly all respects, the two men were exact equals. They lived in the same threadbare village, shared the same hard-scrabble life, and hoed the same rocky turnip fields. At night they returned to identical hovels. The only difference between them was that Boris had a goat and Ivan didn't. One day God looked down from heaven and took pity on poor Ivan. "You're a good man," God told Ivan, "hard working and uncomplaining. Therefore, I will grant you a single wish. You can have anything you desire. What is it you want, my son?" and Ivan replied, "I want you to kill Boris's goat."

Wisconsin's governor won a recall election by promising to kill Boris's goat. The goat was whatever somebody else had—a pension, health insurance, a good public school, a different language—that other voters didn't. The politics of divide-and-conquer isn't about policy or even ideology. It's about stoking the widening gaps between the working poor and middle class, between countryside and city, union and non-union, between people who went to college and those who didn't. And it works. The morning after Election Day, my friends and I would all scratch our heads and wonder how things could go so wrong. How could so many people vote against their own best interests? How could a state that was so progressive—so nice—end up so terribly divided? *Why can't it be like it was when we all got along?*

In my neighborhood people pride themselves on being inclusive, on their open-mindedness and kinship with the greater world. They even have doormats that say "Welcome" in different languages. But sometimes I think we're kidding ourselves. If one rain-lashed night, Nick the mechanic or the tattooed bartender showed up at their door soaking wet and out of breath, needing a sparkplug wrench or shelter from the storm, would my neighbors say "Welcome" and take him in? Would I?

~~~~~~~~~~~~~~~~

22

The Good Ol' Days was dark when I carried my gear down to the beach early the next morning. I'd hoped to buy a cup of coffee before heading out but didn't want to risk another chance of being caught on Lake Puckaway in a wind. The water was absolutely calm beneath a curtain of fog. As the mist burned off, the shoreline materialized in pieces: pontoon boats moored to long white docks, duck blinds on stilts above the reeds, a solitary cormorant on a piling with wings outstretched to dry.

Halfway down the lake, I tied up at a public dock in the village of Marquette to look for the elusive cup of coffee. The café kitty-corner to the post office was closed and the whole village still asleep. Walking the deserted streets, I came across the former home of the Caw-Caw Club. The three-story Greek Revival mansion with cobblestone veneer was the oldest and most celebrated of Wisconsin's private hunting clubs. Men with names like Pabst, Allis, and Pfister once looked out on the lake from the upper white porches to plan the day's hunt.

"Duck shooting at the Caw-Caw Club on Puckaway Lake was improving," *Forest and Stream Magazine* reported in 1898. "Major Cunningham and party bagged ninety ducks during their stay this week." No seasons, no bag limits, live decoys, and a rigid hierarchy of "sports" and guides—it was the Gilded Age of hunting. Private shooting clubs waned with the dwindling numbers of ducks and loss of exclusive control over waterways. Younger members took up urban pursuits like golf at country clubs where exclusivity was guaranteed. The Caw-Caw clubhouse was all that remained, but its present owners were still in bed; otherwise I might have asked them for a cup of coffee.

Lake Puckaway funneled into its eastern outlet to become the Fox River again, corkscrewing north through marsh and farmland before pausing at another nineteenth-century artifact, a lock and dam upstream of Princeton. The Fox-Wisconsin Waterway with its extensive lock and dam system had been designed to be another Erie Canal. Promoters envisioned a stream of vessels bearing the products from the Atlantic seaboard to the Mississippi, and the reverse traffic would transform the sleepy little towns along the Fox into busy manufacturing centers. But steamboats couldn't navigate either river without constant dredging and railroads made shipping by water obsolete, so the small towns along the waterway remained small and the lock chambers filled with stagnant water. Only one of the seven stone locks built along the upper river was still operating and then only on summer weekends. As far as I could tell, its sole purpose was providing old men with places to fish.

Two old men were fishing below the dam, one black and one white. As I portaged gear to the end of the lock, the white fisherman was leaving with a single walleye. I asked what he'd caught it on.

"Got him on a leech. Hey Sam, what are you using? Cut bait or stink bait?"

"Stink bait."

Rail-thin and overdressed for the heat in blue overalls, blue base-ball cap, and a blue flannel shirt, Sam was all business. He monitored a pair of fishing rods held upright in metal holders pounded into the soft ground. Heavy sinkers kept the baited lines in the fast water below the spillway. One rod looked capable of landing a marlin. Sam was angling for catfish. Five of them glistened in the bottom of the plastic bucket, channel cats, about a pound each. They had cream-colored bellies and scaleless golden sides speckled like trout. Once you got past the whiskered head, a catfish was a thing of beauty. Sam had another half-dozen fish in a cooler in his car.

"I've caught 'em on worms. I've caught 'em on leeches. But mostly I use stink bait."

Sam produced a jar of "Sonny's Super Sticky Channel Catfish Bait." It was concocted of cheese, blood, meat, and flour and when he unscrewed the lid, my head jerked back. He showed how to apply the stink bait to a plastic mesh tube above the treble hook.

"You just spoon it on like you're putting peanut butter on a sandwich."

Catfishing is the common man's sport because it doesn't require a boat, just a riverbank and time to kill. Catfish will tolerate water conditions other fish can't, so they're widespread on the Fox. Bass put up more of a fight and walleye taste sweeter, but nothing fills a freezer like catfish.

"I catch 'em mostly for my family. The little ones are better eating but I do like catching the big ones. I skin 'em and bake 'em. My daughter likes 'em filleted, not baked. Her kids don't know how to clean fish, but they sure like eating fish! Hah! I'd a had one more today but a damn turtle came along and took it off my stringer."

I followed Sam back to his car when he called it quits and con-solidated the fish in his bucket with those in a Styrofoam cooler. At the bottom of the cooler, massive head and tail curled up on the sides, lay a five-pound monster. It wasn't a channel cat but a flat-head. A full-grown flathead is a fish of mythic proportions. There's a memorable passage in *Huckleberry Finn* in which Huck and Jim hook onto "a cat-fish that was as big as a man, being six foot two inches long, and weighed over two hundred pounds. We couldn't handle him, of course; he would a flung us into the Illinois. We just set there and watched him rip and tear around till he drowned."

"What's the largest catfish you ever caught?"

Sam peered over the rims of his glasses. "Oh, about forty-eight pounds. It was a flathead cat. Caught him on fifty-pound test line right down at that point. My cousin was with me and when I got the fish close to shore I gave him the landing net. That net was a big hoop on the end of a long pole. Man, that fish took off! It like to pull him in the river if I hadn't helped land 'im!"

Princeton is a pretty little town, at least from its backside, a row of brick boutiques and antique shops crowding the riverbank. "Born on the Bayou" was playing on the jukebox when I tied up to the back deck of the Buckhorn Bar and Grill. I ordered the long-awaited cup of coffee and sat in the sunshine enjoying it. Princeton's prosperity was due, no doubt, to it's being sandwiched between two lakes ringed with summer cottages and retirement homes. I couldn't help but over-hearing a foursome of retirees at the next table. The woman speaking was either exasperated or being mock indignant.

"I heard on the news somewhere that there's going to be a new twenty dollar bill with a *woman* on it!"

"Oh for goodness sake! That seems like such a waste."

I slowly turned around to see a pair of couples, silver hair and pink skin. The men were nicely turned out in golf shirts and white shorts, the women in bright summer dresses.

"It has to do with counterfeiters," one of the husbands volunteered. "To make it harder for them to copy a bill."

"Oh well, that's different," the other wife replied. "I don't see why they don't just change a little detail of the bill we got now and not tell anyone."

Then the first woman said: "I think the new bill is supposed to have a colored woman on it."

"Oh sure, that or a *Mexican*!"

They all wheezed with laughter.

I scribbled this down, not because the conversation had a nasty tone but because it was delivered so nonchalantly.

I was so busy taking notes that I didn't notice one of the women leave her table and stand beside mine. She'd seen me tie my canoe to the lower deck and wanted to know how far I was going.

"To Oshkosh," I said, "and then on to the Bad River." I recited the whole itinerary while trying to shove the notebook into my shirt pocket.

"My goodness! That sounds very exciting," the woman said, gently laying a hand on my shoulder. "I want to give you something."

She took something out of her purse and placed it in the palm of my hand. It was a tiny wooden cross.

"I want you to have this. I want you to keep this because God loves you and will watch over you."

God Loves You was, in fact, burned into one side of the cross.

My notebook safely stowed, I fumbled for a response. What should I do—admit to eavesdropping and read the woman's incriminating words back to her? Pull out my St. Christopher medal and tell her to keep the cross? Lecture her on white privilege? What *do* you say when someone makes an ugly comment in private then treats you kindly in person? I try to take people at face value even when I disagree with them. The woman had offered me a gift with the best of intentions, so that's how I took it. I thanked her and tucked the little cross in my wallet for safekeeping. It's still there.

23

As the Fox flowed northeast and closer to the industrialized Fox River Valley, the overlap between city and country became more apparent. I entered a transition zone between agriculture and manufacturing, a landscape where grain elevators and silos give way to small factories. The switch is not as great as it might seem since the mechanical skills required to operate farm machinery are easily transferable to a factory. My first experience of this rural diaspora came the summer I graduated from high school and worked the swing shift at a Ford assembly plant in southeastern Michigan. Every afternoon I'd leave my suburban home and drive to the factory through a borderland of marginal farms and urban sprawl, places where boys my age wore duck's-ass haircuts and pointy shoes with white socks, the *boonies* as I considered it then. Nobody at the car assembly plant called me "college boy"—at least not to my face. Money, not education, was the big dividing line at the time, and we were all making good wages. That summer was the first time in my life that I was around people who didn't *sound* like me. The small town locals seemed hopelessly out of date in their references to "hoods" and "babes," while the inner city patois of the black workers sounded like the distant future and was known to me chiefly from the radio. The people who commuted the farthest to work fascinated me the most, the Kentuckians who drove back to Appalachia every weekend and lived God-knows-where the rest of the week. I remember one fellow in particular who looked like the country singer Porter Wagoner with his pale bony face and slicked-back yellow hair. He couldn't have been much older than I was but already had a wife, two kids, and car payments. At coffee breaks, he'd sit by himself and smoke with a sort of religious intensity. One day I asked how his weekend had gone. He took a long, thoughtful drag, letting the smoke drift from his mouth, and said he and the wife had gone to an "El-vis pic-ture show."

What I'd learned that summer, other than never wanting to work in another factory, was that country people are everywhere, not just on farms or small towns but in big cities and anywhere else there's work.

Berlin (pronounced *Ber*-line) arrived after a sequence of bridges that revealed the town's history. The first span ended in the empty parking lot of an abandoned tannery. The second bridge led to cream-brick apartment buildings with wooden staircases running down the backside and a church spire in the distance. At the third bridge, over the Main Street, was a sign peeling from the side of an old building.

BERLIN

Fur and Leather Capital

Shop, Dine and Refresh

The word "refresh" struck a chord in the afternoon heat and a few blocks later I tied up at the Riverside Motel. It was an old-fashioned motor lodge in the heart of town with a row of numbered rooms, a set of wrought iron patio chairs flanking each door, and a fishing pier on the river. I didn't bother to unload my canoe and asked the woman at the front desk for a room by the pier so I could keep an eye on the boat. It was probably a needless worry. In the countryside, I'd often left the canoe unattended, but I was in a city now, albeit a small one. The motel room predated the electrical amenities that came with it, so the mini-fridge, microwave, and coffee maker were stacked atop each other. But there was air-conditioning! I showered, changed into fresh clothes, and strolled downtown.

Berlin has the best combination a small town can hope for—new schools and a handsome old downtown that hadn't been gutted by the Walmart Supercenter up by the highway. Population is one indicator of a town's economic vitality; another is retail occupancy and a lack of tattoo parlors. The storefronts on Huron Street had colorful turrets and bay windows, and the two stately bank buildings still held banks. After dinner at Bellisomo Ristorante Italiano that included a nice glass of merlot, I walked back to my air-conditioned room and turned on the evening news.

The news was not good for our governor. After an initial burst in Iowa, he was floundering in the polls. He was steadily losing ground to a political outsider, a real estate magnate from New York. It must have been frustrating because the outsider had taken several pages from the governor's own playbook. He was more divisive, more vitriolic than any of his opponents and primary voters ate it up. It was also puzzling. Here was a brash, fast-talking New Yorker, the quintessential big city slicker, the antithesis of midwestern self-restraint, rocketing ahead in the polls. He insulted other primary candidates. He called them names. Why would rural voters prefer a huckster who was so demonstrably un-nice? Just as puzzling was why his anti-immigration message played so well in a region far removed from any border.

Donald Trump understood better than our governor that Midwest Nice can be a thin veneer covering up a great deal of pent-up frustration. Every year there are fewer ways to make a living in the countryside and while immigrants might view an Iowa milking parlor or meatpacking plant as a gateway to the land of opportunity, the locals don't. Many rural Americans feel like immigrants in reverse, standing dockside and watching their country sail away from them. The solutions Trump proposed—a border wall, tariffs—are quixotic and beside the point, but he was selling attitude rather than solutions. He said in public what others only whispered in private. He gave people license to exercise their own worst instincts. He was promising to take the country back to the good old days, to make us separate from the world. He was promising to kill Boris's goat—only he called it Miguel's goat—and put its bloody head on a stake. That he might actually win the nomination was inconceivable.

I crawled between the sheets and was half asleep when there was a sharp knock on the door. I turned on the bedside lamp and stepped barefoot into the motel parking lot. The knocker stood under the porch light in baggy shorts, flip-flops, and a black T-shirt that didn't quite cover the tattoo spiraling up his thick neck.

"Excuse me, sir. I just want to let you know that we've moved your boat a little—" He stepped aside so that I could see the canoe still tied to the dock. "—so my friend could get to his bait bucket." a barrel-chested Hispanic with a buzz-cut held a fishing pole in one hand and waved to us with the other. Now I immediately distrust anyone who calls me as "sir," a form of address I associate with telemarketers and policemen. But I was tired and said "Okay" then went back in my room and locked the door.

In the morning, the two heavies were still fishing. They worked the afternoon shift at the iron foundry and fished at night behind the motel. They had guessed, correctly, that if I had spotted them untying my canoe the night before, I'd jump to the conclusion that they were stealing it. Hence the knock on the door. I made a cup of coffee and walked out to see if they'd caught anything. The guy in the baggy shorts pulled up a stringer with a pair of white-bellied channel catfish dangling from it.

"That's why we had to move your boat, sir. We couldn't get to the stringer or the bait."

His name was Wesley and he was originally from Arkansas, which explained the excessive politeness. He asked where I was going with the canoe. When I told him, he shot a glance to his buddy.

"I knew it! I said to my friend here, he's probably dying of cancer and this trip is on his bucket list. No offense, sir, but that's what we thought last night."

I hadn't been the only one jumping to conclusions. Wesley had assumed I had one foot in the River Styx.

"Look, I'm not dying. I'm a teacher and I've got the summer off."

A look of happy vindication came over Wesley's broad face.

"I could *tell* you was a teacher!"

Wesley clearly had my number. Was there something pedantic in my voice? Blackboard chalk embedded in my hair?

"My mother was a teacher. She taught grade school all the way through college back in Arkansas."

Wesley had inherited a bit of the schoolteacher himself. He informed me that the Fox was one of only three rivers in the world that flow north. "That's why the fishing here is so good. It has something to do with the river running north."

"What are the other two?"

"The Nile, the Ganges, and the . . ." He flipped open a Smartphone. ". . . the Rhine."

"Well, I can think of two just in Wisconsin," I told him. "One is the Bad River. It flows north into Lake Superior. That's where I'm heading next, the Bad River Chippewa Reservation."

"My grandparents are part Cherokee. People think the Cherokee were a very peaceful tribe. They weren't. They fought like everyone else. People *think* Indians started scalping. They didn't. It was white people. They did it to collect the bounty. The Indians used to burn their enemy's hair off."

With that thought hanging in the air, I went back to my room and made Wesley a cup of coffee. Then we sat in the wrought iron patio chairs outside my door and Wesley fired up a cigarette. Turns out the foundry where he worked would be closing at the end of the year. The company had been acquired by a private-equity group, which was shuttering some of its foundries and consolidating others to achieve, in the CEO's words, a more "cost-effective manufacturing footprint."

Wesley seemed unfazed by the imminent prospect of unemployment. He had his own bucket list to check off and at the top of it was a return to Arkansas and fishing for flathead catfish.

"I grew up three blocks from the Arkansas River. There's holes in that river over 250 feet deep, places where a depth-meter just bottoms out. Me, I'm a flathead fisherman. My friends call me the Flathead Runner because I love fishing for them. I love the fight in them. There's some flatheads wider than the two of us."

"If you liked it so much, why did you leave?"

"Good question." He lit another cigarette. "Two reasons. Fighting addiction is one and the other is to avoid child support. At the time I thought maybe getting away was a blessing 'cause I know too many people fall behind in child support and end up in jail. Then my girlfriend said, either you move back to Arkansas with me or you're not going to see your son. He's twelve now, going on thirteen soon. So now I'm going back to see if I can play a part in my son's life. I'm hoping it's not too late."

Wesley's homesickness only aggravated my own, and when he and his friend packed up, so did I. The weeks I'd been away from home suddenly seemed like years. Before leaving the motel, I called Bob Elkins and asked him to pick me up at Oshkosh before the river flowed into Lake Winnebago. The next call was to my wife to tell her I was taking a break from rivers and coming home for a while. Then I listened very carefully to hear if there was any new edge to her voice.

The Fox did indeed flow north after Berlin. I followed it past cottonwoods and willows, under bridges and past dairy farms with tall Harvestore silos of the kind called Big Blues, past big houses and small openings where someone had mowed the tall grass and put in a fire pit and folding chairs, past three young women paddling kayaks— all without stopping. I kept going past the little towns of Eureka and Omro while the river grew wider and slower and finally emptied into Lake Butte Des Mortes with its distant blue shores and ominous name.

A Brief Intermission

Bad River

~~~~~~~~~~~~

24

E arly in the fall of 1848, Chief Oshkaabewis of the Lake Superior Chippewa led a delegation of six chiefs, four braves, and two women on a six-week journey by water and land to Washington, DC. They paddled away from Madeline Island in "three birch canoes of exquisite workmanship" and headed west, hugging Lake Superior's southern shore for forty miles until they reached the mouth of the Bois Brule. Ascending that swift staircase of a river to its headwaters, they portaged their canoes overland to the source of the St. Croix River and descended its 169-mile length to the Mississippi River. At St. Paul they boarded a steamer that took them to Rock Island, Illinois. The Rock Island Line connecting the Mississippi to the East Coast had yet to be built, so the party continued by river on a second steamer to St. Louis and then a third up the Ohio River to Cincinnati, where they switched to stagecoach and railroads.

The epic journey had been triggered by rumors that the United States government was preparing to remove the Chippewa from

Wisconsin and Michigan and move them west of the Mississippi River. Chief Oshkaabewis hoped to convince President James Polk to declare the tribal homelands a permanent reservation. To avoid the pitfalls of translation and the U.S. government's tendency to divide-and-conquer by pitting band against band, the delegation carried a symbolic petition inscribed on the inner bark of a paper birch to make their argument. It showed a row of animal figures (crane, marten, bear, catfish, man-fish) representing the clans or doodems of the principal chiefs of the Chippewa. A tangle of lines originate in the eye and heart of the crane and lead back to the other figures, to the southern shore of Lake Superior, and to small inland lakes. At first glance, the pictograph is simply drawings of animals superimposed on a map of the south shore of Lake Superior, but its message is more pointed. The Indian agent Henry Rowe Schoolcraft reproduced the pictograph in *Historical and Statistical Information Respecting the History, Condition, and Prospects of the Indian Tribes of the United States* (1851) and explained its meaning:

> It commences with the totem of the chief, called Oshcabawis [*sic*], who headed the party, who is seen to be of the *Ad-ji-jauk*, or Crane clan. To the eye of the bird standing for this chief, the eyes of each of the other totemic animals are directed as denoted by lines, to symbolize *union of views*. The heart of each animal is also connected by lines with the heart of the Crane chief, to denote *unity of feeling and purpose*. If these symbols are successful, they denote that the whole forty-four persons both *see* and *feel* alike—THAT THEY ARE ONE.

When Chief Oshkaabewis's delegation arrived at the nation's capital, they attracted a fair amount of interest not only for their dress, "full feather, paint and blanket," but their formal bearing and "easy manners." They also learned that Polk was no longer president. He had been succeeded by Zachary Taylor, a former general who had made his reputation fighting the Sauk in Wisconsin and the

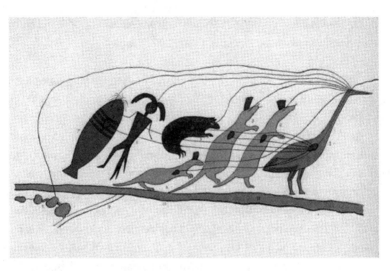

"Symbolic petition of Chippewa chiefs presented at Washington, January 28th, 1849, headed by Oshcabawis [*sic*] of Monomonecau, Wisconsin." From Henry Schoolcraft, *Historical and Statistical Information Respecting the History, Condition, and Prospects of the Indian Tribes of the United States* (1851).

Seminole in Florida. When presented with the Chippewa's petition, President Taylor appeared sympathetic.

A year later, however, Taylor issued an order to relocate the Lake Superior Chippewa from their homelands by means of a cruel ruse. The government moved the tribe's fall annuity payments from Madeline Island 140 miles west to Sandy Lake, Minnesota. By November, with winter closing in, four thousand Chippewa had gathered at Sandy Lake and waited. When the Indian agent finally arrived, he told them that the government lacked supplies to make the payments. The little food he brought was spoiled. As many as four hundred Chippewa died of starvation and disease at Sandy Lake or on the long trek home through the snow. Four years later, the Chippewa signed a treaty ceding most of their remaining land in Wisconsin to the United States in return for four reservations including one for the Bad River Band of Chippewa. After the Treaty of 1854, government policy toward the Chippewa switched from removing Indians from their land to removing the land's natural resources.

In 2011, Gogebic Taconite Ltd., a Florida-based mining company, leased a twenty-two-mile stretch of the Penokee Hills a few miles south of the Bad River Chippewa Reservation and announced plans to dig a $1.5 billion open-pit iron mine. At four miles in length and nine hundred feet deep, it would have been the largest such mine in the world. Governor Walker hailed the proposed mine at the time as a "lifeline to people in northeastern Wisconsin" and urged the legislature to pass a new mining bill to get the process rolling. He did not mention that the mining company had donated $700,000 to his reelection campaign. Lord knows the local economy needed a shot in the arm, but open pit mining at the headwaters of the Bad River posed unique environmental risks. The mining bill, largely drafted by Gogebic Taconite lawyers, attempted to sidestep the risks by shortening the permitting process, eliminating public challenges during that period, and assuming a "significant adverse impact on wetlands" as an unavoidable consequence of mining iron ore.

I first heard of the proposed mine when the tribal chair of the Bad River Chippewa delivered an impromptu speech at my university. Mike Wiggins Jr. had been traveling around the state forming alliances with environmentalists and other groups concerned about water resources. Short-haired and barrel-chested, Wiggins began his remarks by referencing Aldo Leopold and John Muir. He explained that the Bad River watershed receives prodigious amounts of rain and snow, and sulfuric acid from the millions of tons of waste rock produced from an open pit mine could leach into the river and its tributaries and ultimately poison the vast estuary where the Bad empties into Lake Superior and which holds wild rice beds and fish spawning grounds on which the Chippewa have depended since time immemorial. He enumerated Maslov's Hierarchy of Needs, which he said included clean air and clean water. Wiggins went on to say that these basic needs were part of the usufructuary rights guaranteed in the treaties the Chippewa had signed with the United States government over the course of the nineteenth century. After a brief tutorial on federal treaty law, Wiggins concluded his speech by saying that the state needed to see its water resources through the eyes of the sturgeon.

In the winter of 2013 I traveled to the northeastern corner of Wisconsin and interviewed Wiggin, the head of Gogebic Taconite, and protesters camped out in the snow near the proposed mine site. I wanted to write about the mining conflict because it encapsulated so much of what seemed wrong with our state: the corruption of government by dark money from outside interests, the blatant disregard for the environment, the pitting of one group of citizens—in this case Chippewa Indians—against another—white residents looking for an economic revival. It was a dramatic story, in some ways the oldest story in America.

Then, incredibly, in the spring of 2015, Gogebic Taconite withdrew its application. The mining company, despite its deep pockets and the governor's unwavering support, turned tail and ran back to Florida. In taverns across northern Wisconsin various theories were offered for the retreat: competition on the global market, a decline in the price of iron ore, or that the whole thing had been an elaborate ruse for some other project. But the reason I heard over and over in the taverns of northern Wisconsin was simply "the Indians." The Lake Superior Chippewa had scared off G-Tac. They were going to fight the mine in the courts, at the EPA, and in the woods if necessary. It was a remarkable turnaround. So remarkable that I added the Bad River to my itinerary because I wanted to see what an ecological victory looked like and what spoils, if any, went to the victors.

Years ago I canoed the navigable stretch of the Bad River between Copper Falls and the Highway 2 bridge. What I recall of that weekend were red clay banks, a high wooden trestle that looked leftover from the Civil War, and an evening rainstorm that turned the river into an ocher wash. I didn't plan to repeat that trip but to fill in parts of the watershed that I'd missed—a tributary at the headwaters and the river's mouth at Lake Superior. I wanted to see both ends of the slender thread connecting the Bad River Chippewa to their land.

Mike Wiggins Jr. was no longer the tribal chair. Having won the fight against the open pit iron mine, he'd narrowly lost reelection. "He didn't run," one of his supporters told me after the loss. "He more or less walked." (Later, the mayor of the nearby town of Mellen told me: "That guy, Wiggins, stopped the mine by himself. How could he lose an election when they should've put up a statue of him, for Christ's sake?") Wiggins's office was in the Tribal Health Center at New Odanah, seat of tribal government for the Bad River Band of Lake Superior Chippewa and home to its casino along Highway 2.

Wiggins opened the door to his office wearing a tight black T-shirt with the outline of a sturgeon stenciled in white. A criminal justice major in college, he retained the policeman's look of restrained energy. The iron mine now in his rearview mirror, Wiggins was focused on a new threat—hog manure. An Iowa-based pork producer had applied to the state to build a twenty-six-thousand-hog Concentrated Animal Feeding Operation (CAFO) across Chequamegon Bay from the vast estuary formed by the mouths of the Bad River and Kakagon Slough.

"Right now we're poised for a water rights litigation battle. We're fighting a company that wants to put a CAFO on Fish Creek and that could mean nine million gallons of pig shit in the bay. Once you start giving away water rights to corporations, you're in trouble. The Bad River delta is the absolute perfect spot for wild rice. That place takes care of my family. It takes care of my people. Everything is rooted to this place. How do the sturgeon know to come up the same river every year to spawn? It's in their DNA. Same with us. Our water resources aren't looked at in the framework of recreation. It's deeper and goes far beyond that. We view them as our relatives. And whether we're removed from the land or the land and water is removed from us, it's all the same thing."

Wiggins asked if I had time for a short drive. "I want to show you something."

We got in my car and bumped down a dirt road that dead-ended at Longfellow's Gitche Gumee. By surface, Lake Superior is the largest body of freshwater in the world and looked like an inland sea when we walked along the shore in the wind. Normally the lake is crystal clear but runoff from heavy rains had turned the pounding surf a ruddy pink, as if someone had chummed the water with blood. A wave crashed up the inclined beach and soaked my shoes. Finally, Wiggins called a halt.

"Got any tobacco?"

Forewarned, I produced a cellophane-wrapped Macanudo and handed it to Wiggins. He broke the dainty cigar in half and placed one piece on the beach where a wave quickly took it. The other he put in his pocket.

"Macanudo is a nice cigar. I may smoke this later."

Tobacco is a traditional offering to spirits as well as a sign of respect to an elder telling a tribal story. Wiggins picked up a piece of driftwood and began to draw. First he drew a straight line with a bump in the middle. Then a parallel wavy line. Finally, he drew a meandering axis connecting the two lines. It was a map of the Bad River watershed. A pictograph inscribed in wet sand on a windy beach.

"Here are the Penokees," Wiggins said, pointing to the straight line with the bump in the center. "And here," the wavy line, "is Lake Superior." The intersecting axis was the Bad River.

He added some short squiggles between the two lines.

"By the time water from the Penokee Hills reaches the reservation, it hits these oxbows, what I call snakeskins, small lake basins that act like a sponge to absorb excess water. If a mine had been built up here, the toxic wastes would have been stored in a tailings basin. Tailings basins are not built to withstand a thousand-year flood. We've had two in the last decade. Those storms were terrible but from another point of view they were an indication, a warning of nature's power."

Sketching Wiggins's map in my notebook, I was at a loss to keep up with his spate of words. He told me to give the scribbling a rest.

"Look, man, I need to see your face when I talk to you."

I put my pen down.

Wiggins moved to a fresh patch of sand and drew a circle with a bull's-eye.

"This is the earth and at its core is hot, molten lava. It's the beating heart of the earth. That core is mostly iron and a thousand miles down, but in places it comes close to the surface. The deepest part of Lake Superior is where we're closest to the core. The lava also flows along fault lines and when it cools it turns into basalt. That's what underlies the Penokees. So you have this connectivity between air, land, water, and fire. You watch Doppler radar when a storm comes in and you'll see a long finger reach into the Penokees. There's a reason for that connectivity. The Penokees are the home of the Thunderbirds."

Wiggins notched four compass points on the circle. He was no longer drawing a map of the region but a cosmology, a picture of the universe with Bad River squarely at its center.

"You have the first humans. Red. White. Black. Yellow. Each were given instructions from the creator and sent forth. Some people forgot the instructions they were given. The white man can't ask the Indian, 'What are we supposed to do?' because we don't know."

~~~~~~~~~~~~~~~~~

25

Looking south from the Lake Superior shore, you could mistake the Penokee Range for a low chain of mountains, a blue smudge rising above the forest green. The line of elliptical hills runs across a corner of northeastern Wisconsin and into the Upper Peninsula of Michigan, where it's called the Gogebic Range. Technically, it's a monadnock, an isolated ridge of hard rock that remains after millions of years of erosion have leveled the more porous rock around it. The Bad River rises in the Penokees then runs through a gap in the range on its way to the big lake. Tyler Forks, one of its tributaries, retains the splash-and-dazzle of a mountain stream.

After the heat of the car, the forest was cool and shady and smelled pleasantly of cedar. Nick VanderPuy plunged ahead in tennis shoes, climbing briskly over windfalls and splashing through muddy fern-covered rivulets while I wallowed behind in hip boots. I carried a fishing rod in one hand and a plastic container of angleworms in the other. I heard the river before I saw it. Then the path fell away to a steep ravine with a ribbon of water at the bottom. Tyler Forks. It seemed less a river than a crack in the earth.

After a hand-over-hand, tree-grabbing slide to the mossy bottom, we rigged up. Nick threaded a worm onto a tiny hook and let it sink into a pool. There was a flash of white as Nick set the hook and hoisted a small brook trout wriggling from the tea-colored water. The trout was slippery and beautiful: gray and green vermiculation on its back, yellow and carmine coronas along its side. In a short time, he had another. When he had a third, he unsheathed a small knife dangling from a rawhide thong around his neck and began to clean the fish. Nick has a long, deeply tanned, vulpine face—a hunter's face—with a beard going gray along the edges.

"'Once there were brook trout in the streams in the mountains,'" Nick recited as he slit the white bellies and shucked the entrails into the woods. "'In the deep glens where they lived all things were older than man and they hummed of mystery.'"

He was quoting the final lines of *The Road*, Cormac McCarthy's post-apocalyptic novel. Brook trout are the only trout native to Wisconsin and an indicator species. Brook trout require cold, oxygenated water to survive. Their very presence in a stream is a validation of its health. A river that once held brook trout and no longer does can be said to have suffered its own apocalypse.

While Nick cleaned fish, I waded into Tyler Forks and followed the river downstream as it cut a deep V through the hills. Forty feet above me, sunlight gleamed off the exposed rock face while the river below remained in aquarium light. Even in midsummer I could feel the cold through my hip boots. The banks were lined with slate-gray rock, not rounded smooth by the constant flow of water but fractured in straight lines with sharp edges. I picked up a chunk of rock and broke it open. The inside was black, fine-grained and heavy with magnetite. A magnet placed on such a rock would stand at attention. The rock was a fragment of the Ironwood Iron Formation.

The Ironwood Iron Formation was discovered by the nineteenth-century polymath Colonel Charles Whittlesey in the summer of 1849. He'd abandoned going up Tyler Forks, "so swift is the current and narrow and crooked are the channels" to travel overland, prospecting along the way by means of "compass deflection," essentially holding his compass to see if the magnetized needle pointed north or swung wildly. When it repeatedly did the latter, he'd found the hard backbone of the range. "There is a continuous mountain chain from the Montreal River to Bladder Lake," Whittlesley wrote in his report. "I have called it the Penokee range, this being the Indian word for iron, which is found in its westerly portion in great force." The report set off a mining rush to the Penokees that lasted nearly a century. Hematite, a pure form of iron ore, was mined in deep underground shafts. Nobody mined the low-grade magnetite, or taconite, because the deposit lay tilted at a 65-degree angle beneath an immense overburden of rock. To get at it would require leveling the north slope of the Penokees, which is exactly what Gogebic Taconite Ltd. had proposed. Had the mine been developed, its eastern boundary would have been Tyler Forks.

Driving back after fishing, Nick asked me to stop at a turnout on Moore Park Road. Traveling on the Round River, I was perpetually a summer sailor, always seeing places under the best of circumstances in full bloom and left to imagine what they might look like in the dead of winter, the true measure of any place in the Midwest. But I didn't have to imagine the turnout at Moore Park Road under snow because I'd been there in winter. It was the winter of 2013, the winter of the polar vortex when 150 inches of snow fell on the Penokees, the coldest in a century. Now the snow was gone and the landscape was a riot of green from the forest canopy above to the tangled undergrowth below. It was almost unrecognizable. We left the car and picked our way through the woods. Searching through chest-high weeds, Nick uncovered a rusting Franklin stove and, further on, a ring of campfire stones. He was like an archeologist reconstructing a vanished civilization from a few pottery shards.

"You had a big lodge here and a wall tent over there," said Nick, pointing to the empty space between trees. "We had a sugar bush here and a wild onion-drying lodge over there. This was our central fire. People fell in love. Babies got made out here. Something got generated from being on this land. We *tribalized!*"

In the winter of 2013 the standoff over the iron mine had entered its phony war stage. Gogebic Taconite Ltd. had declared the entire mine site an "Exclusion Zone" after a handful of Chippewa Indians set up wall tents and homemade wigwams on adjacent county forest land. When outside protesters not connected to the camp noisily confronted G-Tec employees, the company hired a private security firm. Ex-Special Forces personnel patrolled the area in full camouflage and carrying assault rifles. When it was discovered that the security firm wasn't licensed to operate in the state, they withdrew in an armored vehicle.

I'd met Nick VanderPuy and other foot soldiers in the phony war that winter on Moore Park Road. Their encampment was an assertion of Chippewa treaty rights to hunt and gather on ceded territory. It became the focal point of opposition to the mine. In their application to the county for a camping permit, the protesters said their goal was *gidawiidabima didakiiminaan jinaanaagadawenjigewaad*, which translates as "you shall be part of and sit with the land, to be a presence of aki, the earth, in order to seek knowledge through careful, continuous, and pondering thought and reflection in collaboration of the heart and mind." They called it the Harvest Education Learning Project or H.E.L.P. for short. Others simply called it the Indian Camp like the Hemingway story.

Four inches of fresh snow had fallen and the temperature was a few degrees above zero the day I visited. The Super Bowl had been played the night before. When Nick called it the "Stupid Bowl," I immediately liked him. VanderPuy is a Dutch name. Over breakfast in one of the homemade wigwams, he told me this story:

"One summer when I was about ten years old my family stayed at a North Woods resort and my Uncle Connie told me we were going to the Tuesday night powwow at the Lac du Flambeau reservation. He said it was a wonderful event but at the height of the performance an Indian warrior would throw a silver tomahawk into the stands where it would invariably seek out the heart of a young white boy. I worried about this for days. But the time came and when I didn't get assaulted with a tomahawk, I got out on the powwow ring and danced."

I know an origin account when I hear one, and the tomahawk story was Nick's way of explaining why he was spending the winter in a homemade wigwam. He had taken a circuitous path to get there. He'd majored in philosophy in college then dropped out of law school to become a professional fishing guide. Lunker Guide Service. During the Indian treaty rights controversy of the late 1980s, he became a freelance radio journalist covering confrontations at the boat landings. In short order he got a divorce, sold his house, and moved onto the reservation. "Crossed over" was how he put it.

The white-man-who-lives-with-Indians is a staple character in early American literature, usually a captive who elects to stay with his captors, an outlier who switches sides. He is the model for both Natty Bumppo and, to a lesser degree, Hemingway's Nick Adams. Only recently has the character become a figure of inauthenticity, an appropriator, a wannabe. But cultural gatekeeping is its own form of small-mindedness and where would you draw the line—the canoe, the Articles of Confederation, ecology?

Shortly after my visit, the Iron County Board of Supervisors voted on a resolution to evict the Indian camp from the county forest. The board reckoned that the fourteen-day camping ordinance had been violated by nearly a year and voted unanimously for the sheriff to eject occupants of the camp "by any lawful means necessary." Nick had attended the meeting with a member of the Red Cliff Band of Chippewa, a striking young woman with long black hair. She said nothing during the public comment period, but board members couldn't help stealing glances. She wore traditional leggings, a single eagle feather in her hair and had painted her face red and yellow.

After the eviction notice was served, the camp's residents struck their tents, rolled up their tarps, and moved on. The mining company's withdrawal a year later was almost anticlimactic. Nick now lived in an apartment building just north of Mellen. When I dropped him off, he gathered up his fishing gear, then asked, "Do you think the camp mattered? Do you think we made a difference?"

A tricky question. Nick had spent a year of his life living in a tent for what must have seemed at times a hopeless cause. Victory had caught him by surprise. Who knows why the mining company threw in the towel? But what I said was, "Absolutely."

26

I set up my tent at Copper Falls State Park where Tyler Forks plunges into the Bad River. The park was a short drive to both Mellen and New Odanah, and if I ever entertained thoughts of canoeing the upper Bad all I had to do was look at its rumbling falls.

At night I read by flashlight in my tent. One of the books I'd brought along was the collected Nick Adams stories. Hemingway's spare, unsentimental prose still offers a clear dissection of the North Woods, its raw beauty, sometimes strained relations between Indians and whites, and the upheaval that follows a collapsing economy. In the appropriately titled "The End of Something," Hemingway summarizes the demise of Hortons Bay in a single scene as the town's sawmill is disassembled and shipped south, "the sails of the schooner filled and it moved out into the open lake, carrying with it everything that had made the mill a mill and Hortons Bay a town."

In 1961 when 20th Century Fox scouted locations for a movie version of Ernest Hemingway's early stories, the studio skipped over the upscale resort towns of northern Michigan where the author actually spent his youth in favor of the better-preserved Mellen, Wisconsin. Mellen had escaped the fate of Hortons Bay but just barely. Hemlock forests, not iron ore, had put Mellen on the map. The bark of hemlock was the main ingredient in the formula used for tanning leather, so at the beginning of the last century Mellen was home to the largest tannery in the hemisphere. Six trains a day brought hides from all over the country and South America to be made into shoe leather. The trains brought immigrants as well to work in the tannery. Then in the 1920s the tanning formula changed and hemlock bark was no longer needed. The tannery closed and the trains all but stopped coming. And that's why the redbrick and false-front buildings on Mellen's Bennett Street look as if they're still waiting for an Armistice Day parade.

The film crew set up in the school gym where Paul Newman, Richard Beymer, and Arthur Kennedy could change into costume. Locals were hired to play extras and the Penokee Range played itself, the North Woods where Nick Adams learns about Life with a capital L. For the town's big scene, Adams's return from World War I, Bennett Street was made over with gas street lamps and gravel. A crowd of extras assembled beneath a banner stretched across the street that proclaimed, "WELCOME HOME NICK ADAMS."

Hemingway's Adventures of a Young Man flopped at the box office. More than one reviewer noted that the author's recent suicide had at least spared him the sentimental mess Hollywood had made of his stories. The *Mellen Weekly Record* was more sympathetic. The newspaper ran a special edition that included a still from the movie showing Nick Adams stumbling out of a Bennett Street pool hall. "At this point in the movie," the caption reads, "he is quite despondent over his life in a small town."

One evening, tired of my own cooking, I left the state park and drove to Mellen looking for a restaurant. All the institutions of civic life—city hall, local museum, post office, weekly newspaper, a shuttered bank, new public library—can be found on Bennett Street but no restaurant. So I dropped into Bro's Bar and Grill, the pool hall in the movie, to see if I could get supper.

"There's no place to eat in town now," said Bro, "except the Cenex station for pizza and burgers. We have pizza too but our pizza oven isn't working at the moment so all we have is pizza fries."

Everyone in the place seemed to be related. Bro's wife and his parents worked at the bar and his grandmother sat on a stool playing video slots. It was a family operation. An embossed plastic sign hung over the back bar: "If you think our prices are too high, bring in your wife and we'll dicker."

Bro said the proposed iron mine had divided the town fifty-fifty. "I was for it because of the jobs."

"I'm glad they didn't build the mine," a woman told me when I went out to the back deck, "because it was my understanding it was going to be an open pit mine and would have taken all our fall colors." She had on a pink dress and had a friendly, open face. "The Indians really held their ground."

I sat down at her table and watched the sun slip behind the range. As it did, it burnished an old three-story redbrick building that dominated the horizon. Mellen's school wasn't just disproportionately larger than any of the other surrounding structures, it was monumental. It had obviously been built to serve a much larger town. I asked how old it was.

"1910. That's when that fucker was built," said the woman's companion. "'Scuze my language."

"How many people go to school there now?"

He looked it up on his smartphone. "Here it is. Mellen student body: 282. That's K through high school. They didn't have a football team when I went there. Now they play eight-man football. I really missed out because even though I'm small I'm fast and could have played quarterback or receiver."

I had inadvertently opened the door to the glory days. He began reliving his basketball career until he was interrupted.

"Back when I was younger," said the woman, "there were seventeen bars in Mellen. Now there's two, including this place. Where that fence is now there used to be a big old hotel. It was right by the railway depot. My mother worked in the hotel. I grew up in that gray house."

She pointed to a small house with a pair of square windows on the gable end like two astonished eyes. Mellen had its ups and downs over the years, she noted, but for most of her life there had been one constant.

"We've had the same mayor for like twenty-nine years. Before that, his father was the mayor. I think there's only been one other person elected mayor in all this time. If I get in trouble, the first call I make is to Joe Barabe."

The next morning I had an impromptu audience with the mayor over coffee at the Cenex station where we shared a common table across from the cash register. Besides gas and propane, the station also sells liquor, bait, a few groceries, DVDs, garden supplies, and foil-wrapped egg-and-sausage sandwiches hot from the kitchen. Short and heavily browed beneath a Chicago Cubs cap, Barabe has been mayor for nearly three decades. A quarter century ago, a raise brought his monthly salary to $175 a month. For a career politician, he spoke with unusual candor and if he disagreed with something he'd tilt his head forward and do a Buster Keaton double take. He did that when I referred to Mellen as a small town.

"We're a city, not a township," Barabe fired back. "We have our own fire department, police department, EMTs, utilities. A township doesn't have sewer, fire, or police. We have everything Milwaukee has, for Christ's sake, only smaller."

The future mayor was ten years old when the movie studio came to Mellen. His father was hired as an extra to play one of the town's big-wigs, which in fact he was.

"They took over the town. If you wanted to see the stars, you went to the school gym where the costumes were or down by the railroad depot. That's where the action was. You had Paul Newman running around for Christ's sake."

Barabe thought the movie had its good points, which didn't surprise me since he seemed to like everything about his hometown. He'd grown up in the old neighborhood called Tannerytown and often walked the three blocks "downtown" to visit his father in city hall. Along the way he could follow the progress of baseball games from radios perched on front porches or stop at the Bee Hive Café to get the score. When the movie premiered, his father took the whole family to see it, but they had to drive to Ironwood, Michigan, because Mellen's own theater, the Orpheum, had closed a few years before. It took a draft notice to make Joe leave Mellen. When he returned from Vietnam, nobody hung a banner over Bennett Street saying, "WELCOME HOME JOE BARABE." He went off to college and stayed away six years before returning to Mellen after his father died of a heart attack. His father had been on his way to a city council meeting. I asked Joe why he moved back.

"I owed it to the town."

Our coffee break ended when Barabe had to leave for a meeting with the DNR in Ashland. It took all of fifteen minutes for him to cross the street because he stopped to talk to constituents at every step—a woman on the sidewalk with a baby strapped to her chest, another woman coming out of the grocery store, her husband waiting in a pickup truck—and I realized that being mayor of a small town was like being consigned to a never-ending high school reunion, running into the same faces over and over again, the people ahead of you in school and those behind you, smiling and saying "Hello" and "How're you doing?" every single day of your life.

The year Joe Barabe was born, the population of Mellen was not quite twice the 690 that it is today. As mayor, his primary challenge is to bring in new blood or at least stem the tide of attrition. When Barabe returned from Ashland, I dropped by his comfortable old home a block north of City Hall. He said he hated to leave Mellen

even for a day because everything he cared about was right here—
family, friends, a personal history. I asked what the state government
in Madison could do to help a small city.

"The state could help us out by leaving us alone. They don't
bring any money up here. They take property off our tax rolls—like
the state park. They take muskies out of our lakes for stocking in
other lakes, for Christ's sake. They could lower property taxes for
one thing. They could help our police and fire departments with
training and equipment. All we have is the wood industry. There are
three mills in Mellen and they all do wood. Teachers used to say, if
you don't buckle down, you're going to end up working in the veneer
mill. Well, I worked at the mill. It took twenty years for the government to allow logging in the Chequamegon National Forest, so logs
for the veneer mill were coming from Kentucky, Pennsylvania, and
Illinois because we couldn't get logs here. Well, our logging companies
were dying."

"What about the proposed iron mine?" I asked.

"I was pro-mine until I saw the legislation—186 pages of shit.
The worst part was how little they were going to give the city of
Mellen. When the bill was being negotiated in Madison, I tried calling
the governor to find out what was in it and his secretary said, 'the
governor doesn't talk with constituents.' I said, 'I'm not a constituent.
I'm the mayor of Mellen!' Same thing. The state legislature didn't
even *read* the bill and they passed it. Well, we read it in Mellen. We
had a public hearing on the mine in the gym. 150 people talked and
only one was in favor. I said the mine was going to rape us twice.
First, financially, and second, the environment."

Joe was confident the city can hold its own as long as the mills
keep running and that means keeping the school running. Mellen
Public School was, he admitted, a "dinosaur," the last hundred-year-
old school left in the state, but it was also the key to Mellen's survival
because a city without a school has no future.

"If I can save the school, I can save everything else. You lose the
school and that's it. Every year we graduate twenty to thirty kids.

And they're good kids. We've saved our school three times in the last twenty-five years. The school is everything. I quit the school board the year they wanted to consolidate with Glidden. Who's going to buy a house where there's no school?"

If the school held Mellen's future, its past has long been consolidated a short drive north of town on a gently sloping hillside with headstones in neat drill rows. I parked the car and we walked down a blacktop lane through Union Cemetery. Eventually Joe wandered off the pavement and stooped to read an inscription on the polished granite.

Casper Peck
Jan 1867
July 1928

"Casper Peck. He's the one who built my house in 1902. And over here is Freddy Jelich. I played poker with him on Friday nights. Out of seven guys, I was the youngest at the table." We walked a little further. "This guy over here was a postmaster, also a drunk."

Many of the surnames engraved on the stones suggested a whirlwind tour of Europe—Degrovarium, Stein, Mataija, Pawloswski, Listopad, Haugen—and some listed nation of origin but wherever the deceased happened to be when they first opened their eyes to the world, their last glimpse of it was Mellen.

Coppo Pietro
Note in Italia
1893
Morto 1917
Mellen Wis

"Both sides of my family were immigrants," said Joe. "My grampa came from Germany. My grandmother was French-Canadian. I grew up knowing more people who spoke another language. Lithuanian, Polish, Italian. There was a street in town called 'Dago Street' because it was all Italians. Most of them worked in the tannery. When the tannery closed, they stayed."

A wave of immigrants had built Mellen and I suggested that that a new wave could revive its fortunes. Why couldn't the government sponsor resettlement programs in small towns that were shrinking?

"Sure," said Joe, "but first you have to have the jobs."

We continued downhill to the older part of the cemetery where the headstones were limestone rather than granite and the lettering obscured with lichens. Beneath the shade of pines was a family grouping, children flanked by father and mother.

FATHER			MOTHER
THOMAS	NELLY	LOUIS	ANNA
1858–1933	1893–1904	1887–1904	1862–1927

"The kids were rowing across a lake on the way to a fishing spot," said Joe, "when the girl fell out of the boat and her brother dove in to save her. He had hip-boots on and she latched onto his back. Louie was an excellent swimmer, but he couldn't swim for the both of them and they went down together. So many sad stories."

Cemeteries are all about compression, about condensing the many dead into a single space, crowding different generations and social classes together—bluebloods and the indigent, mill owners and mill workers, veterans and octogenarians, reckless youth and stillborn babies—into a single shady neighborhood within driving distance. Cemeteries are also about compressing time. Headstones bring out the mathematician in all of us. Birth dates subtracted from death dates and the sum calculated against our own age. In the end, the numbers always add up to zero. Strolling through a cemetery, we're not just visiting the past but getting a glimpse of our future. I kept thinking of the Stage Manager in *Our Town* who spends Act Three doing pretty much what Joe was doing, walking through a small town cemetery—"a windy hilltop"—pausing now and then to explicate the dead. I told Joe as much.

"My favorite part of that play," he said, "is when they're up in heaven and they're looking down and wondering why people are so troubled."

What the Stage Manager actually says in Act Three is this: "You know as well as I do that the dead don't stay interested in us living people for very long." Of course, this is poetic nonsense. The dead lose interest in everything the moment they stop breathing. It's the living who abandon the dead, not the other way around. The older we get, the more people we have to remember until we hit a memory overload and let some of them slip away. I was impressed that Joe, as Mellen's unofficial historian, had assigned himself the task of remembering people who predated his own life. Retracing our steps, we walked uphill from the older part of the cemetery until Joe stopped in front of a granite slab with a rounded top.

HERMAN C
BONITZ
WISCONSIN
PFC MED DEPT
WORLD WAR II
APRIL 9, 1921
JUNE 6, 1944

"Look at the date of death. D-Day. Herman was a paratrooper with the 101st Airborne. He died in the first wave. He was twenty-three."

Union Cemetery has its own military section. Veterans who died in combat abroad or years later at home in bed are buried at no cost. For a small-town cemetery, the military section is disproportionately large.

JAMES LARS LEDIN
MAY 1944
JULY 1966

"We had two people killed in Vietnam. Jim was a couple years ahead of me in school. He was shot as his platoon helicoptered out of a hot spot. His mother was my high school English teacher and his father sold insurance. Mellen sure cried over that one."

We had slowly gained elevation until we were back at the narrow blacktop road. The cemetery continued to a ridge, then descended into a grassy swale bordered by new housing. For years Joe had tried to purchase the swale to enlarge the cemetery before it ran out of space, but the DNR had classified the swale as a periodic wetland and unbuildable. "F'ng DNR," whispered Joe.

He stopped beside a newer headstone:

JOHN PAUL BARABE
1954–1975

"This is my older brother. He was a senior at UW–Oshkosh when he drowned in the Fox River. Four years ago I lost another brother. I didn't think he'd be buried here, but here is where he is. I was glad when they brought him home. They should all come home."

~~~~~~~~~~~~~~~~

27

Before resuming my Round River trip around the state, I wanted to visit Kakagon Slough. The fight over iron mining at the headwaters of the Bad River had largely been about protecting the great estuary at the river's other end—at least as far as the Indians were concerned. Both the Bad River and Kakagon Slough empty into the cold waters of Lake Superior. Between the two river deltas lay sixteen thousand acres of coastal wetlands, one of the largest and most pristine freshwater estuaries in the world. Sheltered from pounding lake waves by a long barrier spit, the labyrinth of sloughs and coastal lagoons provides a major spawning ground for walleye and lake sturgeon and a critical stopover for migratory birds. It is also the largest natural wild rice bed in the Great Lakes basin and the reason the Bad River Chippewa live where they do. When I learned the Tribal Historic Preservation Officer was taking a party of schoolteachers on a boat tour of Kakagon Slough, I cadged a ride.

The tour assembled at the tribal fish hatchery near Old Odanah and its leader wore a baseball cap with THPO stitched on the crown.

Edith Leoso has a broad, handsome face with finely arched eyebrows and a commanding presence.

"A lot of people associate historic preservation with old buildings," she said while waiting for the schoolteachers to arrive. "Because we try not to leave a footprint on the ground, we preserve those places that become our memories like the pow-wow grounds."

The tribal history Leoso was charged with preserving is permanently housed within the Chippewa language.

"Ninety percent of the Chippewa language is verbs. It's a descriptive language. It describes the purpose of everything based on observation. Each tree, each plant has a name descriptive of its use. If something doesn't have a name, then it didn't come from here. Each river has a name that describes the fish in it or some particular use. We call the Bad River *Mashkiiziibii*. There are two words in the name, *ziibii* means 'river'; the other word, *mashkii*, means both 'swamp' and 'medicine' because we know medicine grows in the swamp. The French had a terrible time going up the river in boats and put that on their maps, so the English called it Bad River."

"So *Odanah* is the word for 'village'?"

Edith's perfect eyebrows flattened.

"You *could* call it that, but every Chippewa village is called *Odanah*. *Oda* means 'heart' and *nah* means 'place.' a place of the heart. What does that mean? You'd have to know the name of the drum, *O-day-way-egun*. 'Heartbeat.' The village is where you hear the heartbeat. Once you understand our language, you understand a little bit about everything."

When the half-dozen schoolteachers had assembled, Edith handed each an orange life jacket. Then she took a pinch of tobacco from a plastic roll-your-own bag, walked to the end of the dock and crumbled the tobacco into the clear, spring-fed water of Kakagon Slough. Piling into two motorboats, we headed downstream. It was nice to be on the water again. We proceeded at trolling speed because the wild rice was at the flowering stage when even a boat wake could dislodge it. Edith sat in the bow of my boat naming trees as they slid past. I could barely hear her voice over the forty-horse Mercury's rumble.

"The sugar maple," Edith said, "is *aninaatig*. It means the 'man tree.'"

One of the schoolteachers asked why.

"Well, when you put a spout in the trunk, what does it look like?"

A stand of white pines marked the slough's outlet to Lake Superior, but the marsh was so flat and the slough so coiled that our boat never seemed to make any forward progress. One minute we'd be heading toward the pines, the next minute we'd be moving away from them. We passed a row of wooden posts in the river. In the spring, hatchery workers drape nets from the posts to catch spawning walleyes. Then they strip the eggs from the females to raise as fingerlings for restocking lakes on the reservation. *Ogaa-kagon-ike*, Edith explained, means "the place where walleyes spawn" and refers to the motion of spawning fish as well as the slough's own serpentine course.

The trees receded and the slough broadened as we entered a bowl of light. The sky was hazy white at the horizon and deepened overhead to a delft blue. Vegetation spread out in successive bands of green—lily pads, cattails, arrowhead, and finally a broad expanse of wild rice that was a shade of spring green so light it seemed an entirely new color. Wild rice is an aquatic grass, the only cereal grain native to North America. It's high in protein, easy to store, and rich in the amino acid lysine. But it's also a finicky plant, a Goldilocks grass that requires just the right conditions to grow—shallow water that's neither too warm nor too hot, a gentle current but not too much, a mucky bottom rich in sediment. The estuary of Kakagon Slough has those perfect conditions. It also fulfills an ancient prophecy in which the Great Spirit told the Chippewa to migrate westward from the Atlantic seaboard until they found *manoomin*, the food that grows on water.

It was now early August and the wild rice harvest would begin as soon as a committee of elders determined the grain was ripe. Edith was a member of that committee. She said the entire slough would have to be checked on a regular basis because the wild rice at the mouth tends to ripen slower than upriver. If the kernels are green and milky, it's too early. If they're black at the top, they're ripe and ready to fall off the stalk. Once the committee gives the go-ahead, Kakagon Slough quickly fills with canoes. Long ago families would put up a wigwam and camp on the shore of Lake Superior for a month processing the rice. Now they run back upriver and process it at home.

Traditionally, ricing was women's work. In Captain Seth Eastman's 1853 watercolor *Gathering Wild Rice* three women sit in a birchbark canoe; the woman in the stern holds the canoe steady with her paddle. The women facing her, or strikers, use flat cedar rods to bend the wild rice stalks over the gunwales and gently knock the kernels into the boat. Apart from the birchbark canoe and women's outfits, the technique of gathering wild rice by hand has changed very little. The real work begins after the rice is gathered. The kernels need to be dried, either air dried or parched in an iron pot over a fire, then walked upon to break the grain's husk, and finally winnowed to separate the grain from the chaff. A one-pound bag of hand-harvested wild rice that sells for $12.50 hardly reflects the labor involved.

In the late 1960s, agricultural scientists from state universities arrived at Old Odanah to develop a more profitable wild rice crop. The project called for sowing genetically improved seed in diked paddies and using combines rather than canoes to harvest the wild rice. The experiment divided the reservation, including Edith's family.

"My uncle was behind the effort to commercially grow wild rice. My grandfather said it wouldn't work. I asked him why and he said, 'Because it's not the same.' The movement of water in the river is not the same in a rice paddy."

After three harvests, the tribe abandoned the commercial paddies.

At last, an hour after leaving the dock, we reached the white pines at the end of the slough. The slough spread out into the great expanse of Lake Superior. Across Chequamegon Bay, I could see the blue headlands of the Bayfield Peninsula, the possible future home of twenty-six thousand hogs. When Edith decided the second boat had probably taken another channel and returned to the fish hatchery, we turned around as well. Along the way we passed a cut-off channel where the river had sliced through its own meander to form a low island. I hadn't noticed it on the trip downriver.

Back at the fish hatchery and the schoolteachers gone, I asked Edith the name of the side channel we'd passed midway down the slough. She showed it to me on a map, a curlicue of water.

"That channel breaks off from Kakagon Slough to the northeast," she said. "It loops around an island and comes back again. We call it the Round River."

Bois Brule River

~~~~~~~~~~~~~~~~~~~

28

Rivers are more fun than lakes," a novelist friend once told me, "because they have, you know, a narrative." He meant that a river is a story because it starts in one place and goes somewhere else. He'd made this observation at the beginning of a canoe trip when the river was deep and promising. Later, when the river got shallower and we were dragging our canoe through interminable riffles, he decided he didn't want to stick around to see how it ended. That was years ago on the Pine River. We should have done the Brule instead.

The Bois Brule has the most dramatic conclusion a river can hope for—shouldering through a green curtain of forest, then a quick dash across an empty beach to spend itself in the oncoming waves of an inland sea. To look back at the mouth of the Brule from Lake Superior in the spangled light of early morning is to glimpse the New World as yet unspoiled, especially if you're the only figure in the landscape. And I was, apart from Bob Elkins.

Elkins had trailered a canary-yellow canoe to the beach that morning and watched as I attempted to stand upright in it. Motors aren't allowed on the Brule and I needed a boat light enough to pole upstream, then hoist on my back and carry over a two-mile portage to the headwaters of the St. Croix. Elkins had found the sixteen-foot double-ender at a garage sale in Hayward. Its previous owner, a Chippewa woman, had used the canoe for harvesting wild rice, and that provenance and single thwart made it the perfect choice for the Brule. It also came with a twelve-foot push-pole instead of a paddle. Never having poled a canoe before, I thought it prudent to start on the calm lake before taking on the Brule's current.

So how does one hold a twelve-foot push-pole exactly—like a pole-vaulter or a tightrope walker? I'd seen pictures of canoeists poling up big rivers in Maine like the Allagash and St. John. They wore tartan-plaid shirts, wide-brimmed hats and looked intrepid. Standing up behind the center thwart, feet apart, my wobbly knees slightly flexed, I used the push-pole to paddle into the river. So far, so good. The pole had a duck-billed metal shoe attached to one end for traction on mucky lake bottoms, but once I hit the cobbled riverbed, the metal shoe was pretty much useless. Worse, it made the pole harder to retrieve. As the river got shallower, I had to constantly readjust my grip while the current attempted to turn my bow. If I misjudged the depth, I'd end up with too much or too little pole in the water and the canoe would lurch forward. Before rounding the first bend, I turned to wave goodbye. Elkins watched from shore with a look of serious concern.

"Piece of cake," I shouted.

I kept losing ground to the current as riffles appeared on the Brule's surface, then rock gardens and finally full-fledged rapids. At one point the pole knocked me backwards into the stern seat. When I was sure Elkins couldn't see me, I retired the pole and got out my paddle.

The Brule is arguably the prettiest river in Wisconsin, maybe the entire Midwest—spring-fed and clear, flowing through a timbered valley of cedar and white pine, big white boulders in midstream, and trout moving against the mottled bottom. The Brule was the first river to point me in the direction of home rather than away from it.

And the only one I'd have to paddle ass-backwards. Most of those other rivers had been unrelentingly flat, but the Brule drops 418 feet over forty-four miles, the bulk in the last third. To avoid the main force of the current, I paddled from one side of the river to another and in the process jumped seasons. In the deep shadows of high banks, it was still late spring, the air cool and the grass silvery from a heavy dew. Across the river where the sun hit, it was late summer, a corona of insects hovering above the Queen Anne's lace and a reminder that I was running late.

The gradient continued to get steeper until I finally couldn't make any headway. Having retired the push-pole, I now reluctantly stowed the paddle, got out of the canoe and began to line it. Lining a canoe up a river is like walking a bicycle up a hill in that both admit to failure. Whatever modest hopes I'd entertained of poling or paddling upriver, of being that intrepid fellow in the plaid shirt and wide-brimmed hat, had been extinguished by the Brule.

Occasionally, canoeists and kayakers shot past, yahooing their way through the Class I and II rapids. Sometimes I caught them looking at me as I waded upstream tugging the yellow canoe behind on a short rope. My legs were cold and my thighs ached from the relentless pounding of current. Sometimes I'd jump back in the canoe and paddle a few yards between rapids. Sometimes, to avoid the violent chute of water where a logjam pinched the river, I'd climb over the pile of bleached logs and haul the canoe after me. Going *down* the Brule must be an adventure, I thought, a beautiful adventure. Going *up* the Brule was just stupid.

I was plodding forward this way when a party of kayakers careened past. I shouted a question that was quickly lost in the roar of whitewater. One of the kayakers executed a nifty eddy turn and came back to find out what I'd asked.

"How far to the lamprey barrier?"

"About two miles up," he replied.

The kayaker paused as if he hadn't really seen me before and was just now absorbing what stood before him—a middle-aged man thigh-deep in water walking a yellow canoe the wrong way up a river.

He pivoted around but not before bellowing, *"Are you fucking nuts?"*
It was more of a statement than a question.

Another hour of walking led me to a more sympathetic fly fisherman. To stay clear of his casting lane, I crossed over to his side of the river. He reeled in anyway.

"That doesn't look like fun," he observed.

"I just wanted to see how the Brule looked from the other end."

"Well, we got rain a day ago and the river's come up. We're up to 221 cubic feet per second. The median is 128, so no wonder you're having trouble."

Only a fly fisherman would know this sort of information. For me, the high water felt like a personal vindication, like it was the river's fault I couldn't go up it.

I asked the fly fishermen the same question: How far upstream was the lamprey barrier? He gave a little sideways nod of his head.

"It's just around the bend."

The barrier turned out to be a low concrete dam, a five-foot concrete waterfall built to prevent sea lampreys from wriggling up the Brule to spawn. Anadromous trout get over the dam by means of a fish ladder but a canoeist has to portage around it. Since the barrier is six and a half miles from the river's mouth, I could calculate my rate of travel, which was roughly one mile per hour. Lamprey speed.

By the time I hauled the pack and canoe over the trail, both sides of the steep valley were in shadow. I climbed up a ridge and pitched my tent, too tired to even worry if it was an active game trail. The next morning, exhausted from lining the canoe to the Highway 13 bridge, I climbed out of the river and flagged a ride on a passing shuttle bus.

Until the late nineteenth century, the Brule regularly functioned as a two-way river. For centuries, the Chippewa and Sioux took turns raiding each other by going up or down the Brule. When Chief Oshkaabewis led his delegation to plead for a federally recognized homeland in 1848, the Brule was the first rung on the route to Washington, DC. Seventeen years earlier, the Indian agent Henry Rowe Schoolcraft wrote upon ascending the river: "Often on looking down its channel there are wreaths of foam constituting a brilliant vista. This stream might appropriately be called Rapid or Mad River." French fur traders had already named the river the Bois Brule or "burnt wood," which may have meant a forest fire had swept the valley. More than likely it referred to the Métis or half-breeds who paddled the freighter canoes up the river. Schoolcraft may have avoided the term because his wife Jane was of mixed blood. Her father was a Scotch-Irish trader and her mother the daughter of a prominent Chippewa chief. She had studied in Ireland and wrote poetry in two languages. The tribal myths and legends her husband collected—that Longfellow later twisted into the tom-tom beat of *The Song of Hiawatha*—came from Jane Schoolcraft. Her Christian name was short and, well, plain, while her Indian name was long and melodious and beautiful to say: *Bamewawagezhikaquay*. It meant "Woman of the Sound the Stars Make Rushing through the Sky."

The sheer beauty of the Brule soon attracted summer people. As early as the 1870s, wealthy men from St. Paul, Chicago, and Milwaukee began buying up tracts of land along the river. Their names read like a roll call of the Gilded Age: Chester Adgate Congdon (mining), Henry Clay Pierce (oil and railroads), Edward N. Saunders (coal), Frederick Weyerhaeuser (timber). Having built fortunes on the slag heaps and stumpage they'd left across the Upper Midwest, the titans of industry wanted a retreat from the city, a place where their families could enjoy sparkling water, towering pines, and unparalleled trout fishing. They erected sprawling, Adirondack-style lodges along the river. Henry Clay Pierce's estate had thirty outbuildings, including a dining hall, servants' quarters, a fish hatchery, even a private zoo. Wealth attracts wealth, and more tycoons arrived to build rustic "camps" along the river, giving them fanciful names borrowed from Longfellow's trochaic version of the Chippewa language, thus *Gitche Gumee, Mik-E-Nok, Winneboujou, Wendigo*.

The new arrivals fenced and posted their estates to keep out locals and other riffraff, prompting one to write an 1895 letter to *The Superior Evening Telegram*: "The public and the clubhouse people on the

Brule do not get on well together. The latter own a great deal of land on the river and their enjoyment would be unalloyed if they could keep all other persons from fishing in the waters of the Brule."

At the turn of the last century, business interests in Duluth looked at the nearby Brule and envisioned a shipping canal linking Lake Superior with the Mississippi River via the St. Croix. The proposed canal would have dammed the Brule and transformed its "brilliant vista" into a ruler-straight ditch eighty-feet wide and six feet deep. Faced with a threat from fellow entrepreneurs, the wealthy summer people saved the river by surrounding it with public land. At a dinner party in St. Paul, Edward Saunders (coal) suggested to his neighbor Frederick Weyerhaeuser (timber) that if the lumberman was to donate land along the Brule to the state of Wisconsin, he could add a stipulation against future dams on the river. Weyerhaeuser's gift of more than four thousand acres of timberland in 1906 became the foundation of the Brule River State Forest.

29

Having cut out the middle of the Brule and most of its rapids, I hopped another shuttle bus to Stone's Bridge, where most canoe trips on the river begin. While other passengers on the shuttle bus retrieved their rental canoes and kayaks from the boat trailer and launched themselves downriver to Lake Superior, I paddled under the bridge and headed upstream toward Brule's headwaters.

The beginnings of rivers are mysterious, almost mythic, places, the source of a great river's flow issuing from some hidden spring deep in the forest or from under a rock. In the nineteenth century, explorers mounted long, arduous expeditions in search of the true source of one major river system after another. It was an elaborate competition, like being the first to summit a previously unclimbed peak. The explorer had to ascend a river's multiple tributaries, and then measure length, flow, and altitude to determine the ultimate point of origin. The explorers saw uncharted waters as a kind of flirtation, a terrific come-on based, as with any romance, on what one doesn't know but is willing to find out.

I wasn't looking for the source of the Brule but a historic portage trail to the St. Croix that was somewhere near it. All I had to do was follow the river seven miles upstream to the trailhead. The upper Brule had little current and meandered aimlessly through a brushy alder thicket, the water black as coffee only because it showed clear to the mucky bottom. As the river's course traced a double helix through the swamp, alder branches on either bank drew closer and closer until they intertwined. With the sky choked off and no room to swing a paddle, I couldn't tell if I was pointed upstream or down or hopelessly stuck in a bog. The only way to move was to grab an alder branch and pull the canoe forward. It was slow, scratchy work.

Then the alder-choked river came to T-bone and I was totally flummoxed. Right or left? The wider channel to the right quickly dead-ended, so I backtracked and turned left. The little stream had a steady current but got narrower and narrower until it reached a cul-de-sac in a grassy meadow rimmed with pines. Where was the damn trail? At this point, the yellow canoe was loaded with alder leaves and broken branches. It was also wider than the river, so I got out and walked, following the pocket stream to the edge of the pines where it disappeared like a rabbit down a hole.

Heat had been building all afternoon and now dark storm clouds massed on the horizon. Abandoning the canoe along with any thought of finding the portage trail, I hauled my pack to the closest timber and pitched camp in the lee of a ridge. The rain arrived at nightfall, one of those explosive August thunderstorms that rides in on a cold wave and announces the end of summer.

I awoke in the dark to the baying of hounds. At first I thought I was having a nightmare, a dream about being pursued through a swamp by men and dogs. But I listened again and it was clearly hounds baying in the distance. They were pursuing the Old Man of the Woods. Black bear season didn't open for another month, so the hunters and their dogs were just getting in a practice run. The yelping grew louder and more frenetic until I expected the pack—or fleeing bear—to rampage through my tent. Then the sound gradually faded and finally died off. I tried going back to sleep and wondered if the bear realized this was only practice.

The rain had stopped when I woke up a second time, but the storm had brought cool weather, so I stayed in my sleeping bag. Finally, when it was light enough to look for the portage trail, I crawled outside the tent into what felt like autumn. Damp leaves and overcast skies—football weather. I made a cup of instant coffee that steamed in the cool air, then I walked stiffly a few yards behind the tent and stumbled on the portage trail in the process of relieving myself.

The muddy path, marked with blue blazes on the sides of trees, ran along a pine ridge dividing the headwaters of the Brule from those of the St. Croix River. Leaving my pack for a second trip, I retrieved the canoe from the meadow, slipped underneath it so the center thwart rested on my shoulders, and slowly lurched forward. Rain had scoured the trail down to tree roots in the steeper sections. There was a slight dip to a streambed then a steady climb back to the ridge. Everything was glistening wet and smelled of dank woods.

I almost didn't notice the stone marker beside the trail because it looked like any lichen-covered rock, only larger with a brass plaque attached: Greysolon Dulhut—1680. (I wrote down his name so later I could look up his comments on the portage.) "After having cut down some trees and broken through about a hundred beaver dams, I went up said river, and then made a carry of half a league to reach a lake which emptied into a fine river which brought me up to the Mississippi."

Further on was another rock, Jonathan Carver—1768. "This river is so scant of water we were obliged to raise it with dams for passage." Another dip and rise and there was Henry R. Schoolcraft—1820. Jane's husband, the Indian agent, reported that the portage took "two pauses." Later, accompanying an 1831 military expedition searching for the source of the Mississippi, he wrote of the Brule portage: "The men toiled like dogs, but willingly and without grumbling."

On the verge of grumbling, I heaved my canoe down on the trail and took my first pause. In the damp, gloomy weather, the stone markers seemed less a Cavalcade of History than a line of staggered tombstones, commemorating not the explorer's transitory passage but his final resting place. Ahead on the trail, history was replaced with something more immediate—a steaming gray mound of bear shit—left, no doubt, by the object of that morning's practice chase. Since I didn't know whether the bear was coming or going, I announced my presence by singing. I sang one of those show tunes that over-the-hill actors tend to sing-speak when they no longer can carry a tune. What would frighten the Old Man of the Woods more—a pack of baying hounds or a musical canoe walking down the trail warbling "Singing in the Rain"?

The trail ended in a cutover field and, below the stumps, a black-top road. I left the canoe in the ferns and doubled back for my pack. There was an overlook on a ridge above the swampy beginnings of the St. Croix. I hadn't noticed it the first time around. The overlook came with a bench and a wooden post on which an ammunition box had been mounted. Inside the metal box was a diary with a flowers-and-butterflies cover and the title: Portage Trail Log. It was left, no doubt, for hikers to record their own travels. Taking my second pause, I sat on the bench and thumbed through the pages.

7/11—So much fun imagining carrying a canoe. I am carrying an Adirondack pack that I hand wove, so I am half-way living in the 1800s.

It is undoubtedly more fun to portage an imaginary canoe than a real one, but what set me off was the line about "half-way living in the 1800s." I don't believe in that kind of time travel, the vicarious experience of history by walking the same ground. "No man ever steps in the same river twice"—even on the Brule. The only insight I'd gathered from following in Schoolcraft's footsteps was that he must have had sore muscles and probably missed his wife whenever he looked up to see the stars rushing overhead.

4/20—My mom and I are here celebrating my 29th birthday. Grateful for this place in my home country of northern Wisconsin and for this day with my mother.

The entries were mostly anonymous. They record the date and weather and maybe a little personal history. With the exception of the imaginary canoe, the visitors had carried only themselves. Unlike the explorers, they weren't trying to get somewhere or make a name for themselves. Their names weren't written in stone. Nobody would remember their passage here except themselves.

7/29—I sat a little longer and said a prayer for my wife who is on the other side now.

In the liturgical calendar of the Catholic Church, of which I am a nominal member, periods of the year that fall between the seasons of Christmas and Easter or Lent and Advent are simply called Ordinary Time. I like the term because most people's lives fall under the same designations, the big moments and everything else. The big events get remembered, births and funerals and such, while the rest of the year, most of it, is lost in the slipstream of days. Yet as they get fewer, the ordinary days are what seem holy, so many moveable feasts. We're all explorers of a sort, bravely putting one foot in front of the other, crossing from youth to middle age to dotage until we reach the Great Divide. That's why the anonymous messages left by strangers seemed so much more poignant than the stone markers scattered along the trail.

7/30—Hi. We were here. Much love.

St. Croix River

~~~~~~~~~~~~~~~~~~~~

30

A cold wind blew whitecaps straight down Upper Lake St. Croix and chucked the bow of the square-stern canoe lashed to the end of the dock. I was sitting on a bar stool looking out a picture window at the canoe and feeling glad I wasn't in it. The Green Bay Packers were losing an exhibition game to the Pittsburgh Steelers on a television screen above the bar. I stopped looking at the lake and settled on the game. The barroom at the inn was paneled in knotty pine. There was a fieldstone fireplace, a pool table, and, best of all, old friends. Bob Elkins and Richard Bell had picked me up at the end of the portage trail and switched out the ricing canoe for the aluminum square-stern so I'd have an outboard for the final leg of my trip. Much ado was made of my having carried the yellow canoe two miles on the portage trail, less of my having skipped most of the Brule by hopping on a shuttle bus. I bought another round at half-time. Then suddenly the game was over and everyone paid up and left for the long drive home, except me. I checked into a room at the inn and slept for eleven hours straight.

The next morning, I carried a cup of coffee down to the white dock. The wind had died down but the weather had definitely turned. Yesterday's football game, the gunmetal sky, the row of empty white docks with boats battened down for the season—everything said fall. I hurried back to my room to pack.

The St. Croix would be the last new river on my trip, the only one that I would see from start to finish. It was a 165-mile straight shot from Upper Lake St. Croix to the Mississippi. Over that distance the St. Croix connects the North Woods to the Twin Cities metropolitan area, tying black bears and timber wolves at one end of the river to 3.5 million people at the other. There's a point on any voyage when the incoming tide exerts a stronger pull than the one that took you out to sea, and I'd reached that point. Once I got down the St. Croix, I'd be only a few days from home. Part of the impetus to get back was a bag of chocolate chip cookies my wife had sent along with a poem. A sweet gesture, the cookies, but the poem was a pointed message.

> A dozen cookies just for you,
> but wait, there's more,
> a list to do.

The list went on to enumerate all the domestic chores I'd neglected during my absence and included several more "to be announced." It was a shot across my bow, as it were, a reminder of the obligations of ordinary time, which I'd pushed aside for a quixotic journey on a river that went in circles.

The ghost of Neddy Merrill hovered close by. He's the main character in "The Swimmer," John Cheever's cautionary tale about another husband who takes the long way home. One bright summer day, Neddy Merrill leaves a suburban cocktail party by announcing he will swim home via the semi-continuous chain of his neighbors' swimming pools. Neddy convinces himself he's "a pilgrim, an explorer, a man with a destiny" instead of a careless husband embarked on a foolish stunt. If you know the story, you know how it ends. Neddy stumbles home after his long watery journey only to find a darkened house, empty and locked. I didn't want to end up like Neddy.

In the afternoon I slipped under highway and railroad bridges, one so low it nearly removed my head, and entered the St. Croix Flowage. The impoundment was large enough to hold a confusing number of islands and hidden bays and when I reached the campground at its western outlet I called it a day.

The flowage was the result of the Gordon dam, and like all dams, this one imposed human intention on a river's natural tendency to flow downhill. The dam had replaced a set of rapids because the natural conditions that form rapids—a constriction in the river and sudden drop in elevation—also make for ideal dam sites. Sometimes successive dams are built on the same site, the way medieval churches were often erected on the ruins of ancient temples. Same spot, slightly different intentions. Three dams have occupied the Gordon site over the past two centuries. The first was a *namai kowagon* or "sturgeon fish dam," built by Indians using rocks and sticks to further bottleneck a natural narrowing in the river. Passing through in 1832, Henry Schoolcraft observed a Chippewa village on the east bank of the river with well-tended gardens of corn, potatoes, and pumpkins. Half a century later, loggers built a log-and-timber dam at the same outlet. Raising the backwaters behind it, the dam flooded what remained of the village to float logs that had been stockpiled all winter. Then the loggers opened the dam's sluice gates to shoot the logs downstream.

The final incarnation of the Gordon dam was the one I was standing on, a concrete structure built as a public works project during the Depression. The current dam has eight steel bulkhead gates and a head of twelve feet, which is the elevation difference between the flowage and the river below. There isn't another obstruction for ninety miles downstream until the hydroelectric dam at St. Croix Falls. Between the two concrete plugs, the St. Croix is a designated Wild and Scenic River. Another human intention.

Next morning I discovered that I wasn't the only person staying in the campground. A van with a whitewater canoe strapped to its top had rolled in overnight. Father and son had driven all day from southern Ohio to canoe the North Woods rivers of Wisconsin. Dad was an accountant, short and balding and a little frog-faced behind his glasses. His son, quiet and beetle-browed, was mostly silent and wore shorts despite the morning cold. They seemed comfortable together. When the son pulled his arms into his Star Wars sweatshirt to warm them, the father joked, "Hey, what happened to your arms?" and tickled him.

Like other accountants I've known, Dad had a secret passion—whitewater canoeing. His résumé of rivers—the Wolf, the St. Louis, Monastery Falls on the Red River, and Boyscout Rapids on the Peshtigo—was impressive. Father and son debated whether to run May's Ledges on the Brule after breakfast or canoe the Totogiac River instead.

"My wife won't go with us on these trips," said Dad. "She's afraid we'll tip."

When I confessed that I was afraid of tipping myself, the two exchanged smiles.

"Don't worry," Dad said. "We've done the St. Croix several times and never overturned."

In my twenties, I was as much a whitewater freak as the accountant. I built a slalom kayak from a pair of fiberglass molds, epoxying the two halves together—orange deck and white hull—so that the boat resembled a plastic Easter egg. Every spring when the rivers ran high with snowmelt, my friends and I put on wetsuits and helmets and kayaked a whitewater river up north. To prepare for these trips, we spent at least one winter weekend in the university pool practicing our Eskimo roll. The Inuit had developed the maneuver in order to self-right an overturned kayak in the frigid waters of the Arctic. The water temperature in the university's indoor pool was a uniform 70 degrees.

One pool session we were joined by a young assistant professor of chemistry. She wore a black tank suit that showed off a lithe figure and muscled arms. Standing at the edge of the pool, hands on hips, feet apart, she appraised our own clumsy attempts at rolling. Then she slid into her own kayak and proceeded to do the Eskimo roll. She'd flip upside down, sweep her paddle blade across the surface of the pool and magically pop up. She rolled once, twice, three times in quick succession. Pausing for air, she followed up with the Pawlata roll, a variation where she gripped one blade and sculled the other across the surface to pop to the surface. Then she did a put-across roll, extending her paddle at a right angle from the kayak and using its full length to lever herself upright. Setting her paddle aside, she flipped her kayak over and used only her hands and a hip-flick to right herself. When she was done, she pulled her spray skirt loose, swam to the side of the pool, and lifted herself dripping from the water like Botticelli's Venus only more ripped. We stared not only because the assistant professor of chemistry was an attractive young woman but because she was so clearly in her element in a way that we would never be.

So it came as a shock a couple of years after the pool sessions ended when I learned that Donna Berglund had drowned in Class IV rapids on the upper reaches of Montana's Swan River. At the time she was one of the top women kayakers in the country, having graduated from Wisconsin's modest rivers to the big waters of the West. It was hard to believe that a paddler as skilled as Berglund could fall to any river.

The International Scale of River Difficulty lists six categories of whitewater, Class I being riffles and small waves; Class VI being for all practical purposes unrunnable. A Class IV stretch of water "may feature large, unavoidable waves and holes or constricted passages demanding fast maneuvers under pressure. . . . Risk of injury to swimmers is moderate to high, and water conditions may make self-rescue difficult." American Whitewater, an organization that keeps a database of canoe and kayaking accidents, stated that Berglund had been training on the Swan for a race the following day and decided on one more run. When rest of her party declined, she went ahead by herself. The following day racers found Berglund's body and her kayak pinned below a logjam. The report theorizes that Berglund had likely glanced off a boulder in midstream and been swept into a "strainer." Strainers are logjams that allow water to pass through even as the hydraulic force traps larger objects and pushes them underneath. Under those circumstances, self-rescue via any form of roll isn't an option. Given Berglund's level of expertise, the American Whitewater report concludes with a warning: "No single incident demonstrates the dangers of solo paddling alone as well as this one. She might have easily been rescued by another person."

The presence of rapids has as much to do with the geology of a riverbed as its gradient. For most of the St. Croix's course, the river cuts through soft Cambrian sandstone, but in the upper stretches the river hits the older, harder igneous rock of the Pre-Cambrian era. It's a game of paper-rock-scissors played over geological time. Rapids form where the rock plays to a draw. Water pushes upward to develop standing waves and in the process becomes aerated and bubbly and turns into "whitewater." The more serious the rapids, the more likely they are to have names. In its first dozen miles, the upper St. Croix has seven named rapids, none over a Grade II. On a map of the river, they appear in this order:

Scout Chute
Scott Rapids
Copper Mine Sluice Dam
Shelldrake Rapids
Bear Trap Rapids
Big Fish Trap Rapids
Little Fish Trap Rapids

A rapids' name doesn't necessarily indicate what to expect; nevertheless, I was a little apprehensive about ones ending in the word "trap."

At Copper Mine Sluice Dam, the river split into five fingers around stone piers from an old logging dam. A red sign indicated a portage trail on the right bank, so I pulled over to scout the rapids. I had earlier unbolted my outboard and strapped it in the canoe with the rest of my gear, so the square-stern was a little heavy in the middle and not very nimble. Other than standing waves, Copper Mine Sluice was a straight chute as long as you didn't hit one of the stone piers or iron spikes in the old spillway. A good whitewater kayaker could have run it blindfolded.

Big Fish Trap Rapids announced itself with white streamers set against a green horizon of trees. The "trap" referred to fish weirs Chippewa families used to build in the spring and place below the rapids to catch migrating suckers. No red sign on the bank indicated a portage, so I didn't stop to scout. Going into a rapids, you look for a smooth tongue of water pointing downstream and align the canoe with it. The idea is to go with the prevailing flow, bearing in mind that rocks, not waves, are the problem. The biggest mistake to make in an open boat is to be indecisive, to change course at the last minute and go for another route. At that point you're likely to hit a rock broadside and stay there until the current conspires to roll you over.

On the very first pitch of Fish Trap, my canoe dropped with a bang onto a large boulder and stuck fast. Waves broke over the gunwales as I paddled and pushed furiously without budging. Planted firmly atop the fulcrum of rock, the canoe slowly began pivoting sideways. In a moment or two, it would present itself broadside to the current and overturn. I made a quick mental inventory of what would float when the canoe rolled—myself, my life preserver, the gear stuffed in a dry bag—and what would sink—trunk, outboard, my notes. Once overturned, the canoe would fill with hundreds of pounds of water and lodge against the rocks, and doubtless remain there without a winch. All this was going through my head as the bow slowly turned.

Years ago, I had found myself in a similar situation while canoeing with my older brother on the East Fork of the Chippewa River. I had just bought an old wooden canoe and was demonstrating my mastery of it to my brother when it lodged on a boulder in midstream and stuck there. The fact that I was in the stern and my brother the bow was a reversal of our customary roles in which he, older by five years, led the way and I followed. "Sit tight," I told him and stepped out of the canoe and onto the boulder to free us. The moment I left the canoe, it shot downstream. The unoccupied stern rose three feet out of the water as the canoe and my brother pinwheeled down the river. "You're on your own!" I shouted after him. Wading ashore, I raced along the bank until I could effect a rescue. We finished that trip without further incident and over the years "You're on your own!" became a shared punchline, something I could say to make both of us laugh. My brother has since moved on, by which I mean that he's no longer living. He died in the spring, on his living room couch alone in a distant state so that I had no chance to say goodbye. After he was gone I could think of nothing to say, no elegy from Catullus (*by ways remote and distant waters sped, Brother, to thy sad grave-side am I come*), only an image of the two of us back on the river and my brother drifting slowly out of sight and me shouting after him, "You're on your own!" although now it's myself that I mean.

This time when I stepped onto the boulder, I remembered to keep a tight grip on the gunwales. The canoe floated free and I climbed back in and ran the rest of Fish Trap Rapids. Then I was in quiet water and the sun came out and my wet clothes started to dry. Four round, whiskered heads popped out of the water and followed the canoe. A family of otters. They dove and surfaced so often at times they looked like one head with three humps. I passed a campsite with wet clothes hanging from a clothesline strung between two trees. The family looked none the worse for having tipped in the rapids. I waved and they waved back and one of the boys held up a stringer of bass. I was hoping for an invitation to dinner, but none was forthcoming so I kept going further downstream to another site where I camped by myself.

31

With the addition of the Namekagon, its largest tributary, the St. Croix became a bigger river, broader with less white pine along its banks and more silver maple and birch. Islands piled with driftwood at their heads broke the river into channels. The river also became the boundary line dividing Wisconsin from Minnesota although that was only apparent on a map. The squiggly blue outline of a river on a map can also serve as a kind of Rorschach Test in that the viewer sees what he wants to see. In the 1930s, a group of businessmen and resort owners in northwestern Wisconsin looked at the sinuous dark line of the St. Croix River on a map and saw the profile of an Indian. It was the same profile as on the nickel except facing left instead of right. The group henceforth promoted the area, which had already undergone successive eras of logging and farming, as a vacationland known as Indian Head Country. By that measure, I had made my way down the Indian's forehead and was approaching the bridge of his nose at Danbury.

I parked my canoe in a slough, crossed a high wooden bridge, and walked a half-mile to Danbury. The St. Croix Band of Chippewa casino, a futuristic building with glass walls and multiple rooflines, looked as if it had crash landed on a direct flight from Las Vegas. There was the same darkness-at-noon feel of any casino, the same flashing neon and electronic pinging that results in an utter sense of dislocation from time and place. Not wanting to gamble, I crossed the street to the Log Cabin Store and Eatery for lunch. The interior was bright and cheerful and all about place, a sense achieved mainly through taxidermy—stuffed fish, a stuffed coyote, and the centerpiece, a 578-pound stuffed black bear "harvested by Wild Bill." The bear was posed upright on its hind legs, paws splayed and raised to swat, jaws agape—every camper's nightmare. In addition to tourist apparel, the store sold bear bait, fifty-five-gallon barrels of bear cookies and cookie dough, so it was entirely possible the bear hadn't been as angry in life as it appeared in death and that it had probably spent its final moments happily muzzling through a tub of chocolate chip cookie dough before "Wild Bill" dispatched it.

The stuffed black bear got me thinking about the meaning of the word "wild" and how much depends upon context. A *wild* bear is one in its natural setting; whereas a *wild* man is someone out of step with polite company. Wildness in a river is in the eye of the beholder. I've never canoed a river that didn't at least *feel* wild, and that includes the Milwaukee River where it passes under the North Avenue bridge. Since leaving the dam at Gordon, I had been traveling on a Wild and Scenic River, a federal designation that meant the ninety-mile stretch of the St. Croix was "free of impoundments and generally inaccessible except by trail with watersheds or shorelines essentially primitive and waters unpolluted." The National Park Service administers the St. Croix Riverway as a whole, but the riparian corridor is pieced together from several state parks, state forests, wildlife refuges, and part of the St. Croix Chippewa Reservation.

Congress has been preserving wild lands since the Grant administration but didn't begin to protect rivers until 1968 after a spate of dam building out West and a year before Ohio's Cuyahoga River caught fire. The Cuyahoga had been regularly catching fire for a century but the country hadn't taken notice until that moment when the environmental movement was building steam. Initially the St. Croix wasn't a candidate for the Wild and Scenic Rivers Act because, unlike Western rivers, most of it didn't flow through public land. Northern States Power owned seventy miles on both sides of the river—from St. Croix Falls all the way upstream to just below the mouth of the Namekagon. It took a political compromise for the St. Croix to become "wild." NSP originally intended to build a series of hydroelectric dams on its land along the upper river but later shelved those plans and proposed a coal-fired generating plant on the lower St. Croix instead. Gaylord Nelson, at the time a U.S. Senator from Wisconsin, led a fight against the proposed power plant, so NSP offered to strike a deal. The company would convey its land along the upper river to the government if Nelson would agree not to oppose the new plant. Nelson took the deal. In 1968 the upper St. Croix was folded into the Wild and Scenic Rivers Act and preserved for future generations, like myself.

All morning I'd passed only a single pair of fishermen flailing the river with stick-baits, and the St. Croix did not seem wild to me so much as deserted. If anything, the lack of people made the river seem strangely artificial, a painted backdrop to a weekend getaway. Perhaps I'd been spoiled by my summer on the Yukon, a true wilderness river that is a vital transportation link while remaining a source of both sustenance and tradition for the people living along it. The closest I'd seen of that combination in Wisconsin was the Bad River. The idea of wilderness as a place apart from human connection, a tabula rasa on which the modern traveler writes his solitary adventure, is itself an illusion. A free-running river may look like a blank slate, but it's really a palimpsest, an ongoing story that keeps being added to over time, layer upon layer, until the narratives are so mixed together you can't tell where one begins and another leaves off. Every tributary of the Round River, even the remotest stretch of water, offered constant reminders that I was following in other people's wakes.

A few years ago I met a woman at a writer's conference in Duluth who'd inherited her father's leather-bound canoe journals and was preparing them for publication. Martha Greene Phillips looked no older than I, so it came as a shock to learn that her father had served in the Spanish-American War. Howard Greene mustered out of the army as a captain and returned home to run the family pharmaceutical business in Milwaukee. He must have missed the logistical challenges of putting men in the field, however, because he soon began mounting canoe expeditions to the North Woods.

Border Country: The Northwoods Canoe Journals of Howard Greene, 1906–1916 offers a unique portrait of northern Wisconsin at the juncture between the end of the logging era and the beginning of the modern epoch of outdoor recreation. Greene's journal for the St. Croix River trip is the usual accounting of weather and meals and who fell into the drink. What made Greene remarkable for the time was that he had not come to the North Woods to log or plow, he came strictly for fun. In that respect, he was a pioneer. Leaky canvas tents and sleeping on the ground weren't necessarily fun in themselves but took on meaning when connected to the new idea of wilderness recreation. Americans had previously viewed wilderness as an impediment to progress; now it was seen as a source of inner renewal. A synchronicity of ideas at the turn of the last century led to this turnabout. In the White House Teddy Roosevelt espoused the outdoor life for instilling "fundamental frontier virtues." Those virtues, not always apparent during the country's settlement, had recently been enumerated by historian Frederick Jackson Turner. Turner's "Frontier Thesis" argued that wild land was the very forge upon which the nation's character had been hammered: "The very fact of the wilderness appealed to men as a fair, blank page on which to write a new chapter in the story of man's struggle for a higher type of society." The frontier had closed, Turner wrote, when the 1890 census revealed there was no longer a consistent line of unsettled land. One way a citizen could recreate its virtues was to go camping. Roosevelt was a great admirer of Turner and vice versa. When Turner studied at the University of Wisconsin, one of his classmates was Howard Greene.

On August 15, 1907, Greene, his two young sons and their schoolmate, and a pair of adult friends arrived in Gordon on the sleeper train from Chicago. Waiting for them at the depot were three rib-and-plank canoes, camping gear, and two unemployed lumberjacks hired on as cooks and "wood butchers." Greene's party pitched their tent above the logging dam and four days later embarked down the St. Croix. The boys swam and fished during the heat of the day and listened to mandolin music and comic recitations around the campfire at night. Howard put a hole in the bottom of his canoe and one boy broke a paddle at Fish Trap Rapids, necessitating an impromptu repair job. They took potshots at ducks along the river and stopped at two unnamed Indian villages, including one "on a high plateau overlooking the river" that sounds a lot like Danbury.

Greene illustrated his journal with photographs taken with a large-format Graflex camera. Looking at the black-and-white pictures a century later, you can't help noticing the number and variety of people along the river: log drivers and homesteaders, Swedes and ferrymen, and, of course, the Indians. Not that they shared equal standing. A man of his times, Greene wrote of "bucks" and "squaws" and "half-breeds" and described the small grave houses in a village cemetery as "the survival of barbarism." in one photograph a pair of Chippewa men pose warily in ornate beadwork sashes as if they know the camera lens will transform them into something other than who they are.

Greene's party caught up with "not less than 75 men" where a log drive had jammed in the rapids below the Kettle River. The loggers were impressed when Howard ran the whitewater in a canoe that was lighter and more nimble than their flat-bottomed bateaux. The trip came to an end the first week of September when the party arrived at the horseshoe-shaped dam at St. Croix Falls. The hydroelectric dam had recently come online and its power lines reached to the greater world. Renewed by the summer's adventure, Greene's party boarded a train for Minneapolis, all except the two lumberjacks who stayed behind to ship the camping gear home. In a postscript to the journal, Howard wrote that one of the men later succumbed to alcoholism: "As usual with Martin it was a case of the snakes and he went off in the woods where he was found dead."

Late in the day, I landed at St. Croix State Park on the Minnesota side. It was a weekday and the walk-in camping loop was empty. After supper, I sat at my picnic table and watched the moon inflate like a hot air balloon and float above the trees. A young family arrived at the next site and set up camp according to a strict division of labor. Mom unloaded the car while Dad pegged down the tent and refereed two small boys, who ricocheted all over the place. Here then was the next generation of outdoor enthusiasts. Had they come to the woods to instill frontier virtues or just the chance to burn a few s'mores? I was hoping to hear mandolin music and campfire recitations; instead I listened to the boys pestering their parents and each other. The younger boy in particular was a constant stream of questions. When can we eat? Why does the tent smell funny? Where is the river?

After the family finished supper, they retreated into their tent, as I did into mine. The moon had drifted away, leaving only darkness and the melancholic, end-of-summer chirping of crickets. Then the younger boy's interrogation began all over again. What are we going to do tomorrow? Can I start a fire? How far is the moon? The father responded to each question in a patient and hushed voice, aware perhaps that night air is a perfect conductor of sound.

The younger boy had just settled down when, from just beyond the walk-in loop, came a high-pitched howl. *Arrrooohh . . . oooooo . . . ooow!*

"What's *that*?" asked the boy with all the questions. "Is that a wolf?"

I knew they were coyotes and not wolves because the howling began with a sharp bark then quickly climbed several octaves to an ear-splitting whine that broke into manic yapping as if an air raid siren had been installed in a dog pound. It sounded like a concert hall full of dissonant coyotes although the racket probably came from a single pair with pups.

"I don't think they're wolves," the father whispered. "It's probably some coyotes."

The boy paused to process this new information.

"Are they nice?"

"Nice?"

"The coyotes. Are they nice?"

"Well, I don't think they'd bother you."

The night grew silent again as the coyotes moved on and crickets filled the void. From inside the boy's tent, a thin, wavering voice rose in an unmistakable call of the wild, *"Wooooo . . . Ooooh . . . wwoooooo!!!"*

32

The next morning I ran the rapids below the mouth of the Kettle River and then had mostly flat water all the way to the high dam at St. Croix Falls. The dam marks the end of the Wild St. Croix and the beginning of the strictly Scenic portion of the river. These are legal rather than aesthetic judgments. Below the dam the land-scape hardly changes but there are more access points—bridge cross-ings, intersecting roads, and boat landings—and therefore more boat traffic. The change is almost atmospheric, from silence to the roar of outboards, from too few people to suddenly too many. As in physics, time alters space. A canoeist covering ninety miles of the upper river in three or four days can't help feeling dwarfed by the unbroken forest and steeply canted bluffs; whereas, a speedboat driver hurtling down the lower river measures his distance in hours and horsepower, the landscape flowing behind him like a green cape.

For me, the dam meant one final portage—on Bob Elkins's boat trailer. The last forty miles of the St. Croix widens into a lake before it joins the Mississippi. The small cities strung along this lake—Stillwater, Bayport, Hudson, Afton—all lay within commuting distance of the metropolitan Twin Cities and 3.5 million people. This final stretch of river is designated "Recreational," a word I now understand as synonymous with "speedboats." Lake St. Croix on a summer weekend takes on the frenzied atmosphere of a European roundabout, the Piazza Venezia in Rome, say, on a busy Sunday afternoon, whirling power yachts instead of Fiats and Alfa Romeos jockeying for position, the blast of air horns instead of honking. Put a midwesterner behind the wheel of a speedboat and he suddenly becomes Mario Andretti. Because I was riding in a low-profile canoe painted in camouflage colors, I slipped on a neon yellow T-shirt to be better seen among the whirl of watercraft. It might as well have been the cloak of invisibility.

Approaching a marina above Stillwater, I was nearly swamped by a passing speedboat. I was still roiling in its wake when the boat suddenly swerved toward the marina and cut me off. I swung the canoe around and barely avoided a collision, managing only to make a gesture with my free hand. Then I followed the speedboat to the dock.

"Hey you!"

The driver in wraparound shades evidently couldn't hear any better than he could see. I tried again, "Hey! You almost hit me out there!"

"Sorry, man. Didn't see you." He kept walking.

"Well, that's the point, isn't it? You didn't *see* me!"

He finished tying up his boat and turned to face me, a young guy with a round head. His breath stank of whiskey.

"Hey, man. Look, I said I'm sorry."

Then he walked away.

I was still angry when I climbed back in the canoe and a little taken aback that the speedboat driver had turned out to be Hmong. I don't know why that surprised me, but it did. The near-collision set an alarming tone for the remainder of the afternoon. Speedboats were a threat and I kept my head on a swivel to avoid them. Since most of the shoreline was private, there was the additional problem of where to camp for the night. It would be dark soon and if I didn't find a vacant sandbar by then I'd be truly invisible.

There's an old railroad swing bridge at Hudson and below it a long comma of sand called Swing Bridge Island. The beach resembled a boat show. It was ringed with power cruisers, the kind with bulbous, outsized bows, each tethered to shore with a long anchor line. I slipped my canoe between two lines and started to unload. Three couples sat in camp chairs at the water's edge sharing a cooler of drinks and watching me carry my gear to the beach. A husky, sunburned fellow in his forties motioned to an empty chair.

"Hey, you want a beer? Something to eat?"

He climbed a short stepladder onto his boat, disappeared down the companionway and returned a few minutes later with a cold can of beer and a blueberry muffin. I was surprised at the welcome, given that other boaters had seemed intent on sinking me.

"So what's the deal?" asked the man's wife. "You have to camp every night and cook over a campfire?"

"Not really. As a matter of fact, last night I stayed in a motel. I'm just trying to get to the Mississippi without getting run over."

"Well, I was a corpsman in the Navy," said the husband, "and you wouldn't catch me on a big lake in a canoe. Anyway, you picked a good weekend 'cause it's slow tonight."

It didn't look like a slow night. It looked like Party Central. A steady parade of enormous power yachts cruised up and down the river. They were dwarfed by a four-deck dinner cruise boat strung with so many lights it looked like a city block that had broken off from Hudson and was drifting upstream to Stillwater. The guy who'd given me the beer gave me the rundown on his own boat, a twenty-eight-foot Sea-Ray cabin cruiser with a 250-horse V-6 engine, a cruising range of 140 miles, and top speed of 46 mph. It burned an average of 38 gallons of gas an hour.

"Boats are cheap," he said. "I bought this used for $15,000."

The boat's name was written in large black lettering across the white hull: *Bada-Bing!* Stenciled below the name was the silhouette of a buxom, reclining woman. I didn't get the reference at first and then . . . bada-bing . . . I did. Bada-Bing! was the New Jersey strip club on *The Sopranos*. It was where Tony Soprano could relax and be himself after whacking errant wise-guys. The boat's owner wore a T-shirt with Bada-Bing! printed across the chest, so I decided that was his name as well. Mr. Bada-Bing! switched on the boat's sound system and the feverish falsetto of Maurice Gibbs floated over the beach.

"We knew these guys from before," explained Mrs. Bada-Bing!, "but everybody else we met through boating. We'd come here on weekends and get together and that's how we all became friends."

She was letting me know that she and her friends weren't millionaires, just working stiffs who owned really big boats. In America, the land of brazen consumption, it's always a mistake to size people up based on their possessions. Is the skinny guy wearing patched Carhartts a day laborer or a tenured poet? Is the guy who almost ran you over in a powerboat a raging redneck or the son of Laotian immigrants? Whenever I guessed, I inevitably guessed wrong. That would be the one great takeaway from my long, roundabout trip—not to guess.

"Hey," said Mr. Bada-Bing!, rallying the troops, "where should we go this week?"

"Lake Pepin," one of the other skippers replied. "Let's go to Lake Pepin."

"Nah. I don't want to go to Lake Pepin. I've seen enough lakes. Let's go up to St. Paul. We'll dock at Harriet Island and go dancing. What about it?"

The others shrugged. When I announced my own plans to get up early and beat the Sunday traffic to the Mississippi, Mr. Bada-Bing! looked disappointed. Clearly, I was a party-pooper.

"Hey, you going to Prescott tomorrow?" he asked one of the others. "Why not take John with you? Tie the canoe behind?"

The skipper agreed, a little reluctantly I thought.

"Now you got a ride to Prescott, so you don't have to go to bed so early."

He poured me a shot of rum. The soundtrack of *Saturday Night Fever* ended and Neil Diamond's deep baritone boomed "Sweet Caroline" over Swing Bridge Island. It was a signal. The three women rose from their camp chairs as one and sang along. As the song reached its brassy crescendo, the women fist-pumped the air and shouted the chorus about past times that never seemed . . . "SO GOOD! . . . SO GOOD! . . . SO GOOD!"

"One thing about boat people," said Mrs. Bada-Bing! when the song was over, "is we really like to drink."

The party moved onto a fourth power yacht for a tour of the lights of Stillwater while I promised to keep an eye on their boats. I was encouraged to help myself to more beer. I had traded solitude for Party Island and felt like baby Moses plucked from the Nile by the Pharaoh's daughter. The rum helped too.

Air horns and bottle rockets kept me awake late into the night. Music faded in and out with every passing boat. I decided not to wait for the promised ride to Prescott in the morning once I realized that being towed behind one of the big cruisers would almost certainly turn my canoe into a submarine. Everyone was still sleeping it off when I got up at dawn and loaded the canoe as quietly as possible. I wanted to leave a thank-you note for Mr. and Mrs. Bada-Bing!, but I didn't see how without climbing aboard their yacht and waking them. So I pushed off with my canoe paddle and stole into the pearly morning light as silently as a thief.

by hometown. Over half came from Red Wing, mostly women and children who had boarded a ship here in high spirits on another hot summer day.

On Sunday morning, July 13, 1890, the *Sea Wing* departed Red Wing bound for a National Guard encampment below Lake City. The stern-wheeler was 135 feet long, narrow of beam and taller than she was wide. Her ungainly lines betrayed the ship's origins as a log-hauler on the lake before being refitted as an excursion boat. She steamed out of Red Wing carrying two hundred passengers and a crew of ten spread over three decks; a covered barge lashed to the port side accommodated the overflow crowd. As the *Sea Wing* entered the blue expanse of Lake Pepin, a string orchestra played on her deck.

Passengers disembarked an hour later for a day of marching bands, patriotic songs, and cannon fusillades over the water. After cool breezes on the lake voyage, the heat of the shadeless military camp must have been oppressive, and excursionists bought ice cream and lemonade to quench their thirst. A sudden rain squall late in the afternoon delayed the day's final event, a military dress parade. At seven in the evening, Captain David Wethern blew the *Sea Wing*'s steam whistle for the return voyage. Some passengers expressed concern about black clouds massing to the northeast, but Wethern, whose own wife and eight-year-old son were aboard, headed onto the lake. He reprimanded a few young passengers for donning life jackets. "Take them off," he demanded. "You will frighten the ladies."

Large hail began pummeling the ship, and the ladies were encouraged to shelter in the enclosed cabin on the second deck. Waves running six to eight feet broke over the ship's bow and flooded the lower deck. Wethern would later explain that he was trying to reach the shallows beneath the Wisconsin bluffs and run the *Sea Wing* aground. When that proved impossible, he reversed course and steered directly into the gale. At some point, the barge line broke or was cut and the ship, already top-heavy, listed 45 degrees. In the darkness, an enormous wave smashed the ship broadside, and the *Sea Wing* keeled completely over. Bracing his legs against the ship's wheel and pushing with his back, Wethern broke a window to escape the submerged pilothouse and swam ashore. The women and children trapped in the ship's cabin, including the captain's wife and son, were not as lucky.

Forty-four funerals were held in Red Wing on a single day after the wreck. At the official inquiry, Inspector John D. Sloan warned "that excursions on Lake Pepin should not be made under any circumstances, owing to the dangers from sudden squalls." Most of the *Sea Wing*'s male passengers managed to swim ashore—like the musician who rode his bass viol as a life raft—while nearly all the women and girls aboard drowned. The disparity could be blamed in part on the times. Women weren't taught to swim, and even if they could, their cumbersome clothing would have made it difficult if not impossible. Survivors who clung to the capsized ship would later recall lightning flashes revealing women in long white summer dresses thrashing hopelessly on the dark surface of the lake.

Late in the afternoon, I left Red Wing and chugged beneath Barn Bluff then through a maze of islands until the channel opened into Lake Pepin. The lake was blue and placid beneath an immense sky. On the lake I didn't have to worry about boat traffic, just wind— especially a south wind with twenty-one unimpeded miles to build up steam. There was only the slightest breeze at the moment. To play it safe, though, I camped on a deserted beach on the Wisconsin head of the lake and planned to get an early start before the day's heat could raise a wind.

All night I kept waking in the dark and checking my watch to see if it was time to leave. Once I even rolled up my sleeping bag before realizing I'd misread the luminous hands on the dial so that what seemed like 6:15 was really 2:30. When I finally crawled out of the tent, the far shore had vanished. Lake Pepin in a fog looked like an ocean because there was no end to it, only a thin line separating gray water from gray sky. But the water was calm, so I pushed off before the wind had a chance to change its mind. I kept the Wisconsin shore within swimming distance and puttered south. As the fog slowly lifted, the ghostly outline of Maiden Rock, the landmark Captain Wethern had been steaming toward before the storm overtook him, suddenly materialized as big as a mountain. I rounded the point and ran smack into a stiff headwind. At first the surface of the lake rolled in gentle swells and then broke into whitecaps. My canoe began to shrink among the oncoming waves until it was roughly the size of a bass viol.

Then the shoreline curved in another direction and the wind died as quickly as it had risen. In the tattered fog I passed a "scoop" of white pelicans feeding in the shadows. I took it as a good omen. An hour later I rounded a rocky point that turned out to be a breakwater. Rising behind it was a forest of tall white masts.

I left my canoe moored to a dock at the Pepin marina and walked into town for breakfast. A sign hung in front of a white clapboard restaurant:

THE HOMEMADE CAFÉ
BREAKFAST & LUNCH
PIE

The waitress was a big, healthy-looking girl with her hair in a ponytail and a friendly manner. She seemed to know everyone who walked into the café.

"Go ahead and sit in your favorite spot," she called to a white-haired couple.

My favorite spot was the first available table. The waitress brought eggs, toast, hash browns, and sausage on a big crockery plate and kept returning to top off my coffee. When I'd finished, she asked if I wanted a piece of pie to go. "Our black and blue pie travels well."

Traveling pie was an idea impossible to resist. I told her I was heading up the Chippewa River later in the day. Turns out she had grown up hunting in the Tiffany Bottoms.

"Me and my family been hunting the bottoms since I was a kid," she volunteered. "I like it all, bow and gun, but I like duck hunting the best. The last time my friends and I rode jet skis into the bottoms. We didn't get very far."

I was thinking that the waitress was a good example of the new country woman—hunting and jet skiing and serving up traveling pie—when an image of the old version walked into the café, a girl about ten years old accompanied by her parents. The girl wore a long calico dress and matching sunbonnet that hung from a strap down her back. When the family didn't bow their heads in prayer, I decided they weren't religious fundamentalists but tourists bound for the Laura Ingalls Wilder Museum across the street.

"I read all the Laura books when I was a kid," said the waitress.

"My favorite," I confided, "is *The Long Winter* because it had more plot than the others."

"Well, it doesn't take much imagination to guess where she was writing about," the waitress said, glancing out the window.

The waitress had her geography mixed up. *The Long Winter* takes place in South Dakota, not Wisconsin. At any rate, the Little House books aren't about any one place because the Ingalls family kept moving; they're more about time, specifically the brief span of years called childhood. And to a child, a small-town winter can feel long wherever it happens to be. The continued appeal of the Little House books is that they confirm what children already know—that a year is measured in seasons, not months, that weather is an important event, and family is at the center of an expanding universe.

One of the first books I read to my oldest daughter was *Little House in the Big Woods*. As a parent, I had mixed motives for choosing it for bedtime reading. True, I wanted my daughter to absorb some of Laura's pluck and her ability to see beauty in simple things, but I was also hoping a little of Pa's glory would rub off on me. Pa made a great role model for a first-time father: unflappable, handy with tools, and not so full of himself he couldn't get down on all fours to play "mad dog" with his kids. Pa, not Laura, is the book's hero and the author lavishes long scenes on everything he does: Pa making bullets, Pa greasing his traps, Pa going off to hunt, Pa fiddling, Pa telling stories of his own childhood. Even when Ma swats a bear one night in the barnyard, she comforts her girls by saying that Pa will soon be home. After we finished the book, my daughter and I made a pilgrimage to the Laura Ingalls Wilder Wayside a few miles north of Pepin to see the actual site. But it didn't produce the effect of a pilgrimage, which is a deepening of faith rather than the first crack of skepticism. The replica log cabin was the right size and weathered a silver gray, but it sat on the edge of a large, open cornfield. Where were the Big Woods? Where were the bears, wolves, and wildcats? Where had Laura and her family gone if they had been so happy there?

When I told this story to the waitress, she whispered in a conspiratorial tone, "That's not the *real* site. The real site is off County NN near Plum Creek where I live. The county moved the cabin to a more convenient location, but there's no way the Ingallses would have built a cabin there 'cause there's no water."

The gift shop at the Laura Ingalls Wilder Museum across the street was well stocked with Little House books, long calico dresses, and sunbonnets. There were even kits for making Laura's corncob doll, Susan, surely the saddest doll in American literature. ("It wasn't Susan's fault that she was only a corncob.") The kit consisted one corncob and two buttons to be attached as eyes. Fully assembled, Susan the corncob doll would enable any child with a closet full of toys to pretend to be poor but resourceful.

The museum's docent told me that the waitress at the café was flat wrong about the location of Laura's first home.

"We have Charles Ingalls's tax bill from 1872. Six dollars and sixty-six cents for forty acres of land," she said matter-of-factly. "They left the next year when Ingalls sold the land to a man named Anderson. It's off County C."

She pointed to a wall-size 1877 plat map of Pepin County divided into eight townships that alternated in color between washed-out pink and mint green. A yellow sticker marked the southwest corner of section 27, Pepin Township, an eighty-acre parcel at the end of a wagon road with a small black square indicating a house or cabin. The name inked into the small white rectangle was O. Anderson. The Ingallses had left the property three years earlier.

"The Ingallses' cabin was on this quarter-section. The farmers cleared everything and tore down the log cabin because they weren't using it. But when the owner donated the property to the city, the footprint of the cabin was still there."

Charles Ingalls first sold his property on a land contract to a Swede named Gustaf Gustafson in 1868, when Laura was only two, and packed the family off to Kansas in a failed attempt to preempt Indian land. They returned the next year to live with in-laws until Gustafson vacated the "little house." Laura omits the Kansas interlude in *Little House in the Big Woods* as well as the homecoming, but she describes in great detail a prosperous, happy time when there was plenty of food from garden and forest and a large extended family of aunts and uncles and cousins to share it with. In many respects, the years in Pepin County were the best times for all of them, but they didn't last. In February of 1874, when Laura was just five, the family crossed Lake Pepin on the ice to Minnesota. This move was followed by a move to Iowa in 1876, back to Minnesota in 1877, and on to Dakota Territory in 1879. A chart of the family's travels—five moves in nine years—resembles a campaign map in which nearly every advance is followed by a retreat.

The Ingallses weren't alone in their rootlessness, the docent explained. On the whole, pioneers were a peripatetic bunch.

"That's what my grandfather did—homestead, prove up, and sell. He was from Buffalo County and then moved to South Dakota and then Montana."

"Did you grow up in Pepin?"

"No. I'm not from here. This is where I retired."

Mobility has always been the formula for success in American life—that and hard work. The better job, the bigger spread awaits the risk-taker with the gumption to pull up stakes and head over the horizon. The virtues that Frederick Jackson Turner saw retrospectively in frontier life—independence, self-reliance, fortitude—were the reward for pushing ahead of the line of settlement. The pioneers trusted that prosperity would follow virtue with the same blind faith they believed rain followed the plow. It didn't always work out that way. The Ingallses got all the virtues but none of the financial rewards.

Little House in the Big Woods ends in one of the most poignant—and puzzling—scenes found in any novel, much less a children's book. Laura, safely tucked into her trundle bed, watches Pa fiddling and Ma knitting in the small circle of firelight and trusts that nothing will ever change.

> She was glad that the cosy house, and Pa and Ma and the firelight and the music, were now. They could not be forgotten, she thought, because now is now. It can never be a long time ago.

It's a dream-like scene, the past telescoping into the present, reinforcing the intimacy of the moment while simultaneously jerking the reader out of it. And what did Wilder mean by "now"? Did she mean the "now" of narrative time in which events hang suspended on the page and a reader can get up and fetch of glass of water and return to find Pa still fiddling? Or did she mean the "now" in the ordinary sense of the moment in which she was writing, a sixty-five-year-old woman recounting childhood memories even as the Great Depression worsened around her? I think the scene works both ways. Laura-the-child is doing what children do, bargaining with God, praying to extend one precious moment into forever while Laura-the-writer (along with the reader) knows that change is inevitable, that nothing in life is fixed, that hard times lay ahead, and home can be one place today and somewhere entirely different tomorrow.

The museum only had two items that belonged to the Ingallses, a nine-square quilt sewn by Laura and one of Rose Wilder's lace doilies.

On the other hand, an entire exhibit was devoted to Anna Barry, Laura's first teacher. On display were Barry's double-weave coverlet, her side table, a scuffed copy of a *Fifth Independent Reader*, and an autograph book of tributes by former students.

> Dear teacher, when hills and mountains separate us two
> You think of me and I of you.

Barry would have been in her late twenties when Laura and Mary attended the Barry Corner School a half mile down from the Ingallses' cabin. Given the scarcity of adult women in Laura's childhood and her own stint as a teacher, I'd have thought Barry would have left more of an impression, but she isn't even mentioned in *Little House in the Big Woods*. The Ingallses were Leavers and Anna Barry was a Stayer. Barry stayed in Pepin until she died at age 94. A photograph in the exhibit showed her as a young woman, dark hair coiled in a braid above her head. The schoolmarm's long face looks like a composite. The upper half is delicate, especially the shy, deep-set eyes, while the bottom half is mannish with thin lips and a strong chin.

"And that's her dress from way back when," said the docent. She pointed to a lacey, ivory-colored cotton shift with a sewn-on shawl and apron. It was draped over a mannequin that stood under five feet tall. Pioneer women usually wore black or brown for every day, so the shift must have been for special occasions.

"Was that Barry's wedding gown?" I asked.

"No. She never married. That's probably a summer dress like the kind they used to wear."

The Rivers of Eden

The Chippewa River had been falling all summer, something I didn't notice until a few miles upstream of where the river empties into Lake Pepin. At first there was plenty of water and I ran the outboard wide open. But by Five Mile Bluff the canoe started bottoming out on the shoals and I had to slow down. A riparian topography that had been submerged when I'd come down the Chippewa in June was now laid bare—sunken logs like beach defenses, sand and cobble terraces, sloughs cut off from the main channel. The lower Chippewa was a repeat visit for me, and I'd hoped to race up it and arrive home in a day or two instead of slowly picking my way through shoals.

The only advantage to a falling river is that there are more sandbars to camp on. I pitched my tent on a high wedge of sand and cobble below Durand that must have been low and damp in June and had now dried out enough for violet phlox to get purchase and bloom. And because it was late August the white shards of turtle eggs scattered about the sand could be taken as a sign of newly hatched turtles rather than the sad remains of a skunk's meal.

Summer was over. Not in the astronomical sense—three weeks remained until the autumnal equinox—but with the finality of a schoolboy who realizes that his vacation is over, kaput, and classes begin soon. The Chippewa was the final spoke on my roundabout route home and tonight would be my last night on any river for the foreseeable future. Suddenly I wished it wasn't. I had enjoyed being a jolly flatboatman for the summer. For weeks there had been the exhilaration of being on the move and not knowing what new possibility lay around the bend. Now I knew exactly what lay around the next bend—a very long to-do list. After supper, I crawled into my sleeping bag and listened to a pair of barred owls calling back and forth in the darkness. It sounded like the beginning of a domestic dispute. One owl would inquire, *Whooo-whooo-cooks-for-you?* And the response would come from deeper in the woods, *Whooo-whooo-(do-you-think)-cooks-for-you?*

In the morning, another dense fog. Instead of burning off, the fog clung to the river and turned incandescent as a blinding sun rose behind it. I couldn't see more than a foot upriver. So I was marooned for the time being. I made coffee, packed my tent and sleeping bag, and waited. If I ignored the sound of trucks downshifting on the highway across the river, it was possible to imagine myself totally alone, the only human being on earth.

In 1886 an itinerant preacher from western Wisconsin named Reverend David O. Van Slyke published a treatise locating the biblical Garden of Eden not in the Fertile Crescent of Mesopotamia but in the coulee country of western Wisconsin. He reached this astounding conclusion after close reading of Genesis 2, 8–14: "And the Lord God planted a garden eastward in Eden. . . . And a river went out of Eden. And from there, it was parted and became into four heads. . . . And the fourth river is Euphrates." If you accept Van Slyke's central notion that "Euphrates" simply means "Long River," a name that could apply to any major waterway, then wasn't it possible, even likely, that the Mississippi, five hundred miles longer than the one in Mesopotamia, was Eden's true "fourth river"? Once that idea is swallowed, the other landmarks fall into place. The three tributaries that head east of the "great river" and join it to form the Garden's boundaries are no longer the Pishon, Gihoni, and Chidekel but the La Crosse, Trempealeau, and Black Rivers.

Van Slyke, a staunch abolitionist, had earlier marched off to the Civil War at the age of forty-four. He looked like John Brown, another native prophet with a flowing white beard and a withering gaze. His self-published treatise, *Found at Last: The Veritable GARDEN OF EDEN, or a Place That Answers the Bible Description of That Notable Spot Better Than Anything Yet Discovered*, reads like part scriptural analysis, part real estate brochure. The yellow cover is a map showing the triangle of rivers bounded by tall bluffs that form a curving Garden Wall around Van Slyke's hometown of Galesville.

Placing himself on a blufftop like Moses gazing upon the Promised Land, Van Slyke addresses the reader. Why had the Creator placed Adam and Eve in Trempealeau County on exactly the 90th meridian? Because the Almighty wanted them to take advantage of the moderate climate, the plentiful water, and rich soil that was "easily cultivated and adapted to *gardening*." The scarcity of earthquakes and lack of mineral wealth (which could have corrupted the first man and woman) are offered as further proofs. Even the local rattlesnakes play a role in this divine scheme.

"Look immediately around you, over the hanging gardens on which you stand, *and look out for snakes*, for how could you have a garden without a 'Serpent.'"

Van Slyke's treatise may have been a response to Charles Darwin's *The Descent of Man*, which had set off a wave of counter-efforts to find physical evidence of the Bible's literal truth. Five years earlier, the president of Boston University's Theological School had published a book locating the Garden of Eden at the North Pole. Van Slyke's Eden was "Not too far north, not too far south" and within walking distance of his own home. I don't think Van Slyke was a simple booster or real estate speculator because he didn't own any property. I think he was a man trying to convince himself that he'd already found Paradise.

So where is Eden? Did I miss the turn a few miles back or was it just around the next bend? Truth is, I'd stopped looking for paradise about the same time I took out a mortgage. But in my twenties I'd done a great deal of looking, mainly out West. Like many people at the time, I carried a heavily annotated paperback of *Walden* in my backpack with passages underlined that confirmed things I already believed. One passage was, "Wherever I sat, there I might live and the landscape radiated from me accordingly." at the time I was convinced that the good life required Ansel Adams scenery, a dramatic seashore or a mountain range in the background. So I sat in California for a few years and let the landscape radiate from me and did the same thing in Alaska for a bit longer. I was no happier in one than the other. Then I moved back to the Midwest, a place that had neither seacoast nor mountains, and for the most mundane of reasons—a job. Had I missed out on the good life, the one where I'm walking along a pounding surf or climbing a mountain ridge? I don't think so. Since the space we carve out for our lives is mostly about time rather than geography, and since most lives follow a similar trajectory, it's reasonable to suppose that any place can qualify as Eden. Pick a spot on a map. People, not scenery, are the important part of the equation—family, friends, a team to root for—and people are where you find them.

For all practical purposes, there are only two places in the world— home and everywhere else. I'd spent the summer imagining each town I passed through as a potential home; some required no effort at all while others had such an air of hopelessness about them that I wondered why anyone stayed. But I wasn't seriously looking, only window shopping, because I already have a hometown. I love the the sound of it. *Eau Claire.* "It's French for 'Clear Water,'" I'll say to people who've never been there, reminding them that there are two words in the name, not one. Then I'll correct them if they pronounce my hometown, as I initially had, with a Pepe Lé Pew accent. Almost all the river towns I'd passed through had evocative names, words that are beautiful to say and come from the Chippewa or the French like "Odanah" or "Prairie du Chien" or "Muscoda." Even the humblest towns had been named to commemorate some shining moment in the past or stake a claim to a brighter future. The saddest place name I ever came across on a Wisconsin map was an unincorporated crossroads in the northern part of the state called Imalone. Like other funny place names—Disco, Embarrass, Luck—once heard, it became impossible to forget except that Imalone seems more pathetic than funny. I don't know if it was a real place or a cartographer's joke because the name disappeared from subsequent state highway maps before I had the chance to drive there. All I could do was imagine what it looked like and why it disappeared. I pictured scattered houses in a pine woods, a dying roadhouse, a constant drizzle, people leaving one after another until only a single resident remained. One day the surveyor came through and asked where he was, and the last person answered bitterly, "Imalone."

Sometimes the fog doesn't lift till noon," Dan Langlois told me over a late breakfast at the Corral Bar and Grill in Durand.

Langlois had grown up in Durand and played football as a small but speedy running back for the Durand Panthers. His knees were shot now but he still had the heads-up alertness of someone expecting a handoff. We'd known each other for years but I didn't realize he had commuted thirty miles from Durand to the university every single day so he could sleep in the same house he'd grown up in. I asked why he hadn't just relocated.

"I think we had a high school graduation class of 125. Most of them left. Maybe 10 percent stayed. Why did I stay? It's the quality of life, the outdoors, the hunting and fishing I grew up on. I wanted to stay close to my roots and friends. Money was never really a factor."

We were the only customers besides a foursome of old men playing cards. The wall behind the card party was decorated with framed photographs of deer hunters arranged in two groups, Gun Season and Bow Season. The pictures looked almost interchangeable, a hunter either in blaze orange or camouflage cradling the head of a dead buck to best show its antlers. A similar display in a big city bar would be reserved for photographs of ball players or musicians or other celebrities. The wall of fame at the Corral Bar was more democratic in that anyone could earn a spot on it just by shooting a big buck.

Langlois is the most serious Catholic I know. He wore the medals of Saint Hubert, patron of hunters, and Saint Kateri Tekakwitha, patron of ecologists, around his neck. He'd helped establish a Catholic camp across the river at Round Hill. The previous summer he'd led a group of canoeists on a week-long pilgrimage down the Chippewa and Mississippi to the Shrine of Our Lady of Guadalupe in La Crosse.

He saw me wince at the word "pilgrimage."

"It's a pilgrimage if it has a sacred destination like a shrine and the traveler has a personal reason, a personal intention, to get there."

"And yours was?"

"To give thanks for Round Hill. Anyway, on a pilgrimage something is going to happen, and what happened to us was this vision."

The vision involved, as many religious visions do, what seemed to be an optical illusion. A heavy fog lay on the river that first morning. Nearing the mouth of the Chippewa, the canoeists saw, or thought they saw, the profile of a three-masted ship with square sails and a high sterncastle sailing up the Mississippi toward Lake Pepin. It appeared to be a Spanish galleon. But when the pilgrims paddled the last two hundred yards to the confluence, the phantom ship vanished back into the fog.

"The next day we stopped in a town for coffee and somebody slapped a newspaper down. There was a picture of the ship, a replica of Columbus's the *Nina*. She was coming up the river from Mobile,

Alabama, and headed for display in Hudson. What are the odds of it passing just at the moment we came to the river?"

At this point in the trip, my personal intention was to get home, but a falling river made that increasingly more difficult. As the country flattened out above Durand, the Chippewa became, paradoxically, both shallower *and* faster. Exposed gravel bars accelerated the flow by pinching it between fewer channels, so I was working against the river's own gravity. Despite the surrounding flatness, I had the impression of pushing the canoe uphill.

After Nine Mile Island, I was in the water most of the time, holding onto a bowline and pulling the canoe against the current so I wouldn't bust a shear pin. I might as well have been back on the Brule. Wading felt good in the midday heat until one of my sandal straps broke and let sharp bits of gravel get underfoot. Limping along through the shallows with a floppy sandal and a canoe on a rope, I almost stepped on another pilgrim. A newly hatched turtle, a softshell. It tried to burrow into the gravel when I picked it up. The hatchling was no bigger than a silver dollar with a speckled shell, beaded yellow eyes and a head pointed like a pencil nub. When I put it back in the shallows, four webbed feet came out of the shell and began paddling back to the river. I don't know what intention the turtle had for its journey other than to reach deeper water. Me too.

Back in the canoe, the outboard humming along with less than twenty miles to go, I made a dumb mistake by turning up Meridian Slough. Actually, it was the main channel that turned, curving sharply north around an island, while I blithely continued straight ahead. Meridian Slough is wide but shallow even under normal conditions. By the time I realized my mistake I was on a narrow ribbon of water running through a dry expanse of riverbed across from the Meridian boat landing. A family sunning themselves on the beach looked up from their towels and watched as I repeatedly tried to broach a sandbar stretched across the slough. When I couldn't, I tilted up the outboard and stepped over the gunwale. The water was ankle deep. It would be like that all the way up Meridian Slough. At that point, I gave up. Some children were having a wonderful time splashing through the shallows and I wished they weren't. I dragged the canoe up the concrete boat ramp and called Bob Elkins. Then I sat down at a picnic table to wait.

I felt foolish and stymied but mostly annoyed at myself for making an unforced error that had left me stranded. The Meridian landing was not the finish line I had in mind. I wanted the symmetry of ending where I'd started, at the boat landing below the campus footbridge. I wanted to complete the circle and arrive to a welcoming party of family and friends, not strangers sunbathing on a beach. It was, I realize now, a silly ambition. After all, the Round River was a made-up route with no real destination and it only ends, as Paul Bunyan discovered and I was just learning, the moment you realize you've been circling home all along.

It was the end of August. Classes would begin after Labor Day. The English department would host its usual start-of-the-semester party to introduce new faculty and welcome back others. Some would return with traveler's tales to match the pictures they'd posted on Facebook. Maybe somebody would notice my sunburned face and strike up a conversation. *Where had I gone over summer break?* Not far, I'd say. No more than a few hours drive from where we're now standing. *What had I learned on my trip?* I'm so glad you asked.

I had learned a sense of scale. I had learned, for instance, that the Midwest is larger and more topographically varied when viewed at ground level than from the window of an airplane flying overhead. From a canoe it looks practically like a country unto itself. I had traveled roughly eight hundred river miles, crossed multiple watersheds, and had learned to measure distance by days rather than hours. The slower I went, the more I was aware of the land's permanence and my own fleeting passage through it. I had embarked on this journey hoping to discover who my neighbors might be and what, if anything, we shared in common. On the whole, the people I met were open and welcoming. They gave me directions, free marina slips, a socket wrench. If they sensed I was lost or needed help, they took me in. That so many happened to be unemployed, on disability, or just scraping by only underscored their generosity.

I had learned the obvious, that small towns are getting smaller. The population of the countryside is bleeding out and while I wish I had a solution for this death by a thousand cuts, I don't. A new wave of immigrants would help, but that won't happen without jobs. In the 1930s when the last wave of immigration had already begun to recede, the federal government infused jobs and people into rural America with infrastructure projects like the lock and dam system on the Mississippi River and Civilian Conservation Corps camps in the North Woods. But as the rural population declines, we've come to view the countryside solely for what can be extracted from it—base minerals, pulpwood, corn and soybeans, high school graduates— without much thought as to what can be returned.

I had learned that history doesn't flow in a circle but loops and meanders across the same narrow plain. Events may not repeat exactly, but situations do, over and over again. So immigration can be viewed as a nineteenth-century phenomenon that ended with the arrival of one's forebears and the collective efforts of the New Deal can seem like ancient history while the individual heroics of the pioneer era remain as fresh as last night's dream. And those pioneer virtues that small town residents still hold dear—self-sufficiency, independence, and the deeply ingrained habit of taking whatever's on your plate— have allowed them to quietly go down with the ship, one ship at a time.

Like many Americans who live in cities, I have a sentimental attachment to small towns. Every Christmas season I watch *It's a Wonderful Life* to see George Bailey save Bedford Fall for the ump-teenth time. Even though the little town clearly drives him nuts— the savings and loan, the same faces, the limited opportunities—his sense of duty keeps him there. Only divine intervention allows George to see all the good he's done for Bedford Falls . . . simply by staying put! Even if he doesn't need Bedford Falls, it needs him. Almost singlehandedly he keeps his hometown from becoming Pottersville although the neon-lit dance halls and noisy gin joints of Pottersville look like a fun alternative. But small towns that fail don't turn into Pottersville. They become Imalone.

Time and again on my journey, I had met George Bailey in one incarnation or another—the entrepreneur who bought the oldest hotel in town just to keep it running, the mayor who's been in office for three decades, the tribal chair who beat the out-of-state mining company—each of them had, in a sense, drawn an outline of the universe and put their hometown at the very center of it. These days it's hard to understand why anyone invests an entire lifetime in one place, let alone a place where staying means long drives to the grocery store or drugstore or to the hospital. To an outsider, it might seem like inertia or a lack of ambition, but now I understand that it's something else—love.

When my children were young I would take them on long drives in the countryside, meandering trips to cranberry marshes in early fall or in the heat of summer to roadside grottos fashioned from old beer bottles, concrete, and seashells or to climb on a tank permanently parked in some town square. I considered these trips educational because they were intended to provoke a sense of wonder as well as belonging, to assure the kids that they lived in an interesting place. Not bland or quaint but interesting—as in worthy of attention. I was forearming them against the day when they'd go off to college and encounter some version of Professor Marvel—*"Professor Marvel never guesses, he knows!"*—so keen to defamiliarize them from their surroundings that they'd end up believing that real life begins in New York or L.A. or wherever Professor Marvel went to graduate school. (I'd played Professor Marvel myself over the years.) You want your children to be at home in the world, but first they have to feel at home.

Now, with the kids grown and gone, I had taken myself on the Round River with the same purpose behind those meandering drives, to remember why I live here. Almost every day supplied a good reason or two—people, the towns, the land itself—but it was a river that tied those reasons together like a bow. They were different rivers, seven in all, but after awhile they blurred into one continuous stream, the sum of all its tributaries, a great river that flows forwards and backwards at the same time and carried me far afield even as it steadily brought me home.

Acknowledgments

Writing a book is as much a journey as launching a canoe down an unknown river; there are dead-ends and detours and long periods of being hopelessly lost. So in addition to the people kind enough to share their time and thoughts with me along the rivers, I wish to thank those on the writing end—my editor Gwen Walker, Brady Foust, Jack Bushnell, Nickolas Butler, James Campbell, Dale Peters, Richard Bell, Gregory Orfalea, and most especially my wife, Sharon—for their good advice and support.

Selected Sources

Chippewa River

Jonathan Carver. *The Journals of Jonathan Carver and Related Documents.* Edited by John Parker. St. Paul: Minnesota Historical Society Press, 1976.

John E. Hallwas. *Dime Novel Desperadoes: The Notorious Maxwell Brothers.* Urbana: University of Illinois Press, 2008.

Jonathan Raban. *Old Glory: An American Voyage.* New York: Simon & Schuster, 1981.

Curtis Roseman and Elizabeth Roseman. *Grand Excursions on the Upper Mississippi River: Places, Landscapes, and Regional Identity after 1854.* Iowa City: University of Iowa Press, 2009.

William Warren. *History of the Ojibway People.* St. Paul: Minnesota Historical Society, 1885. Reprint, St. Paul: Minnesota Historical Society Press, 1984.

Mississippi River

Black Hawk. *Life of Black Hawk, or Ma-ka-tai-me-she-kia-kiak, Dictated by Himself.* New edition of 1833 text edited by J. Gerald Kennedy. New York: Penguin, 2008.

Patrick J. Carr and Maria J. Kefalas. *Hollowing Out the Middle: The Rural Brain Drain and What It Means for America.* Boston: Beacon Press, 2009.

Scott Gordon. *The Path Towards Peak Population in Rural Wisconsin: Births, Deaths, Migration and the Economies of Price, Buffalo and Manitowoc Counties.* https://www.wiscontext.org/path-towards-peak-population-rural-wisconsin, September 21, 2016.

Jack Kerouac. *On the Road.* New York: Viking Press, 1957.

Dawn Merritt. "90 Years of Conservation Success: The Roaring 20s." In the Izaak Walton League's *Outdoor America.* Winter 2012.

Kenny Salwey. *Kenny Salwey's Tales of a River Rat: Adventures along the Wild Mississippi.* St. Paul, MN: Voyageur Press, 2005.

Wisconsin River

P. Donan. *The Dells of the Wisconsin.* Chicago: Rollins Publishing Company, 1879. Reprint, Wisconsin Dells, WI: H. H. Bennett Studio, 2015.

Steven D. Hoelscher. *Picturing Indians: Photographic Encounters and Tourist Fantasies in H. H. Bennett's Wisconsin Dells.* Madison: University of Wisconsin Press, 2008.

Aldo Leopold. *A Sand County Almanac and Sketches Here and There.* New York: Oxford University Press, 1949.

Estella B. Leopold. *Stories from the Shack: Sand County Revisited.* New York: Oxford University Press, 2016.

Jacques Marquette. "The Mississippi Voyage of Jolliet and Marquette." In *Early Narratives of the Northwest, 1634–1699.* Edited by Louise P. Kellogg, 223–57. New York: Charles Scribner's Sons, 1917. Available online at http://www.americanjourneys.org/aj-051/.

Reuben Gold Thwaites. *Down Historic Waterways: Six Hundred Miles of Canoeing upon Illinois and Wisconsin Rivers.* Chicago: A.C. McClurg, 1902.

Virgil Vogel. "Wisconsin's Name: A Linguistic Puzzle." *The Wisconsin Magazine of History* 48, 3 (Spring 1965): 181–86.

Fox River

Katherine J. Cramer. *The Politics of Resentment: Rural Consciousness in Wisconsin and the Rise of Scott Walker.* Chicago: University of Chicago Press, 2016.

John Muir. *The Story of My Boyhood and Youth*. Boston: Houghton Mifflin, 1913. Reprint, Madison: University of Wisconsin Press, 1965.

Bad River

Ernest Hemingway. *The Nick Adams Stories*. New York: Charles Scribner's Sons, 1972.

Henry Rowe Schoolcraft. *Historical and Statistical Information Respecting the History, Condition, and Prospects of the Indian Tribes of the United States*. Vol. 1. Philadelphia: Lippincott, 1851.

Charles Whittlesey. *Geological Report on That Portion of Wisconsin Bordering on the South Shore of Lake Superior. Surveyed in the Year 1849 in David Dale Owen's Report of a Geological Survey of Wisconsin, Iowa and Minnesota; and Incidentally of a Portion of Nebraska Territory*. Philadelphia: C. Sherman Printer, 1852.

Bois Brule River

James W. Feldman. *A Storied Wilderness: Rewilding the Apostle Islands*. Seattle: University of Washington Press, 2011.

Judith Koll Healey. *Frederick Weyerhaeuser and the American West*. St. Paul: Minnesota Historical Society Press, 2013.

D. John O'Donnell. *A History of Fishing in the Brule River. Brule River Survey: Paper No. 3*. Madison: Wisconsin Conservation Department, 1944.

Henry Rowe Schoolcraft. *Personal Memoirs of a Residence of Thirty Years with the Indian Tribes on the American Frontiers with Brief Notes of Passing Events, Facts and Opinions, A.D. 1812 to A.D. 1842*. Philadelphia: Lippincott, Granbo & Company, 1851.

St. Croix River

Eileen M. McMahon and Theodore J. Karamanski. *North Woods River: The St. Croix River in Upper Midwest History*. Madison: University of Wisconsin Press, 2009.

Martha Greene Phillips. *Border Country: The Northwoods Canoe Journals of Howard Greene, 1906–1916*. Minneapolis: University of Minnesota Press, 2017.

Frederick Jackson Turner. *The Frontier in American History*. New York: Henry Holt, 1921.

Lake Pepin

"Sea Wing Capsizes on Lake Pepin." *Minneapolis Tribune*. July 14, 1890. Original newspaper account posted on *Minneapolis Star Tribune* website in April 2008 and reposted August 1, 2014.

Caroline Fraser. *Prairie Fires: The American Dreams of Laura Ingalls Wilder*. New York: Henry Holt & Company, 2017.

Frederick L. Johnson. "Unlocking the Mysteries of the Sea Wing." *Minnesota History Magazine*. Summer 1990.

Laura Ingalls Wilder. *Little House in the Big Woods*. New York: Harper & Row, 1932.

Laura Ingalls Wilder. *Pioneer Girl: The Annotated Autobiography*. Edited by Pamela Smith Hill. Pierre: South Dakota Historical Society Press, 2014.

The Rivers of Eden

Reverend D. O. Van Slyke. *Found at Last: The Veritable GARDEN OF EDEN, or a Place That Answers the Bible Description of That Notable Spot Better Than Anything Yet Discovered*. Galesville, WI: Independent Printing House, 1886.